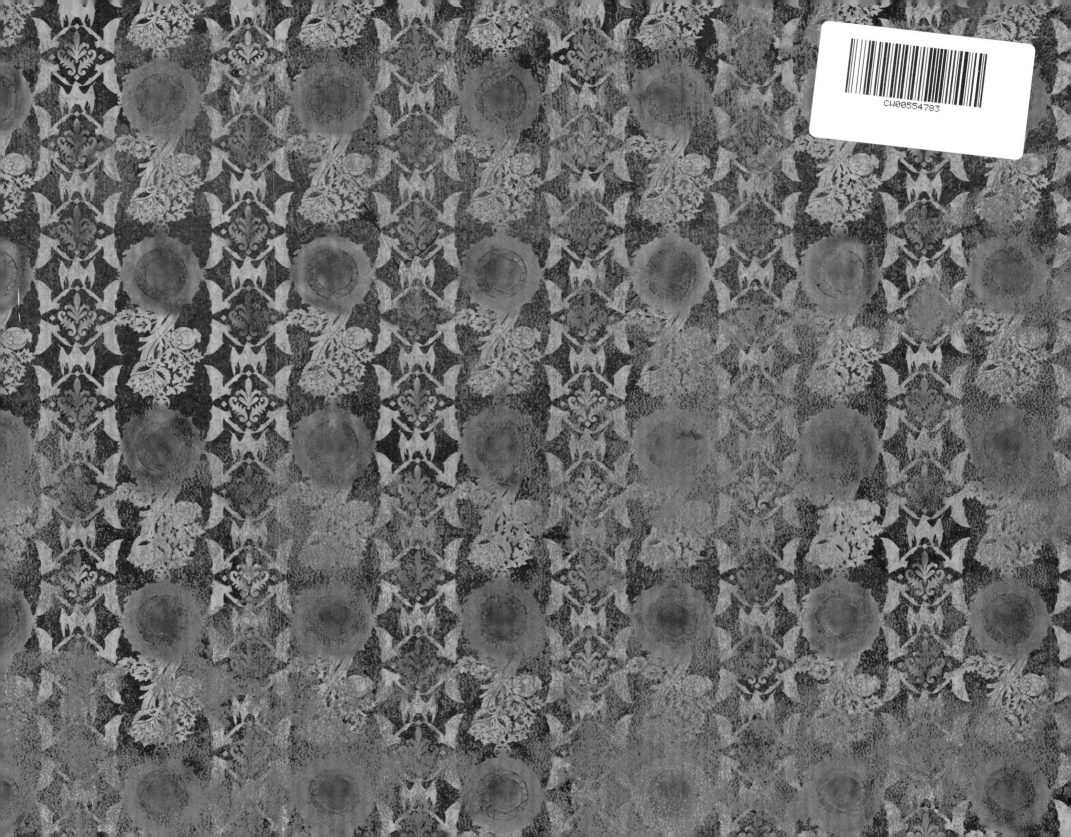

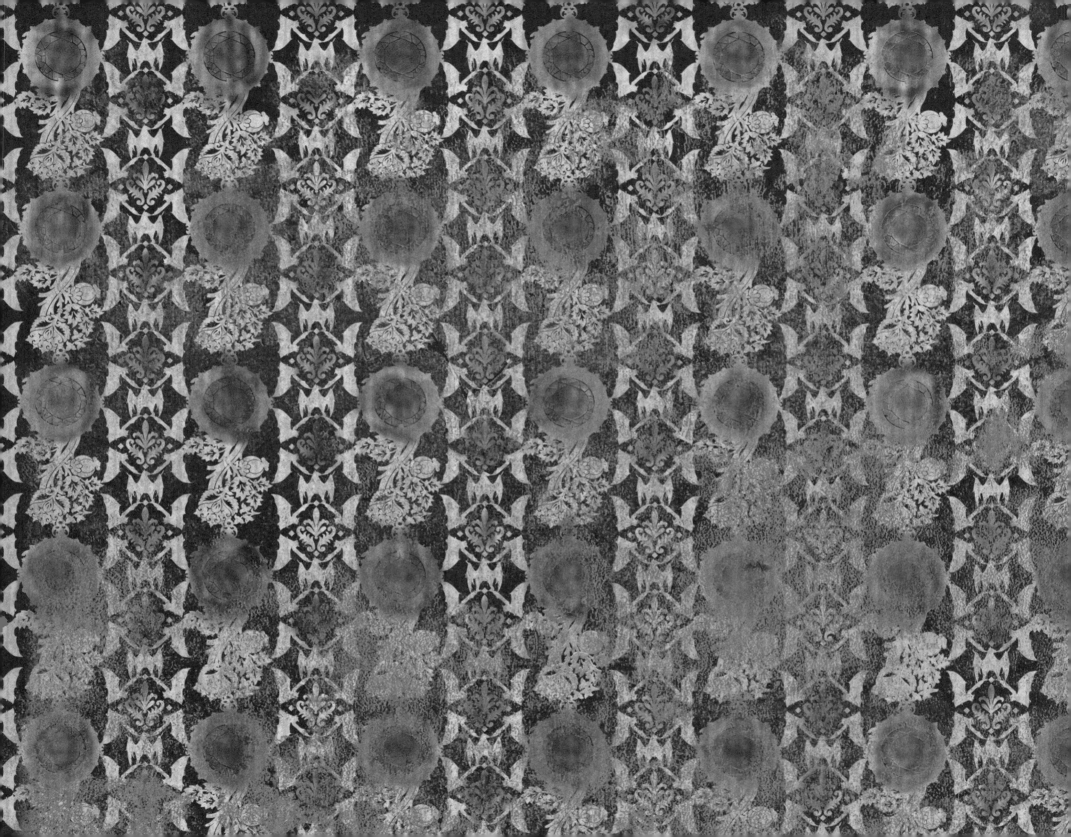

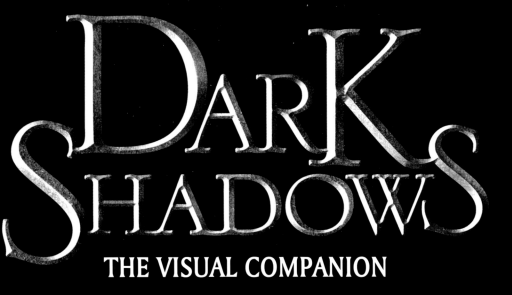

DARK SHADOWS

THE VISUAL COMPANION

MARK SALISBURY

Foreword by JOHNNY DEPP
Introduction by TIM BURTON
Afterword by RICHARD D. ZANUCK

Based on the television series created by DAN CURTIS

Edited by Leah Gallo   Designed by Holly C. Kempf

Titan Books

Acknowledgments

The author would like to express his gratitude to Tim Burton, Derek Frey, Richard D. Zanuck, Rick Heinrichs for their gracious hospitality during my many visits to Collinsport; Sarah Clark for her unparalleled skills as tour guide; Holly and Leah, for making this adventure smooth and fun; Stephen Deuters and Christi Dembrowski for their wrangling skills; Adam Newell at Titan Books, for his keen eyes and editorial assistance; my Mum, for her constant love and support; Cal McCrystal, for the loan of his precious *Dark Shadows* DVDs; Jayne Trotman at Warner Bros.; and, finally, the talented cast and crew of *Dark Shadows*, too many to list here, but whose dedication and creativity brought this world to life.

The editor & designer would like to thank Derek Frey, for his guidance throughout this process. He was an invaluable resource, answering any question thrown his way, as well as offering many bloody good bits of information. There are several others who deserve our gratitude - Charlotte Piddington, who was our point woman on the film long after her job had finished; Tommy Kemplen, JC Bond and Barrie Hemsley for pulling the film stills we needed; Jim Pierson, for graciously providing us with an assortment of photos from the Dan Curtis estate; Jess Garcia and Diane Sponsler at Warner Bros. for sending us the Polaroids and grading guidelines; John Stanford and Ariadne Chucholowski at Warner Bros. for speedily providing us with all of the Print Marketing material; Stephen Deuters, Brenda Berrisford, Kate Buckley, Nicky English, Teri and Trevor Moretz and Leslie Rice for helping to coordinate approvals; and finally to Tim Burton, for his amazing vision, and for incorporating us into his mad world.

Photographs by Leah Gallo and Peter Mountain. Also: Mary Ellen Mark p.2 & p.186-189, Joel Harlow p.143 & 145, Roy Morris p.108, Derek Frey p.152. Artwork by Tim Burton, Rick Heinrichs, Dermot Power, Adam Brockbank, Chris Rosewarne, Kim Fredericksen, Mauro Borelli and Jim Carson. Costume concepts by Colleen Atwood (p. 128, p.132-135).

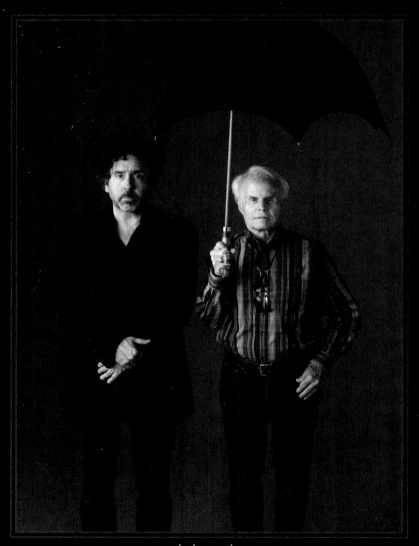

dedicated to
Richard D. Zanuck
1934-2012

TABLE OF CONTENTS

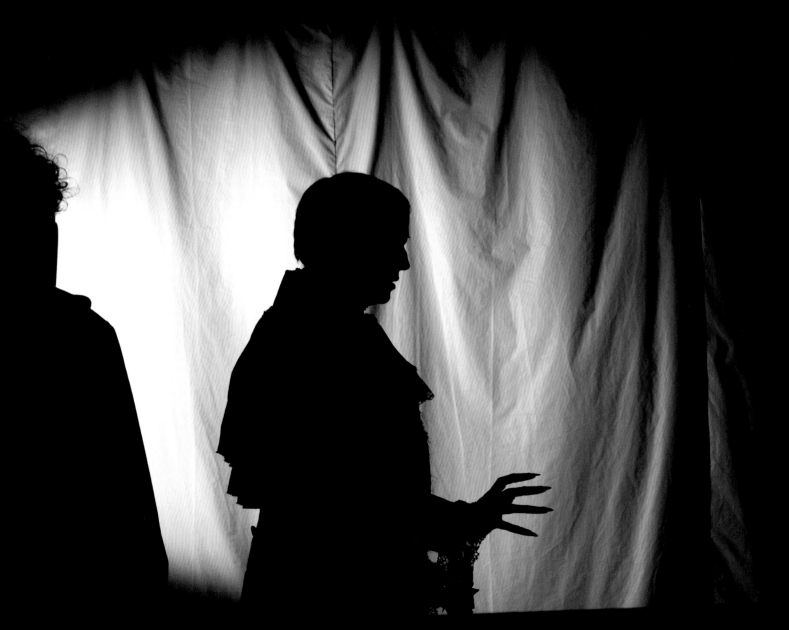

$\mathcal{A}$s a child, I had always been a huge fan of horror films and monster movies. *Frankenstein, Dracula, The Mummy*, and on and on. I found solace in these outsider creatures, brilliantly portrayed by the likes of Bela Lugosi, Boris Karloff, Christopher Lee and on and on and on – one of my all time heroes being the chameleonic Lon Chaney, Sr.

From my early elementary school days, I would sprint home to catch *Dark Shadows*. The character of Barnabas Collins possessed a sense of elegance that bewitched me. Another fringe dweller, his was a strange and haunting presence. I felt as though I were the one under a spell. Specifically, for this film, it was the idea of the cursed gentleman, locked in a box for some two hundred years, only to arrive back at a time when the twin union of taste and aesthetics were at their very worst, which both intrigued and made Tim and I laugh the most. The possibilities seemed endless. We felt like it would probably be the ultimate culture shock, coming from the ornate, puritanical nature of America of the late 1700s to the reign of fast food, super-charged muscle cars and hokey radio, curious fashions, macramé owls and all that the early 1970s had to offer. We used this as our springboard, our wallpaper. The perfect backdrop for a tale of long lost love, witches, curses and supernatural vendettas.

In terms of developing the film with Tim, it is without question the most we've put into any film we've done together. Tim's suggestion of Seth Grahame-Smith was sheer perfection. He understood exactly where we were going, right off the bat. The collaboration was a giggling, absurdist fantasy. Every morning, every evening, we would sit and hone and sculpt and re-sculpt the following week's work.

Bringing one of my childhood heroes to life was a task, to be sure, but one that I felt worthy; and given the canvas that Tim provides with all of the magick colors of the immensely talented and inventive cast and crew, made the dream all the more special.

Johnny Depp

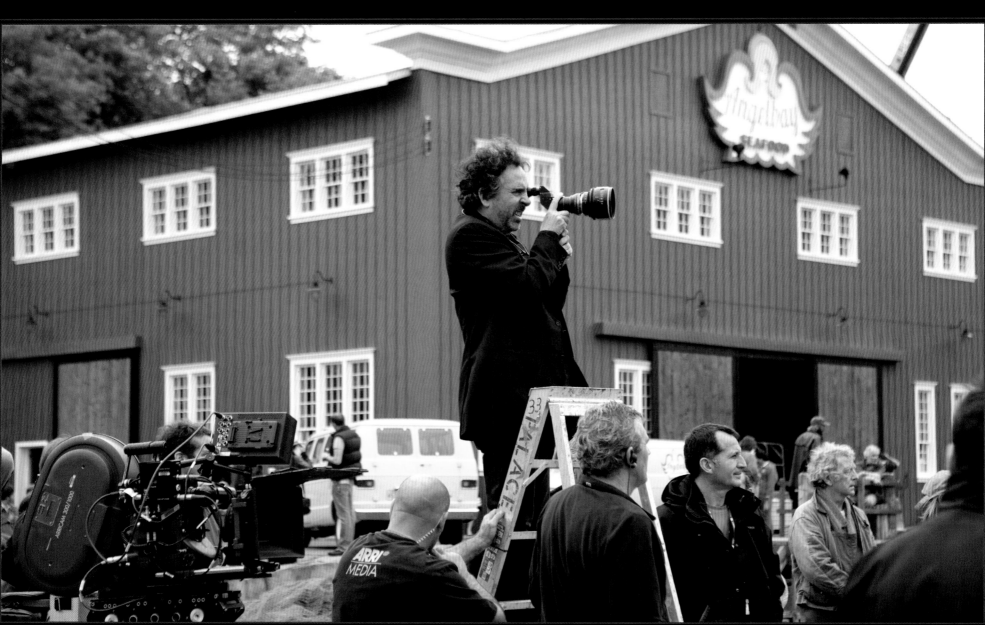

Dark Shadows was a strange cultural phenomenon. Racing home from school to watch this odd Gothic soap opera on TV every afternoon was a very memorable experience for me (it also made me a lousy student because I avoided doing my homework).

Johnny mentioned the possibility of doing Dark Shadows many years ago. I could tell playing Barnabas was something deep in his heart. Also it allowed me the opportunity to spray him with blood, water, and vomit.

I want to thank the amazing cast. Each and every one captured the unique spirit of the film. They are Dark Shadows (whether they like it or not)!

Of course none of this would have been possible without the crew, who worked so hard to capture the unusual blend of the gothic and the early 1970s. It's not an easy thing to represent, but they created it so beautifully.

And thanks to all of you, the viewers, for being interested in seeing more of the world of Dark Shadows. These photos and artwork help convey the time spent, the many details, and the funny and quirky moments that are all part of the process of filmmaking. Hope you enjoy.

Tim Burton

HISTORY

Dark Shadows debuted on US network television on June 27, 1966. Created by Dan Curtis, the series broke the mold of daytime TV and shook up the soap opera status quo with its unique blend of Gothic romance, melodrama and mystery. At a time when afternoon serials mostly involved the affairs of handsome doctors and pretty nurses, here was a daily soap that featured vampires, werewolves and ghosts, not to mention the occasional pirate and a spot of time travel.

"It was a very unusual thing, a supernatural soap in the afternoon," remembers Tim Burton who, like so many kids of his generation, would race home from school to watch the strange story of the Collins family, who lived in a spooky, rundown mansion overlooking the Maine fishing village of Collinsport. "It had such a weird vibe, like a weird dream, a kind of nightmare in the afternoon. It was more about this weird vibe that it created than it was about the actual thing itself. It's like watching an Ed Wood movie every day.

"There was something about the music, the languid pace, and the seriousness of the way the actors were taking it," Burton continues, "that gave it this unique quality. It was serious, but at the same time I found it kind of funny. But it's not meant to be funny. It was also the first thing in the modern era to kind of mix things like witches, ghosts, vampires in one property, and it was very unusual to have that kind of mash up, especially on TV, in the afternoon. It had a lot of strange elements thrown into the brew."

Initially aimed at young housewives, *Dark Shadows* wasn't an immediate hit with its constituent audience. But, in April 1967, Curtis introduced a character who would prove to be the spark the show needed. Played by Canadian stage actor Jonathan Frid, Barnabas Collins made his debut in

episode 202. A reluctant vampire who returns to his familial home of Collinwood after two centuries buried in a coffin, Frid's bloodsucker was only meant to appear in a handful of episodes but the ratings soared upon his arrival and his presence opened up an entirely new section of audience. Barnabas was written into the show and soon came to define *Dark Shadows*.

In an era before home video, *Dark Shadows* became the very definition of "appointment television" for its devoted fans. "I used to watch it religiously," recalls Johnny Depp, who has similar memories of sprinting home to

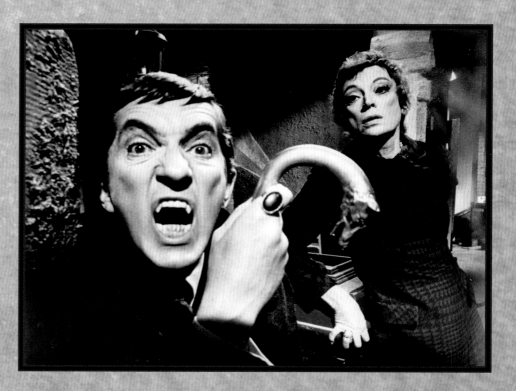

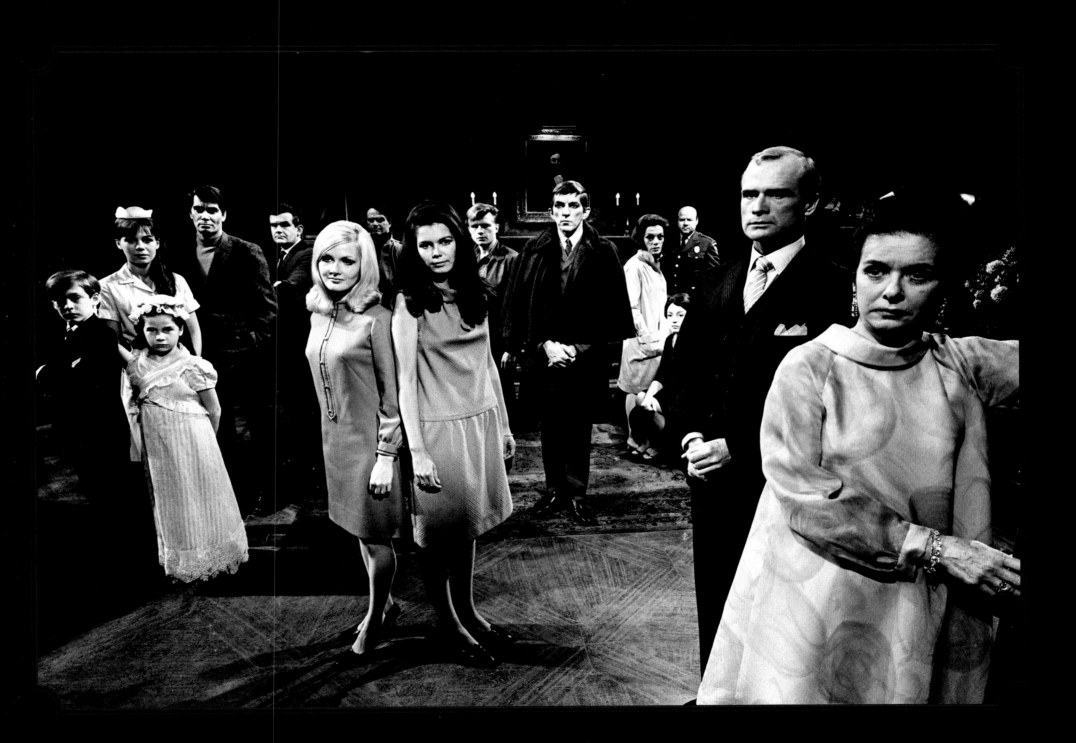

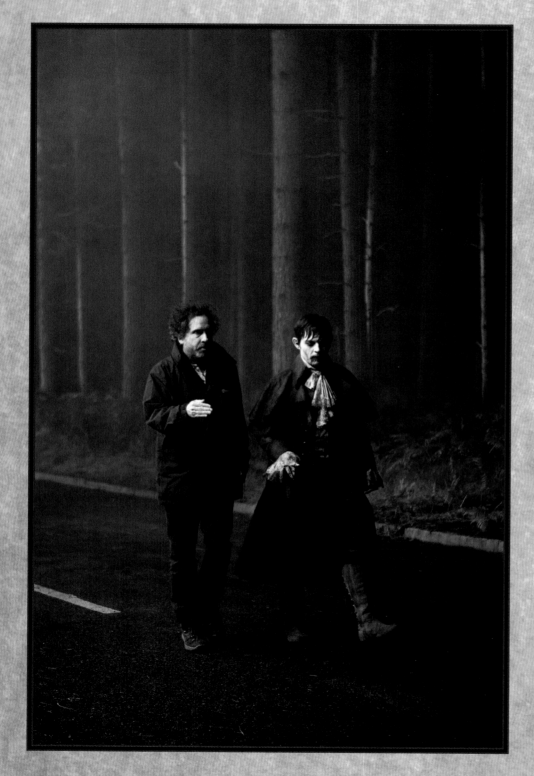

see it. "There was certainly nothing like a Gothic soap opera that had vampires and ghouls and werewolves. So when I got a hold of *Dark Shadows*, you don't let go. I loved it. I was obsessed with Barnabas Collins to the point I had posters and would buy *Dark Shadows* magazines and comic books. He had a very upright, elegant approach to things."

Long before TV's Angel or *Twilight*'s Edward cornered the market in brooding bloodsuckers, Barnabas Collins was the original self-loathing, guilt-ridden, tortured vampire. "He was a ground-breaking character," says novelist/screenwriter Seth Grahame-Smith. "If you think about Dracula and all the vampires leading up to Barnabas, they were all 'I want to suck your blood' types. They had no guilt about the lives they were taking. Along comes this complex, reluctant vampire who has this deep concern for his family's well-being, who has these romantic entanglements, and who hates himself on some deep level for being a bloodsucker."

"I liked that he was a reluctant vampire," says Burton. "That was different territory, that was interesting. I liked the fact he had these sides to him, and had that tragic, bad poetry way of speaking. There was something very appealing about that. It spoke to me. It was a character I could identify with."

Another huge *Dark Shadows* fan was Oscar-nominated actress Michelle Pfeiffer, who had starred in Burton's *Batman Returns*. "I was obsessed," she admits. "It was the first vampire show ever on television and was sort of sexy, too. I'm not sure my mother quite knew what to think of it. She probably assumed, given that it was on in the afternoon, it was safe for me to be watching, but I always had this feeling I was somehow breaking the rules watching it. And it was scary for the time. It was really kind of terrifying."

ABC, which broadcast *Dark Shadows* had, initially, tried to discourage creator Curtis from adding a supernatural element to the daily soap "but his own children told him it was a good idea to bring in the spooky stuff," reveals Kathryn Leigh Scott, who played four roles in the series, including that of Barnabas's long-lost love Josette DuPres. "As soon as Jonathan came on, after we shot maybe two weeks of episodes, there was a crowd of children that would come over, after school, and stand outside the front door and ask for autographs. Within a month there was a huge crowd. Getting out of the studio to walk home became an impossibility."

Dark Shadows ran for five years, clocking up 1,225 episodes, as well as two theatrical movies, *House Of Dark Shadows* and *Night Of Dark Shadows*, with the final episode airing on network television on April 2, 1971. Yet the show refused to die, eventually finding a new lease of life in syndication and later on

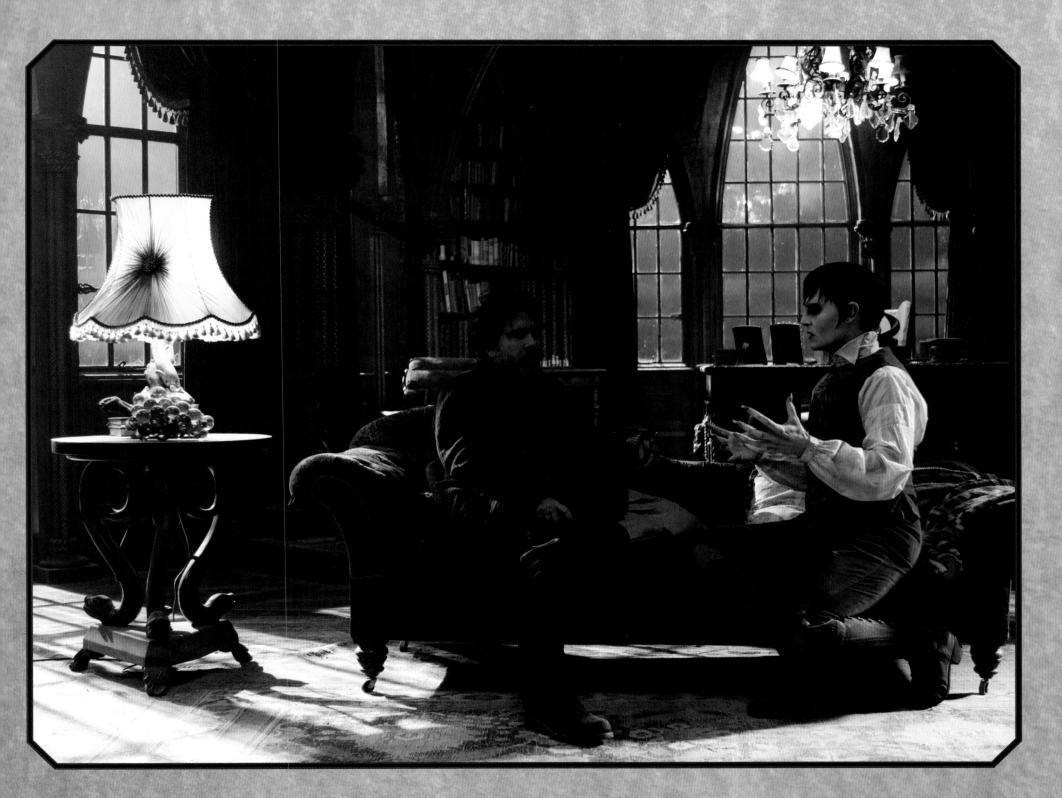

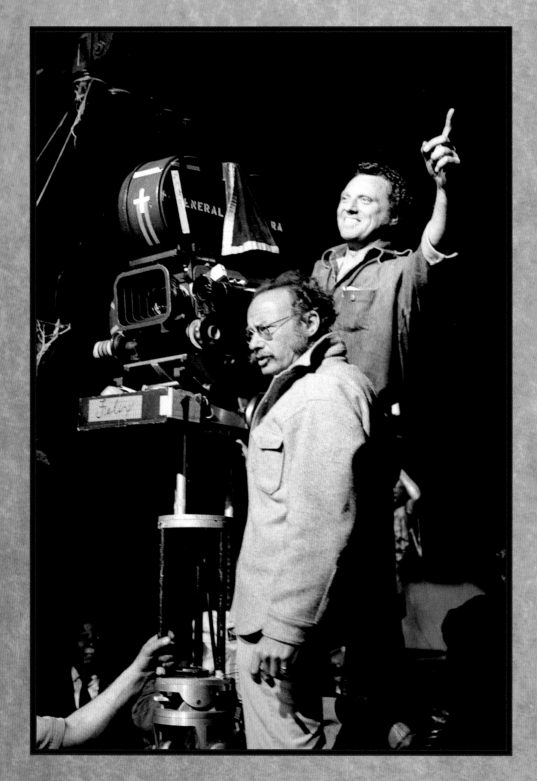

home video. In 1991, there was a short-lived primetime TV revival on NBC with English actor Ben Cross as Barnabas. But creator Curtis and his producing partner David Kennedy were always keen to resurrect *Dark Shadows* for the big screen, and in the early 2000s approached Depp with the idea of him starring as Barnabas in a feature film. At the time the actor was busy with several movie projects, and was unable to commit. Curtis passed away in 2006, and shortly afterwards Depp's production company, Infinitum Nihil, joined with Kennedy and the Curtis Estate to produce a *Dark Shadows* film — one that would star Depp. "If Dan Curtis saw me as Barnabas, I would be honored to play Barnabas," Depp notes. "Obviously the one person that came to mind to bring this thing to life was Tim."

Depp first worked with Burton on *Edward Scissorhands* in 1989, playing the eponymous razor-fingered Edward. Since then, Depp has frequently transformed himself to essay Burton's brand of oddballs, misfits and outsiders, be it cross-dressing filmmaker Ed Wood, Willy Wonka in *Charlie And The Chocolate Factory*, *Sleepy Hollow*'s nervy detective Ichabod Crane, or *Alice In Wonderland*'s mercury-affected Mad Hatter. It was while they were filming Burton's blood-drenched adaptation of Stephen Sondheim's musical *Sweeney Todd: The Demon Barber Of Fleet Street* in 2007 at England's Pinewood Studios that Depp raised the idea of him directing *Dark Shadows*.

"It was one of those off-the-cuff kind of remarks," Depp recalls. "We were standing around talking and laughing, as we normally do, and I said something like, 'Man, we should do a vampire movie together, like *Nosferatu*, a real vampire movie, where the vampire looks like a vampire.' Then it popped into my head — *Dark Shadows*. We started talking about how much we had loved it, and about all the absurdities of that period combined with the Gothic nature, combined with this 200-year-old vampire out of time. We laughed about it, because it was made on such a tight budget. It was like an Ed Wood film: walls would move, flies would land on people's noses, there'd be boom shadows and bad camera moves. The next thing, we were full steam ahead."

"I could see right away he had a passion for it and really wanted to do it," says Burton. "This was something that was very close to him, that inspired him. It was stewing inside of him for a long period of time. He always puts 100 percent into his characters, so I was excited to see what this one would be. Anytime we dip into the horror genre it's fun."

In bringing *Dark Shadows* to the big screen Burton was keen to retain the spirit of the show, but recognized translating its soap opera-y, melodramatic tone was always going to be tricky. "It's a hard thing to try to capture. It's

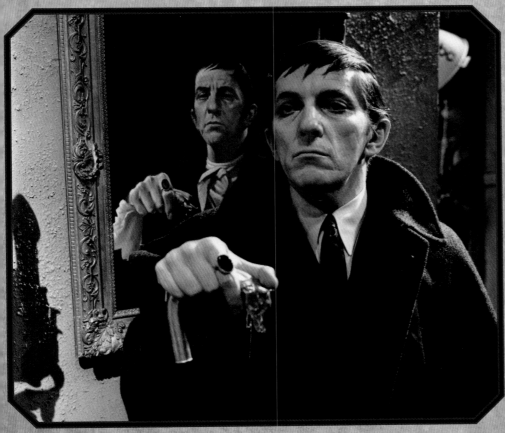

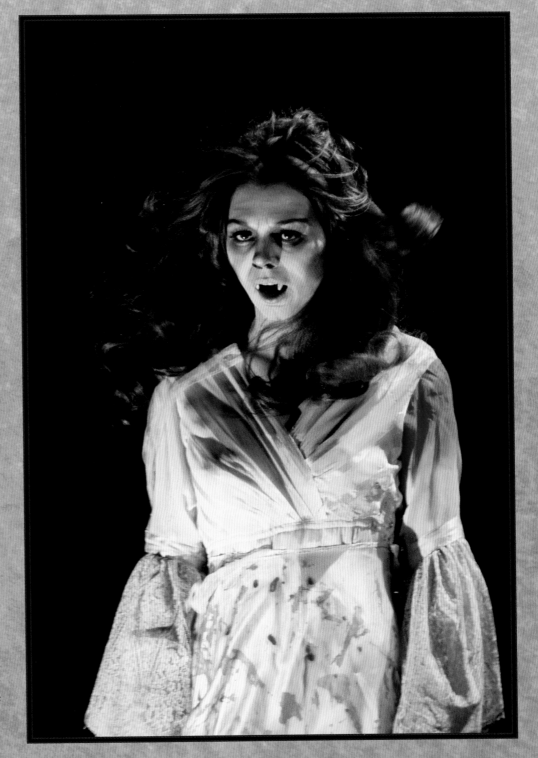

not the kind of thing you can remake because there were more than 1,200 episodes and there was such an elusive tone to it. I've done things where you could say it's a remake but I never considered this to be one, because there's nothing to *re*-make. To be honest, it was more of a perverse challenge, trying to capture something where the tone was so unidentifiable. We were inspired by the show. I mean, if most people looked at it now, they'd think it's a really bad soap opera. It had a whole weird vibe; you wouldn't necessarily want to remake that. So we had to sort of capture the spirit of that elusive thing of why you love something."

For Burton, the show was always about family. "When you're thinking out a whole series and there are all these plot lines and characters, it's quite daunting," he notes. "In the end, it all boiled down to just trying to capture the weird dynamics that happen in any family. Whether they're rich or poor or supernatural, there's a certain kind of internal dynamic that happens. That was the thing that interested me, the workings and the melodramas of a family."

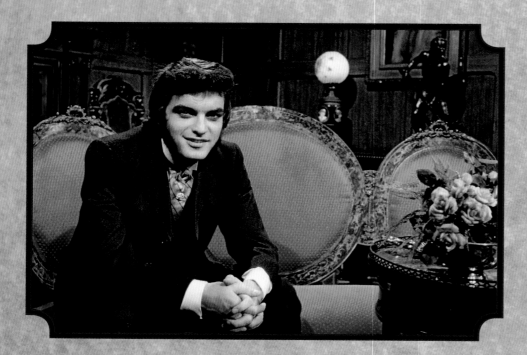

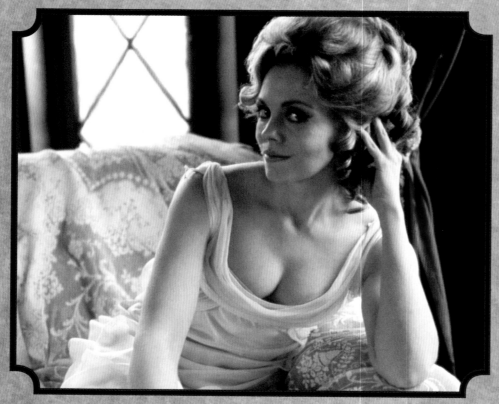

The task of adapting *Dark Shadows* into a two-hour movie initially fell to screenwriter John August, who'd collaborated with Burton on *Big Fish*, *Charlie And The Chocolate Factory*, *Corpse Bride* and *Frankenweenie*. "I went *The Godfather* route and really synthesised a lot of plot lines into it, so it was a very, very busy script, trying to get the full experience of what *Dark Shadows* was," August recalls. "My *Dark Shadows* was about a really messed up, crazy family in Maine and then a vampire shows up. It was very much a family drama/vampire epic, a big, Gothic romance set in 1970. I was really happy with it, and I think everyone was really happy while we first had the script." The plan had been to film *Dark Shadows* during post-production on *Alice In Wonderland*, but the sheer amount of visual effects involved required Burton's undivided attention, and so the idea was ultimately scrapped.

As Depp set sail on a fourth *Pirates of the Caribbean* adventure, a slew of vampire movies and TV shows sapped the lifeblood from August's script. "When I wrote it, *Twilight* hadn't come out, *True Blood* hadn't come out," he says. "I think there was a feeling we're going to be so late telling the big, Gothic, vampire romance it became, 'There's some funny stuff here, what if we went into a funnier direction?' And that's the direction they ultimately went in."

"The thing with *Dark Shadows*, even if you're trying to make it serious, you can't help but have humor," says Burton. "With families there's always tragedy, but there's a humorous side to all tragedy and family dynamics, that's both funny and not funny at the same time, so [John's script] had a certain tone which we actually didn't veer off too much."

"In fairness to John, and in fairness to Tim and myself it was really embryonic," says Depp of that development period. "Tim and I, although we had a very specific tone, were still working out the ins and outs and the various shades of the characters and the complexities and the idea of a dysfunctional family story and building that alongside the tragic love story."

They began again, drafting in Seth Grahame-Smith to write a new script. (August shares a "story by" credit on the final film.) Grahame-Smith had recently adapted his best-selling historical mash-up novel *Abraham Lincoln Vampire Hunter* for Burton to produce. "Tim came up with the idea of Seth," says Depp. "I read his book and was, 'Absolutely. This guy gets it.'"

Grahame-Smith wasn't even born when *Dark Shadows* first aired on TV but was familiar with it in a peripheral way because his mother was a fan. "I have a vague memory of her watching it in re-runs when I was a child. But the one thing I specifically remember was my mother describing Barnabas Collins as a reluctant vampire and how that was so interesting and unique and new. He was a vampire who didn't like being a vampire, who had a conscience and was not proud of the things he'd done."

The young screenwriter's first task was to immerse himself in the world of *Dark Shadows.* "I researched the series as best I could, getting the broad strokes of it, all the key names, places, dates, figures. I read John's draft and there were some really fantastic, descriptive bits and a couple of lines I thought were too clever to part with, so I saved those, then set out writing a treatment for an entirely new story. That was done in collaboration with Tim and with Johnny. I started meeting with both of them, very early in the process, making sure the direction I was going was the direction they wanted to go in. My job was to add humor to the story. They both have wicked, dark senses of humor and a lot of the same influences in terms of films and art, and they're both very excitable. When you're sitting around with them, talking about ideas, they'll jump out of their chairs and act something out. Their enthusiasm is infectious."

"It was almost like a jazz jam session," recalls Depp of those early script meetings. "Tim would riff on something and that would feed me and then it would feed Seth. Ideas would start piling up. Seth made these incredibly specific notes and it all happened really quickly, because Tim and I had finally arrived at where we needed to be, in terms of the film, in terms of the story, in terms of the characters."

Based on these brainstorming sessions, Grahame-Smith first wrote a detailed 14-page outline with sample dialogue and every beat of the story spelled out, before he started scripting. "It's very rare a screenwriter gets to start a script knowing exactly who he is writing for. I knew I was writing for Johnny, I knew I was writing for Tim, and talking to them about the tone of the movie and how Johnny wanted to play Barnabas, this very proper yet almost child-like character who's a man out of time and very earnest and very old world, was a real gift. I was able to tailor it to the things Johnny does extraordinarily well. He's a genius at the subtlety of humor. He can make a joke with a look, with a pause, and, in this case, with an outdated word or a phrase. Frankly, a lot of the turns of phrase come from the times we would get together. He hurls a lot of old world insults — 'You lying strumpet' — and when he first steps on asphalt he says, 'My, what curious terrain.' Those are things that come from Johnny play acting with Tim and I, which in and of itself was an extraordinary experience for me."

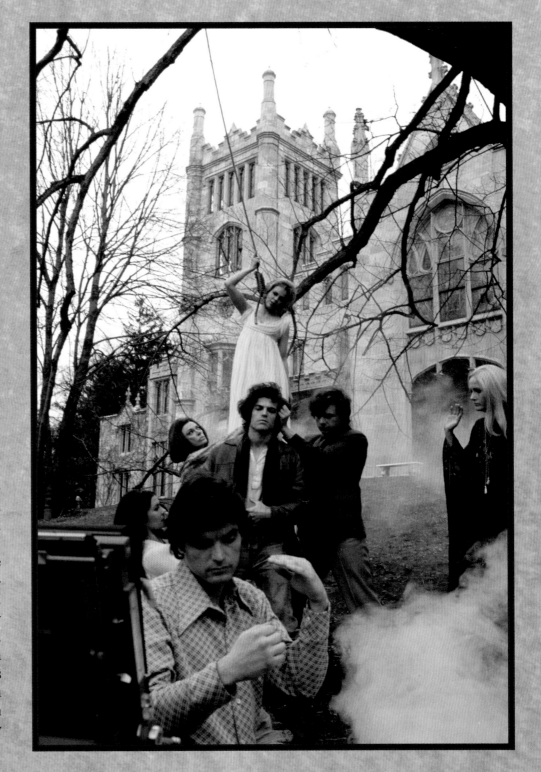

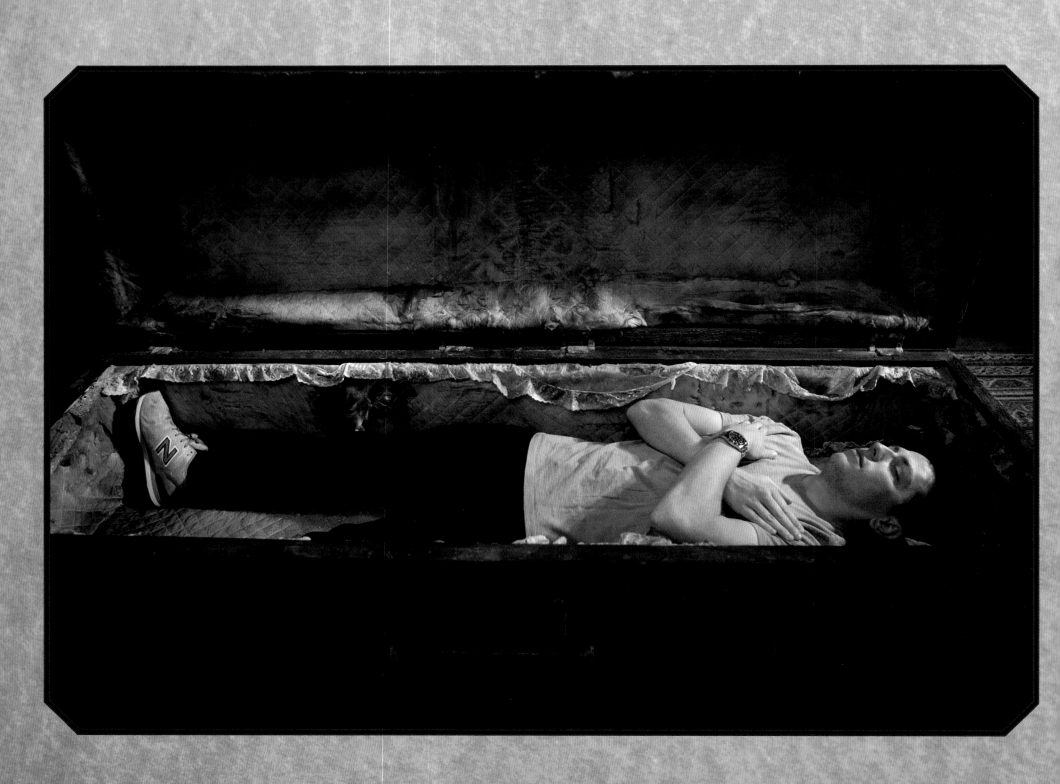

"One of the things Seth brought to it was really digging in and finding that voice of Barnabas," says Burton, "in the sense of somebody who's been locked in a box for 200 years and just how he would see things and not see things, and how he would speak, and how he would not really be with it, so to speak."

Despite their numerous collaborations, *Dark Shadows* marked the first time Burton and Depp had "developed something from the ground up together," says the latter. "Certainly he was always incredibly collaborative, in terms of character and in terms of story, but on this we were in it together from day one. It was a great experience to have Tim, every morning, come into the trailer, and we would discuss the day's work. If something felt odd, in terms of a scene, we would change it, and we would do that at the end of the day as well, for the following day's work. Being that close to Tim with regard to story, and with regard to not just my character but other characters, was a real pleasure."

"Tim would give me the bigger, broader notes about tone," reveals Grahame-Smith. "An image would flash into his mind, and he'd say, 'Work it in somehow if you can.' Not surprisingly he approaches things in a very visual way. Whereas Johnny would really, really delve into the subtext of what's going on as an actor, and would send me pages and pages of single space, typewritten thoughts. Some of it was praise: 'I love what you've done here.' Some of it was: 'I'm not so sure about this.' Some of it was: 'What if?' And many of those 'what ifs' turned into things that are in the film."

Both Burton and Depp felt that humor was an important element in their *Dark Shadows*. "That was the only real approach to take with this, that it needed to be loaded with humor," says Depp. "I'm not exactly sure that was Dan Curtis' intention, but his partner David Kennedy was there quite a lot and he was very happy with everything we were doing. In fact, Dan Curtis' daughters visited and we got their approval. Because that version of *Dark Shadows* had been done, and they did it well within the confines of the restrictions they had, it was time to take it to another level, taking what they did and heightening the universe, heightening the reality of things, heightening the dramatic approach. It's not the original series. There are salutes to the original, and it was done with great respect for the series and for Dan Curtis, because you don't get more die-hard fans than myself, Michelle or Tim."

"One of the first conclusions we reached was that we shouldn't be afraid to be funny," concurs Grahame-Smith. "We wanted the movie to have some of that campiness that was in the original series, but didn't want it to go so far it became a parody of itself. We wanted to make sure in addition to humor you had suspense. You had moments of real fright. You had moments of real drama. You had moments of real longing and even tears. We decided as long as the story of the family was strong enough, you had room to be funny and give the audience something to laugh at."

Much of the film's humor derives from Barnabas, the man-out-of-time. An 18th century lothario cursed by a scorned witch, transformed into a vampire, then buried in a coffin for almost 200 years. When he's finally released it's 1972, a time markedly different from the one he left behind: socially, politically, culturally, sexually and aesthetically. "It was a strange transitional period in American history and world history," reflects Grahame-Smith. "Vietnam was still going on. Nixon was running for re-election but Watergate hadn't happened yet, so there was still this optimistic political spirit. But the hippies are dying on the vine and the disco era is looming. So when Barnabas sits down with hippies and they say, 'We're relics, man!' Barnabas can identify with the idea of being a relic and an outsider. Of course, he kills all the hippies. But let's not judge. Man has to eat."

"The thought of this very elegant man of the 1700s, having been cursed and locked away for 200 years, coming back to 1972 — maybe the worst time, aesthetically, in human existence, where people accepted everything from macramé jewelry and resin grapes to lava lamps — sparked a whole series of ideas," says

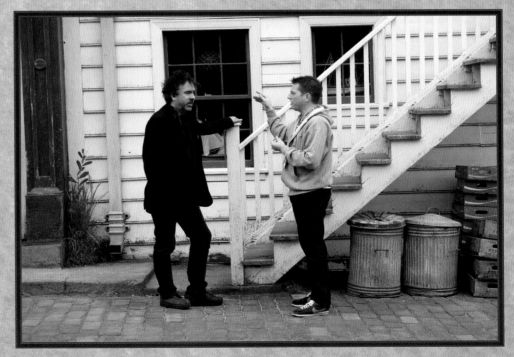

Depp. "We thought, what a great way to incorporate this vampire, being the eyes we never had back then, the eyes that can see the absurdity in those things."

"That was a very uneasy, strange period. It was a time that was strange then and it's strange now," Burton agrees. "I guess you can say that about any era, but that was weird then and it's remained weird to me. Everything was in a slight transitional state at that time too. Music, war, everything was changing and so it just felt like a time that Barnabas, being an out of place person, felt right, like a weird bubble of time. Rather than making it modern day, it was a way for an audience to see things the way Barnabas did. It was more a feeling than an intellectual decision."

Burton endeavors to find a personal connection with his main character on every film, a way to identify with them. "You always try to find those personal things you can latch onto." He was a teenager in 1972 and doesn't remember the time with any fondness. "I was a person feeling very isolated and dislocated from my world. Part of why I liked the show was you feel like a weirdo, you feel like a freak, then you go home and you watch it and somehow you connect with it. I think that's why a lot of kids who liked it were outsider types."

"There's more Tim in this than in a number of his movies," insists Depp. "I mean, walking through the world looking at everything like it's totally bizarre, but for everyone else it's completely normal — that's Tim."

Burton found researching the period for *Dark Shadows* "quite upsetting and alarming. Going back and looking at the fashions and listening to the music and reading magazines from that time made me physically ill. Going back to that time when you're changing from a kid to a teenager and your body is changing. Having that happen in the '70s was particularly unpleasant and strange. I had these flashbacks of lying in bed with pneumonia, with a fever, listening to AM radio all day long."

Inspiration of another kind came from a series of early '70s horror films, among them blaxploitation classic *Scream Blacula Scream*, Hammer's *Dracula A.D. 1972 —* "It's got the rocks, it's got the music," says Burton of the London-set vampire film whose star, Christopher Lee, is a favorite of the director, and has a cameo in *Dark Shadows* — and, in particular, *The Legend Of Hell House*, another British horror movie directed by John Hough and starring Pamela Franklin and Roddy McDowall. "It had such a great tone to it, the sound, and the overall vibe. It's got a seriousness and a spookiness to it that I love. Also I was interested in how close the '70s fashions and Gothic fashions were to being one and the same, because it doesn't sound like they were meant to be, but they were. That I found quite interesting. There's something about hippies and vampires and '70s Gothic horror that feels right."

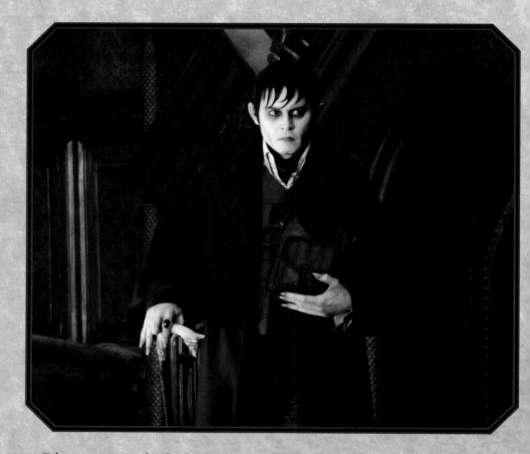

Filming on *Dark Shadows* began on March 18, 2011 at Pinewood Studios, with Burton's creative team including several long-time collaborators, among them Richard D. Zanuck, who has produced every live-action film for Burton since *Planet Of The Apes*; production designer Rick Heinrichs, who was a colleague of Burton's at Disney in the late '70s and later won an Oscar for his work on *Sleepy Hollow*; editor/executive producer Chris Lebenzon; *Alice In Wonderland*'s Oscar-winning costume designer Colleen Atwood; and composer Danny Elfman, who has scored every Burton film bar *Ed Wood* and *Sweeney Todd*. Joining Johnny Depp and Michelle Pfeiffer in front of the camera were an eclectic ensemble of actors, including Helena Bonham Carter, Eva Green, Bella Heathcote, Jackie Earle Haley and Jonny Lee Miller. "Everybody in the movie was, for me, a *Dark Shadows* person, whether they like it or not," says Burton. "Susie Figgis the casting director would come up with these great actors but I'd say, 'That's not a *Dark Shadows* person.' I couldn't put it into words, it was more a feeling — that person is and that person isn't. They could be equally good actors, but there was something about certain people, that they felt more *Dark Shadows*."

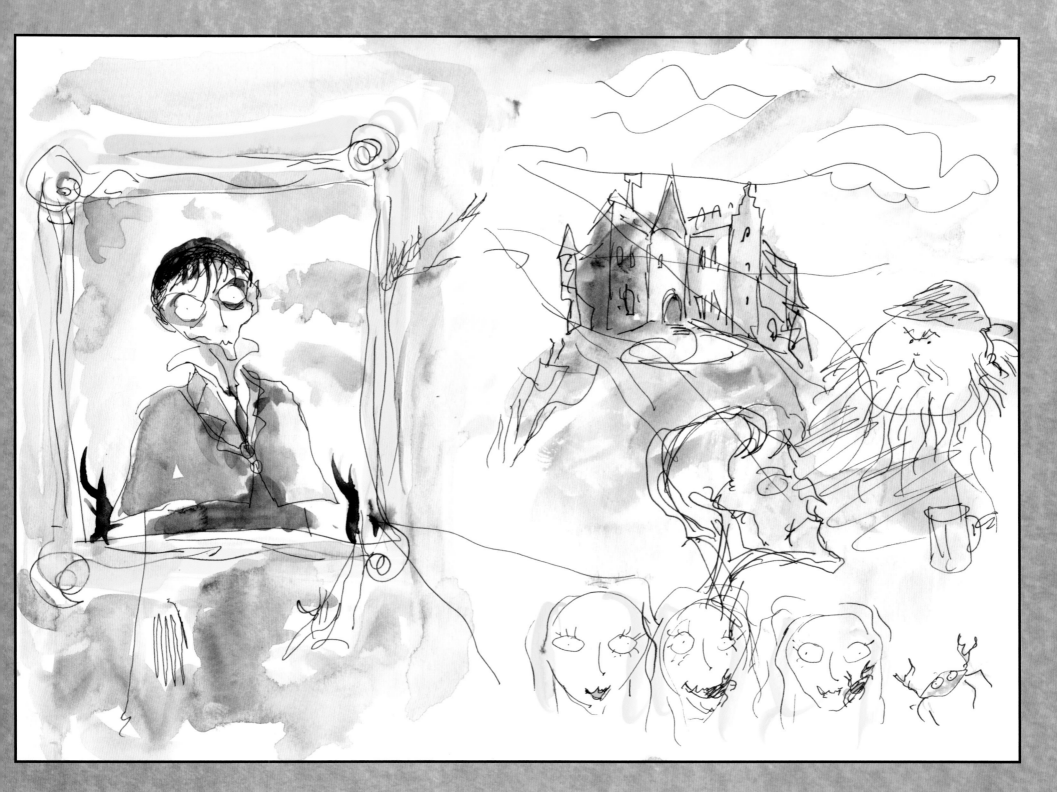

CHAPTER 1

CAST

Just prior to principal photography, Tim Burton got all his main cast together for a photo session in which they would replicate an iconic image of the original TV cast, standing in the lobby of Collinwood Manor. "We didn't have any rehearsals, because we couldn't get the actors all at the same time," he reveals. "So we had everyone come in, get into costume and we recreated that photo. It was like a rehearsal in a way. All the actors could see each other and get a vibe off one another. In about 30 seconds, people found their character, which was really great."

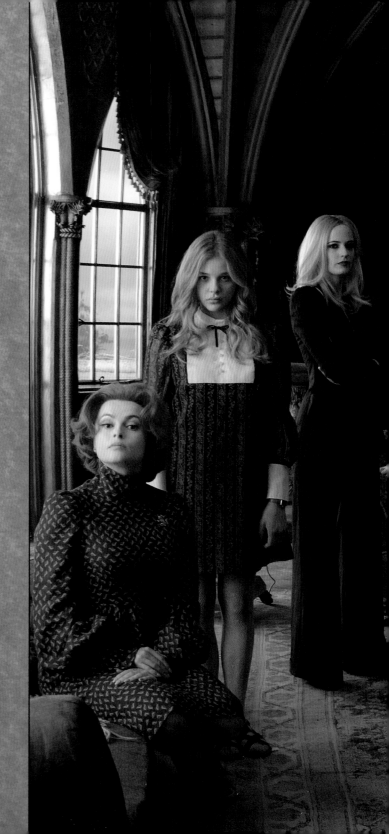

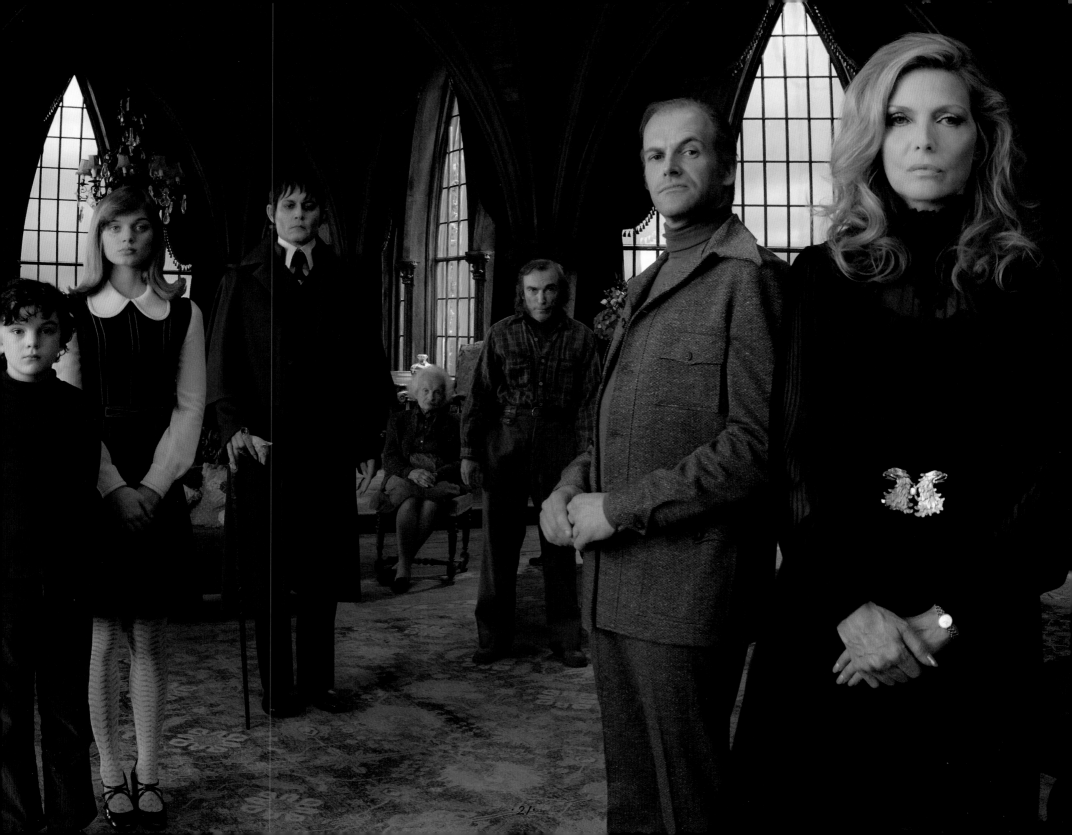

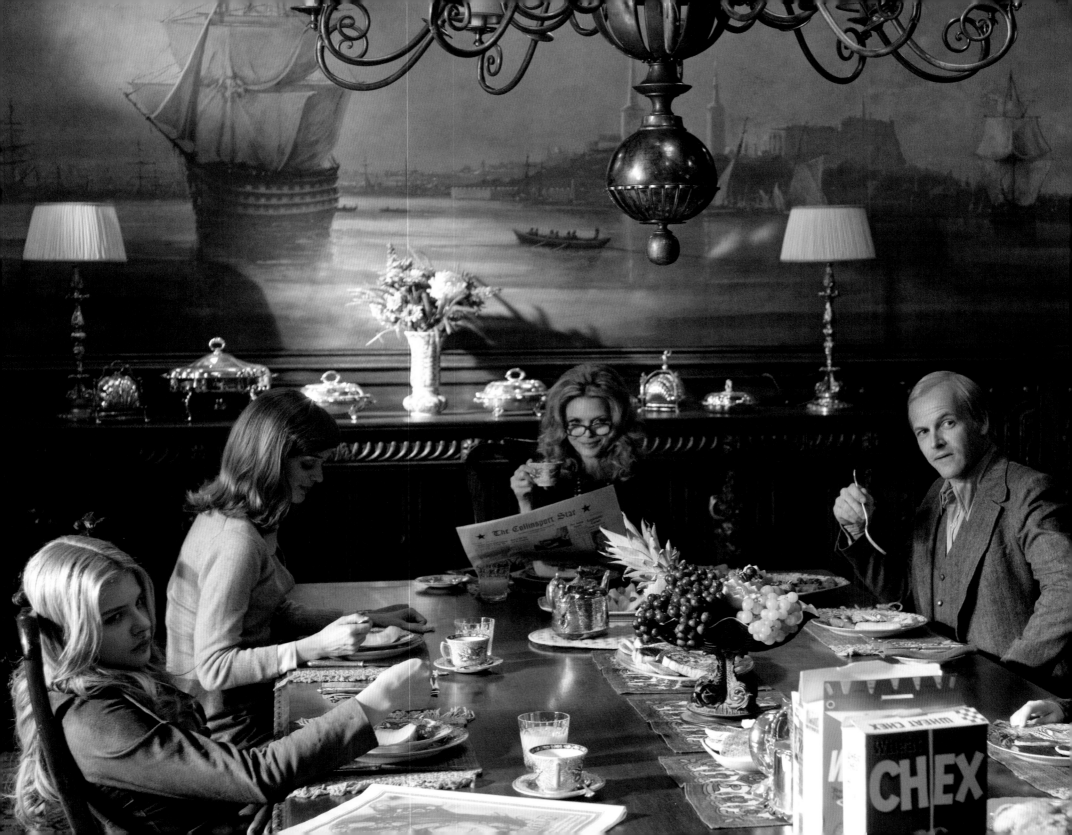

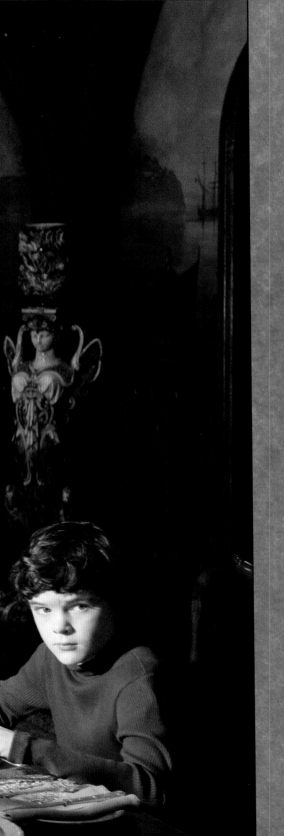

![Cast photo in front of Collins Canning Co. sign]

"The Collins family is odd," says Michelle Pfeiffer who plays its matriarch, Elizabeth Collins Stoddard. "It's an understatement to say they're that family the neighborhood talks about — the weird family. But they have no idea just how weird we are. In fact, I don't think any of us realize just how weird we are. Keeping up appearances is very important to my character and she's very proud and very protective of the family name."

JOHNNY DEPP as
Barnabas Collins

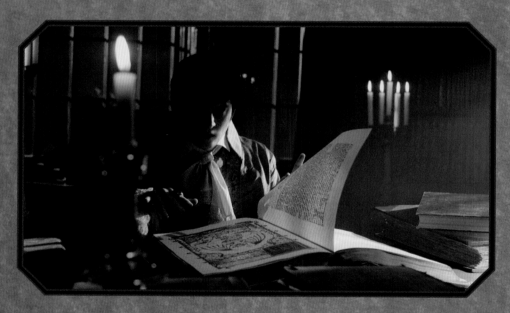

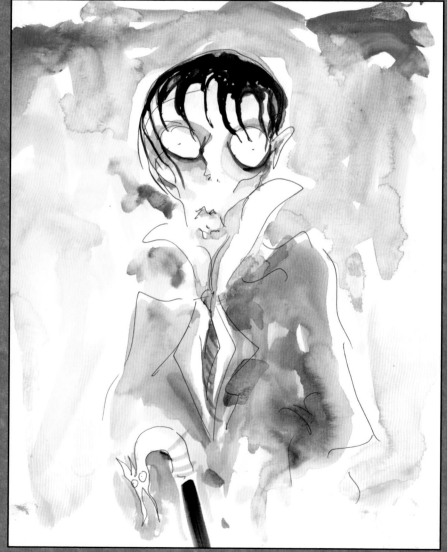

"Everywhere I searched character wise, everywhere I looked character wise, every angle I tried outside of what Jonathan Frid had established very well on the series, I kept coming back to Jonathan Frid," reflects Johnny Depp. "He really did something beautiful with that character. So my Barnabas is based on Jonathan Frid's with maybe a few other ingredients thrown in, and slightly more flowery language, a little bit more of a vocal style in terms of enunciation, almost like Richard Burton in the way he wrapped himself around the words. There's an amazing recording of Richard Burton reading Dylan Thomas' *Under Milk Wood*, which I would often use to fall asleep to, because there was such elegance in his voice, and such power, so I borrowed that for this. A bit of John Gielgud as well. Gielgud doing Shakespeare."

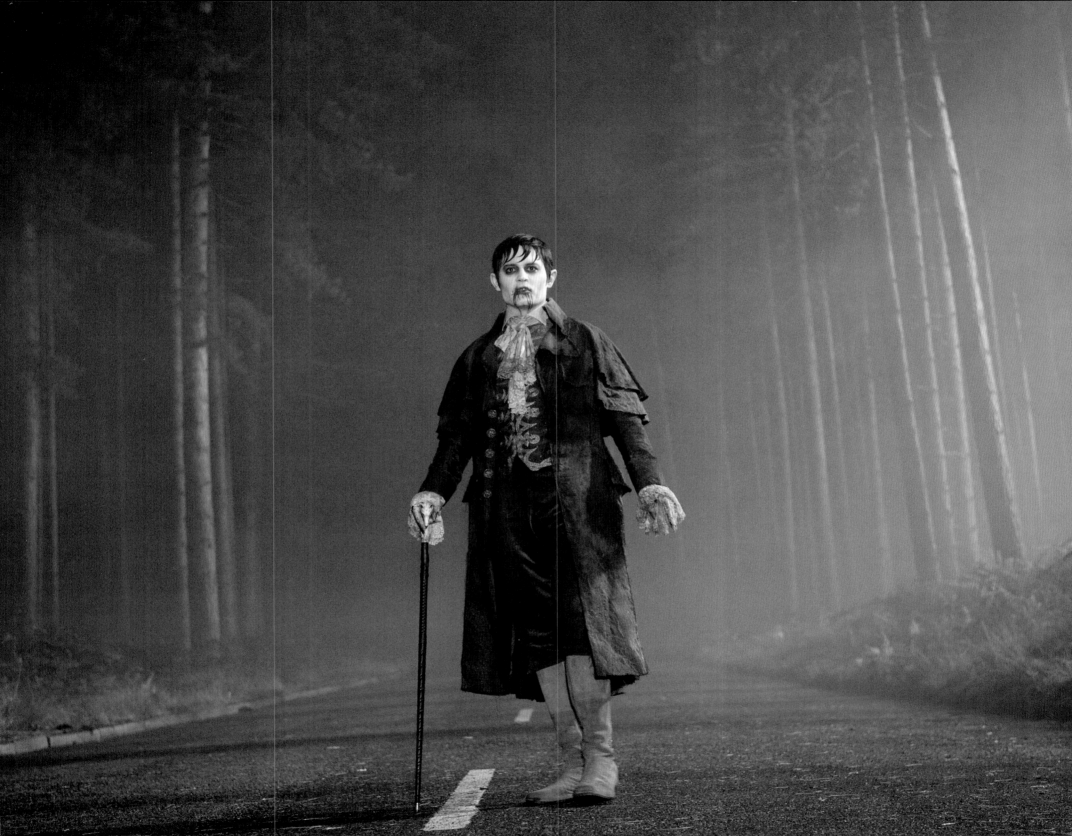

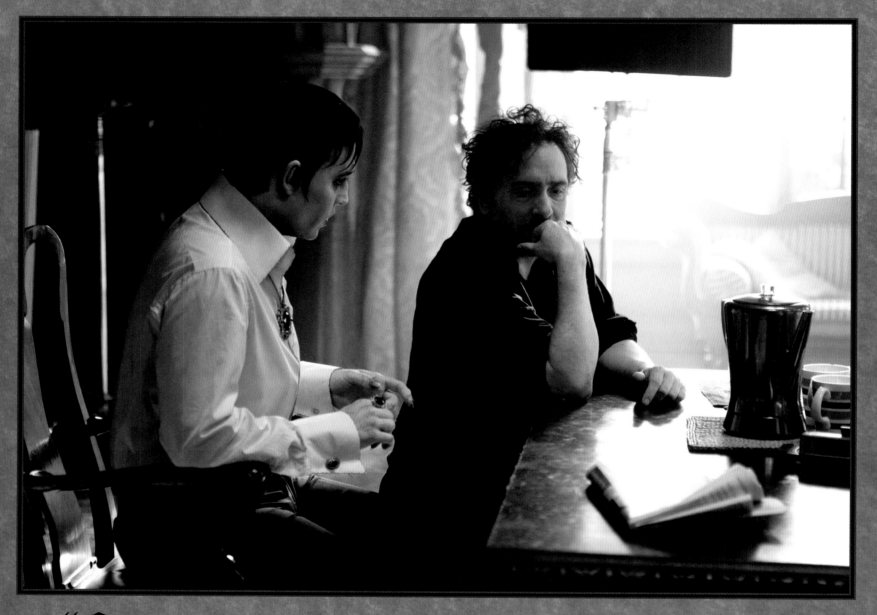

"From the first second Tim and I agreed what Jonathan Frid had established all those years ago, we had to respect that and use that as our basis for Barnabas," reveals Johnny Depp. "We talked about different looks and different hairstyles and ended up going back to what Barnabas was in the series, paying tribute to that look to some degree," says Burton. "There was something about that weird hairstyle and voice and the kind of Shakespearean, romantic dialogue that made that character unique. Again, that was part of the reasons for wanting to do it, to try to capture that reluctant vampire."

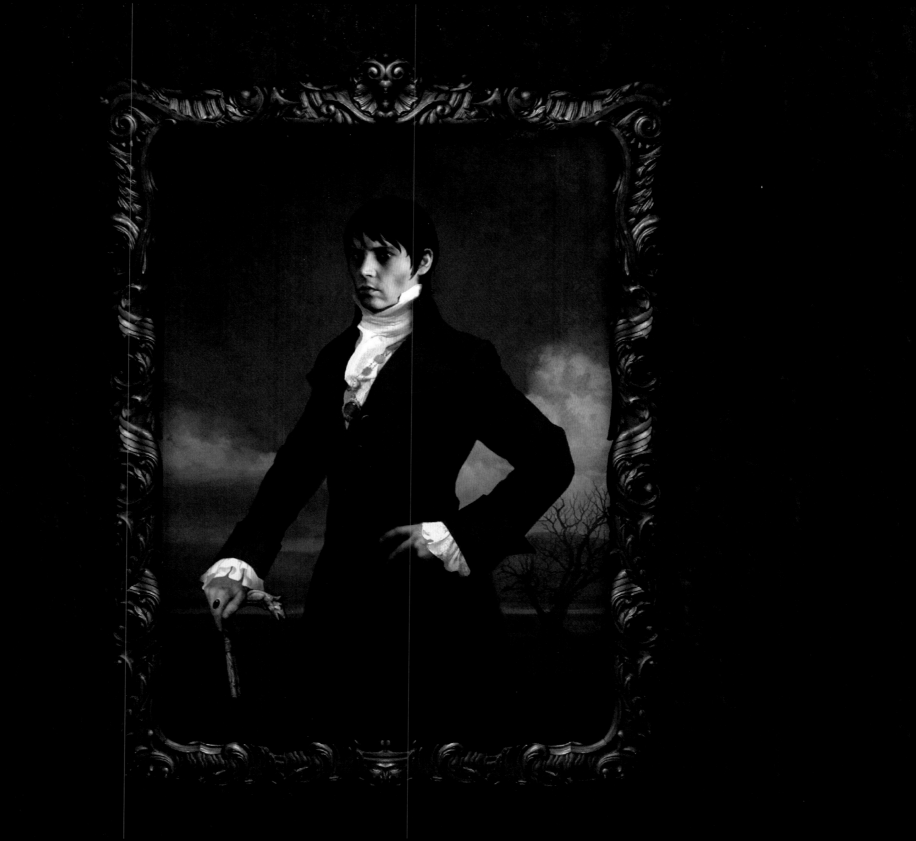

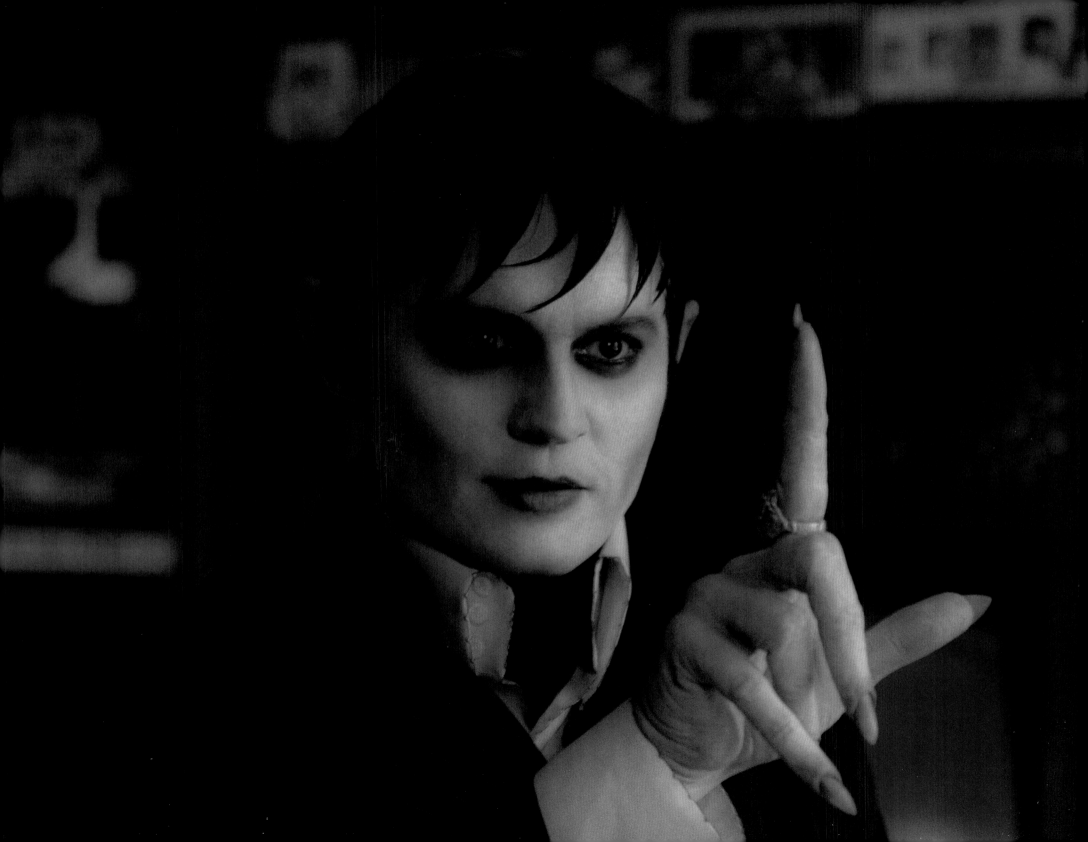

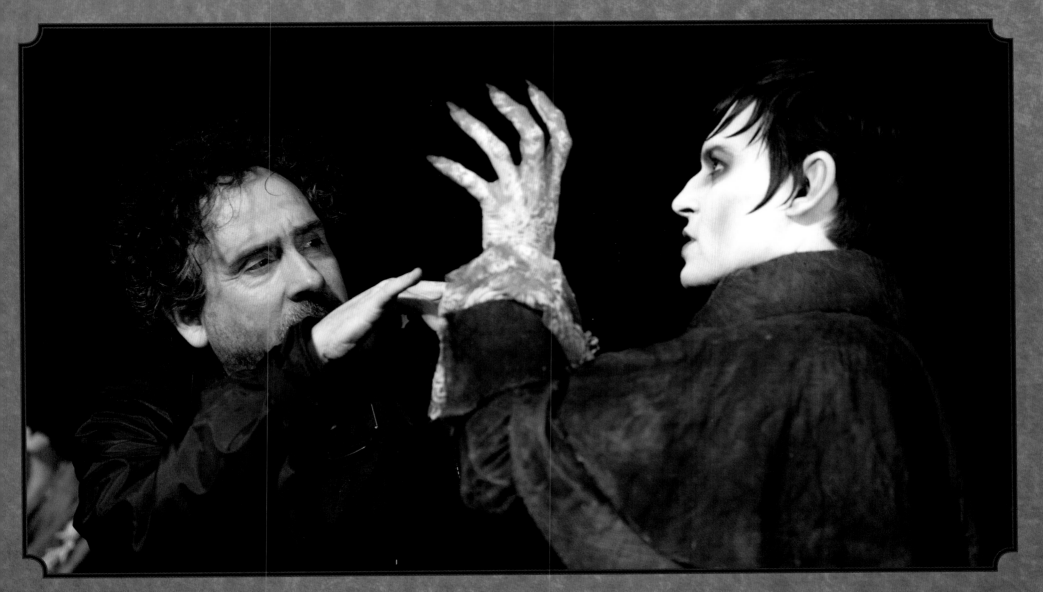

Makeup artist Joel Harlow was responsible for physically transforming Depp into Barnabas, working closely with the actor and Burton to create the character's distinct look. "We went through nine different makeup tests. Nine different tests of this cheek, that nose, these ears, these brows," recalls Harlow. "We had a chin piece at one point, different wigs. Johnny's very enthusiastic when it comes to testing. He was an advocate for trying as many different versions as possible, just to see what the pieces would look like." Says Depp, "Tim felt very strongly a vampire should look like a vampire. What we were all going for was a classic monster, the classic monster look, like something you would have seen on the cover of *Famous Monsters Of Filmland*, and that's what we got. We tried different things, initially, thinking we would mess around with the idea of how emaciated he might have been, and how his death would have affected his pallor. So we went through a few tests to try to get it right, because it had to be perfect."

During production both Michelle Pfeiffer and Johnny Depp would rewatch old episodes of the TV show. "I certainly got a lot out of it, in terms of the character and in terms of tone," says Depp. "Sometimes I'd fall asleep watching the episodes, especially with Barnabas, just to engrain that, to instil that into my brain for the next morning's shoot." Pfeiffer would watch DVDs in her trailer or while in the makeup chair. "It was the most fun I've ever had getting ready for a movie," she says. "There were questions I had about my character and something would come up in the show that would answer them. We really became obsessed with watching the show and would send clips of our favorite footage of the day to the set."

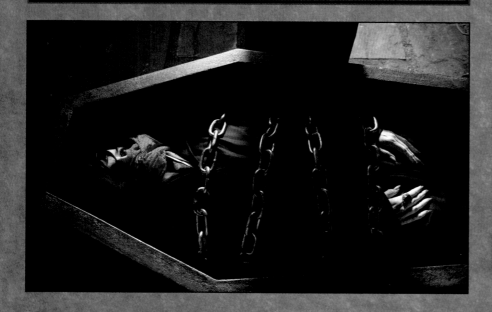

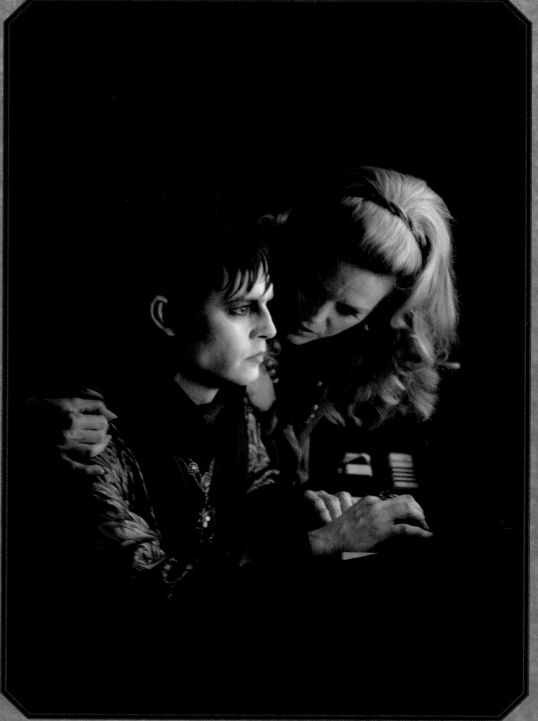

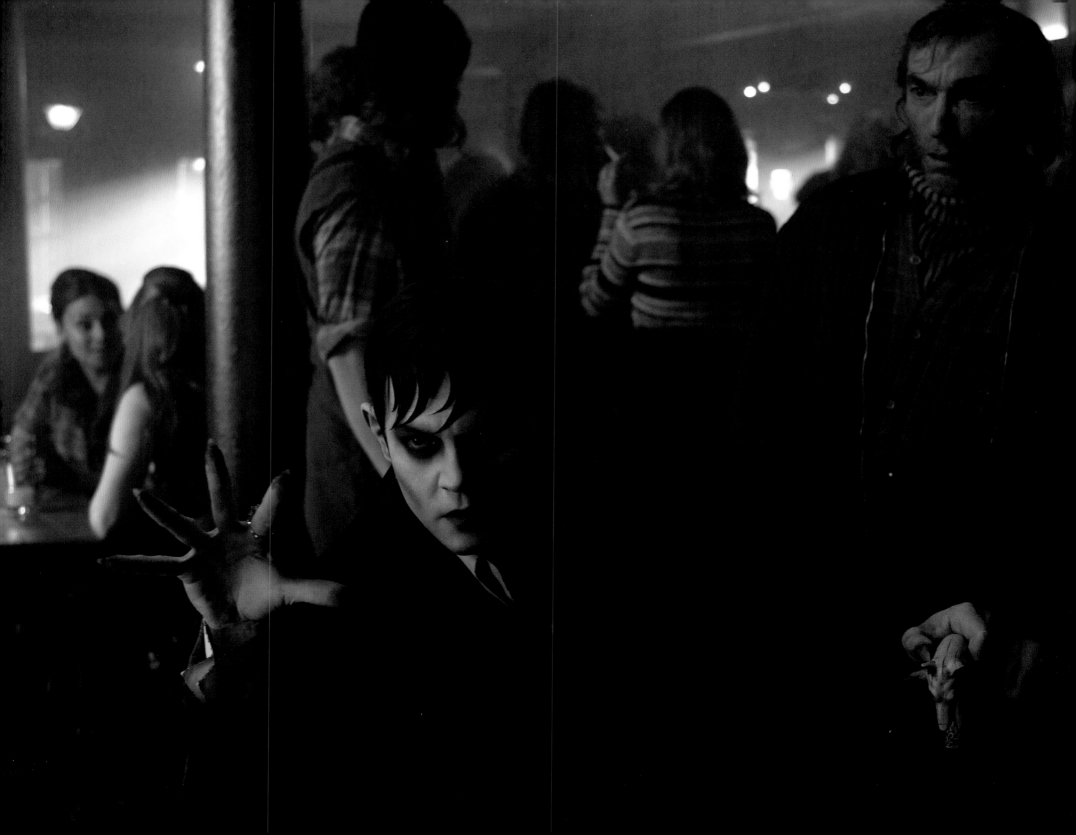

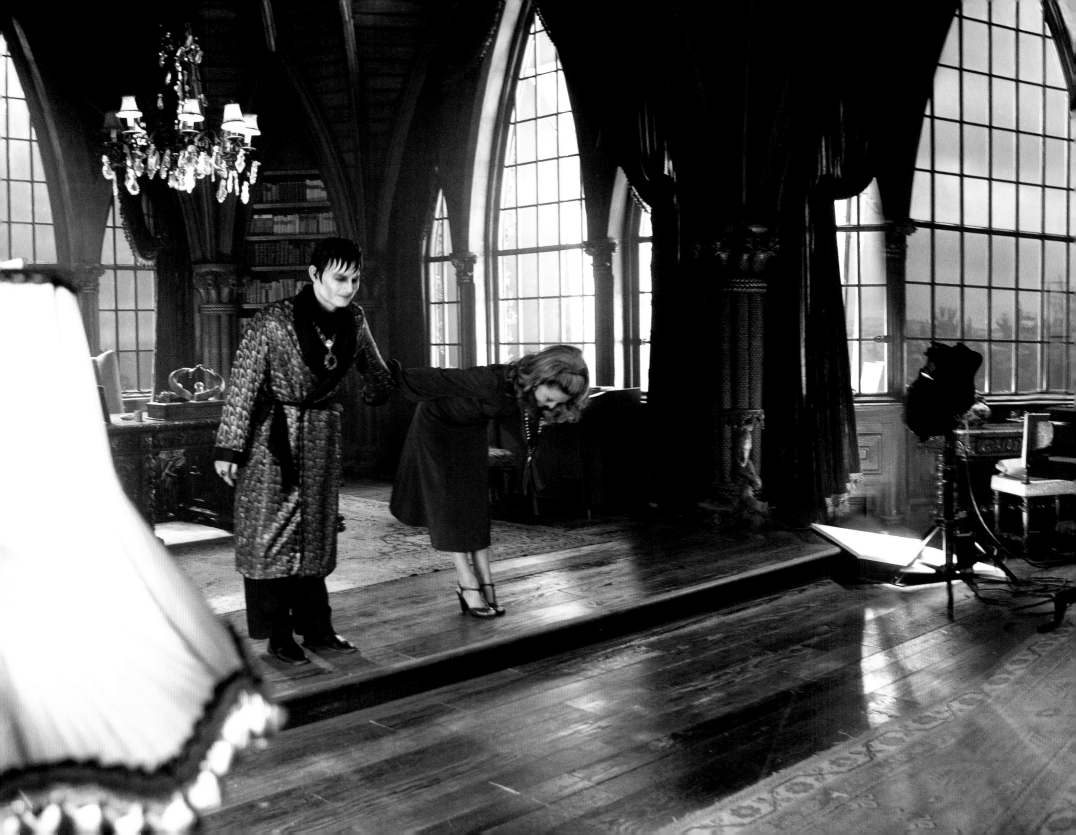

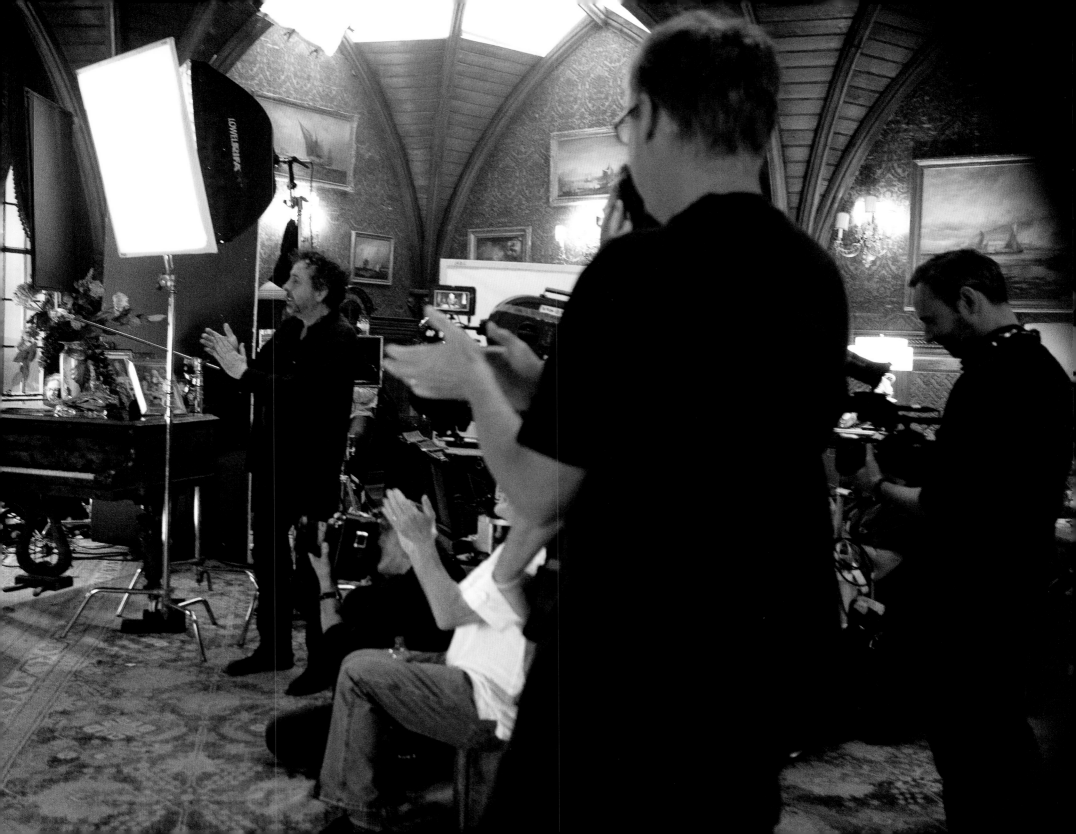

MICHELLE PFEIFFER as
Elizabeth Collins Stoddard

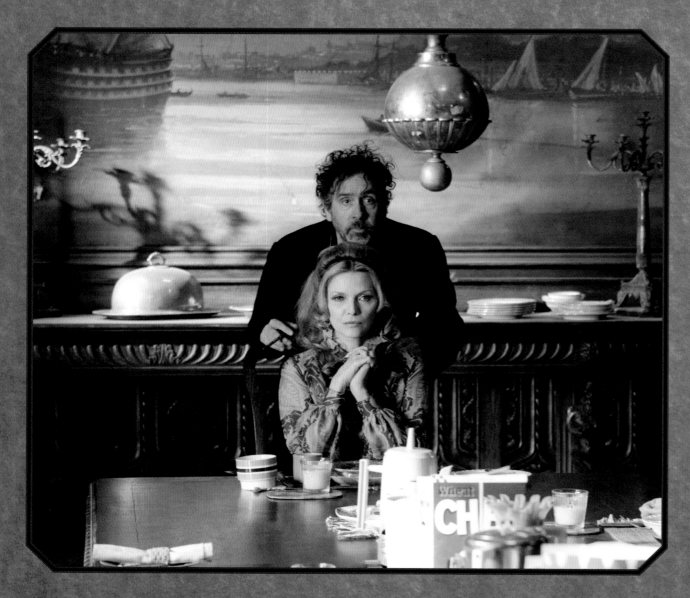

When Pfeiffer read Burton was making *Dark Shadows*, she called him up, asking for a role. "I got so excited, I did something I never do," she recalls. "I basically grovelled for a part in the movie. There was no script at that point — Tim and Johnny were attached — and I said, 'I don't know if there's anything remotely right for me in this, but I want you to know I'm a huge fan of this show.' I felt so uncomfortable but I knew I would kick myself if I didn't because I know how these things are, people are attached before you even know about it, so I thought I really have to do this." The pair had last worked together on *Batman Returns* in 1992. "Her Catwoman was one of my favorite performances of anybody I've worked with," Burton notes. "She was very impressive in it, letting a live bird come out of her mouth, cracking a whip with high heels on."

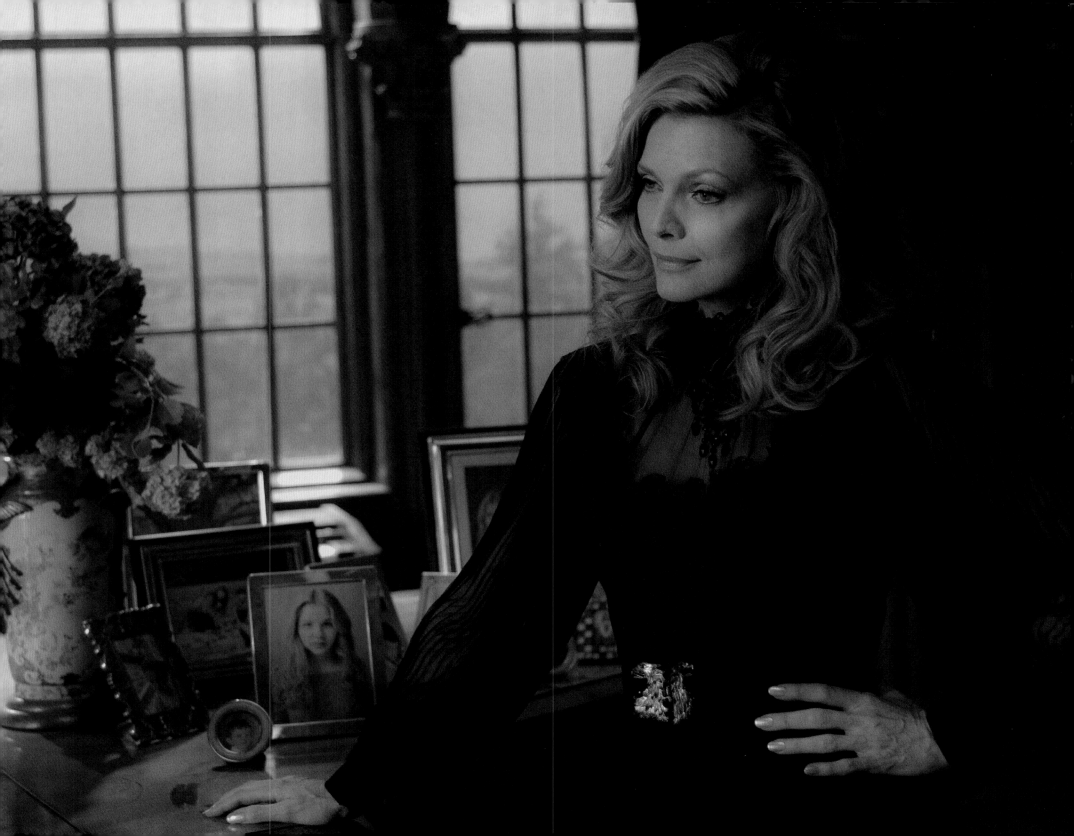

"She's the head of this wealthy family that's hit hard times," says Burton of Pfeiffer's Elizabeth. "And like with a lot of families, it's a very hermetically-sealed world. They don't seem to get out much. They're kind of in their own world, so to speak. And even though there's a supernatural history to the family, she's probably the most grounded of them. But she's got her eccentricities. She likes to make her dramatic entrances on the staircase. It's probably her favorite place in the house."

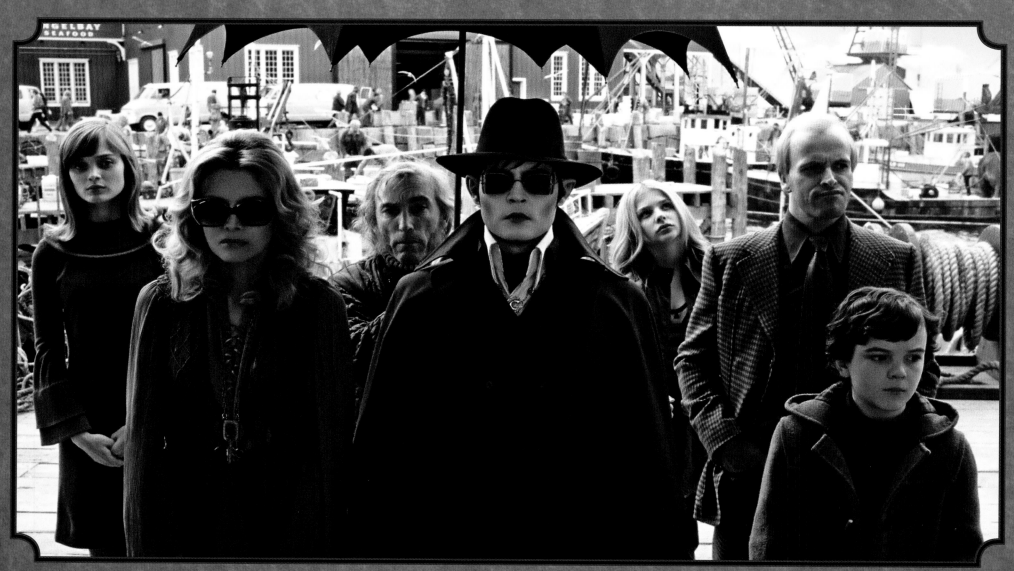

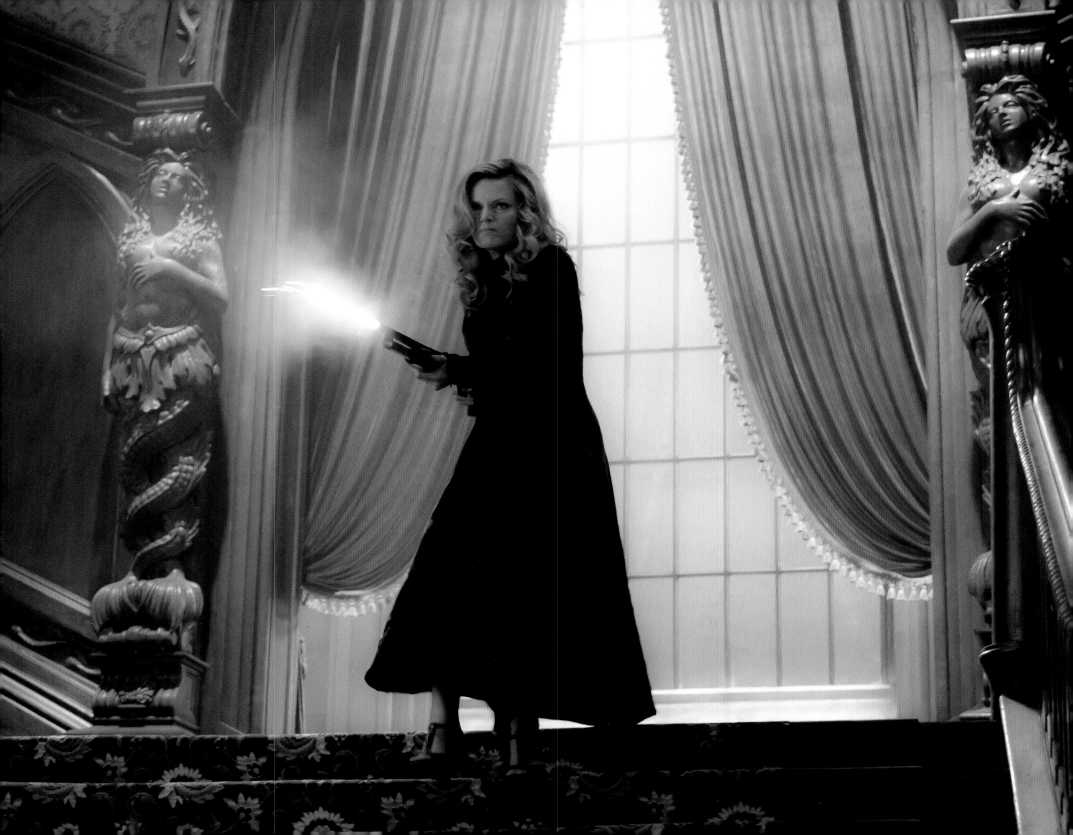

HELENA BONHAM CARTER as
Dr. Julia Hoffman

"**W**hen I look at the original series there's something about the actress who played [Dr. Hoffman] that reminds me of Helena," says Burton. "Helena is a bit younger than that, but a certain kind of look that I felt was strangely similar. She's good. She's always good. I don't know how flattered she was to be offered the role of an aging, alcoholic psychiatrist, but somebody's got to do it, right? The only thing I was worried about... I see her prepare for roles and so I was a bit worried about living with an alcoholic, for several months, but she didn't take it that far this time. Luckily."

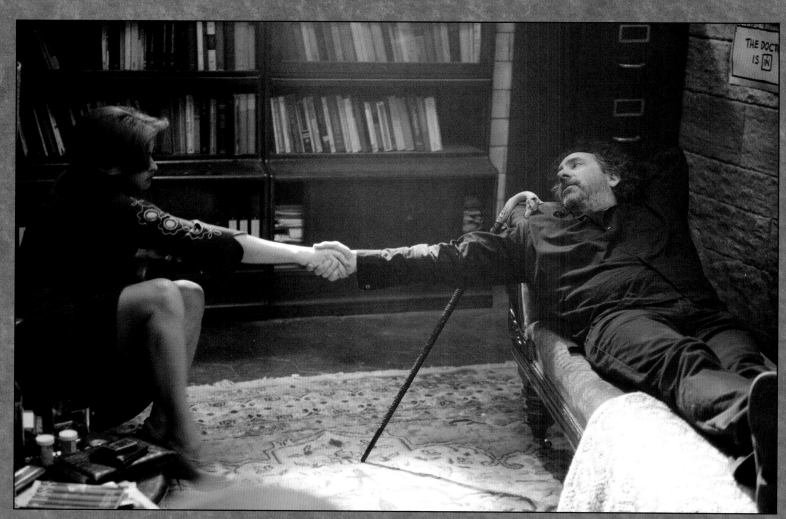

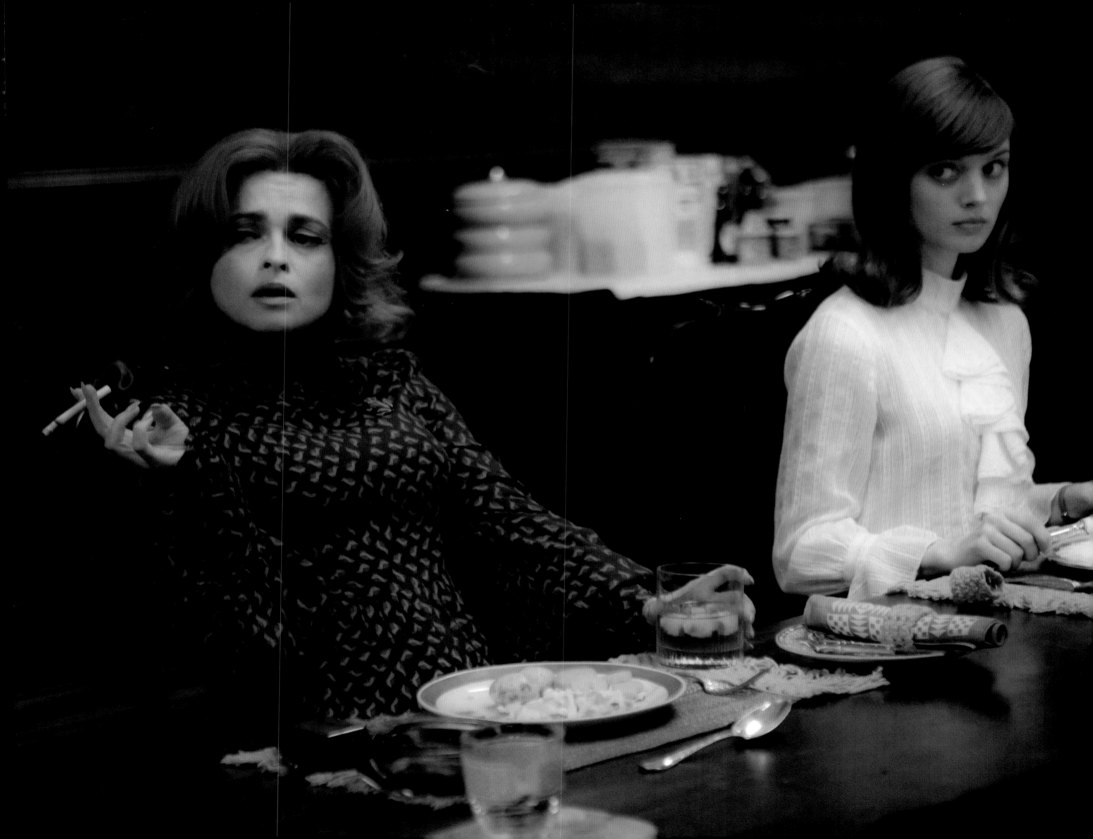

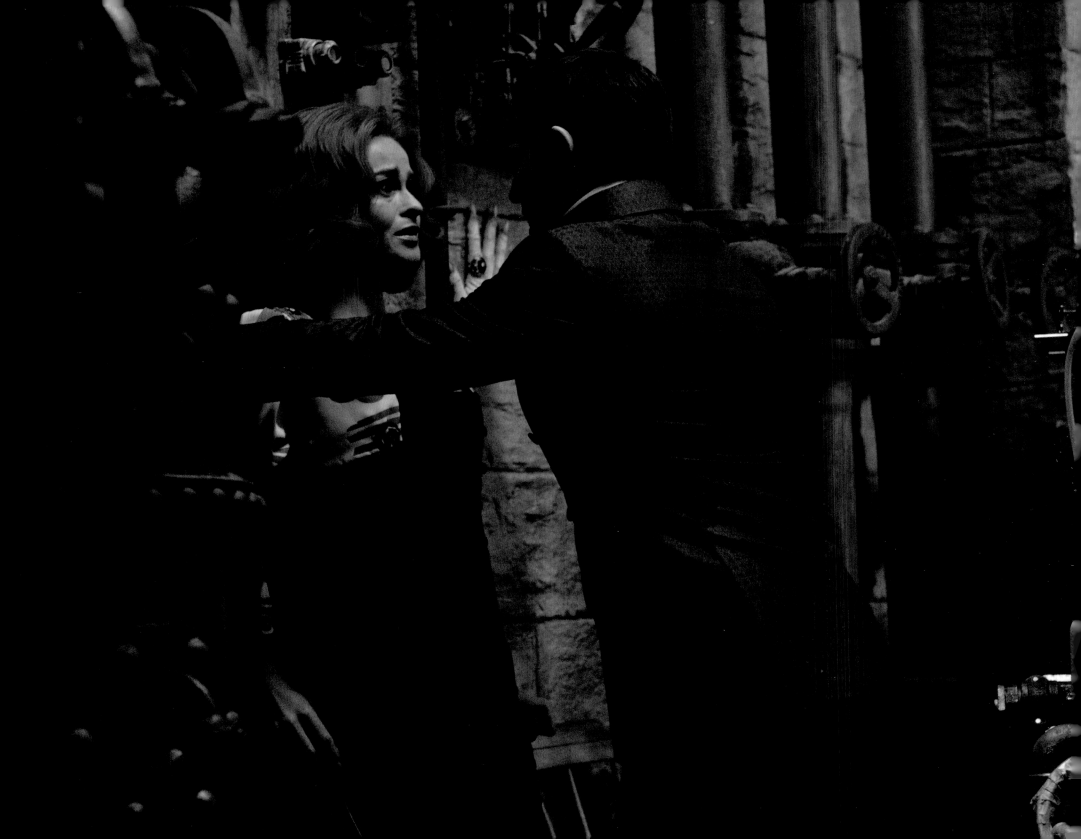

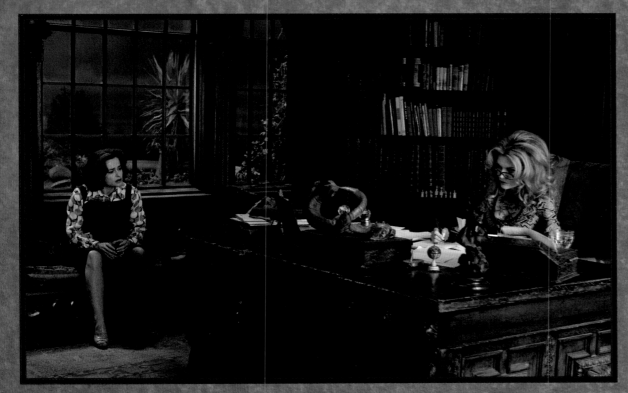

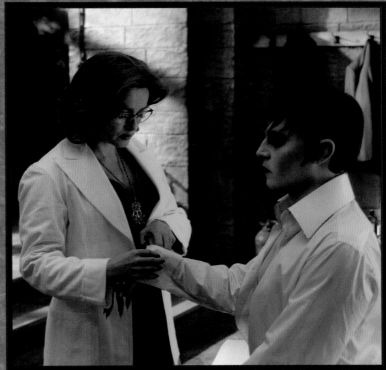

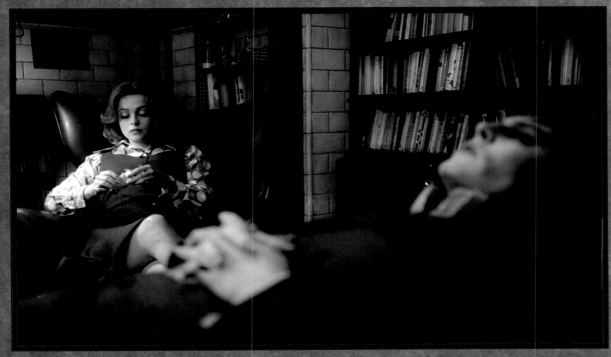

Hired to treat David, the youngest member of the Collins family, following the untimely death of his mother, psychiatrist Dr. Julia Hoffman was only supposed to stay a month but has since taken up permanent residence in the manor, where she has an unlimited supply of alcohol. "She may have just reached the point where she's overstayed her welcome," says Bonham Carter. "Then, into this household, comes this really curious character, Barnabas, this so-called distant relation. Dr. Hoffman prides herself on seeing through people. She's instantly suspicious, quite rightly, that he's not who he says he is. Desperate to remain young, she sees in Barnabas a means to that end."

EVA GREEN AS
Angelique Bouchard

A former servant girl and erstwhile lover of Barnabas, Angelique knows how to hold a grudge. When Barnabas dumps her for Josette, she kills his latest paramour, transforms him into a vampire, then locks him in a coffin for almost 200 years. "She's quite cuckoo," says Green. "She's madly in love with Barnabas. But he breaks her heart. Everything is magnified with her — her pain, her desire, her vengeance. It's such an outrageous character, but I don't see her as necessarily evil. And when Barnabas re-emerges, it's overwhelming for Angelique. She's at the height of her power and yet she's very vulnerable because Barnabas is her weak point. She's convinced he loves her as much as she loves him, but won't admit it. She wants to own him, to possess every bit of him." Says Burton, "She felt spurned by Barnabas and never let it go. We've all had relationships like that, where it's hard to let go, and she does that in the extreme."

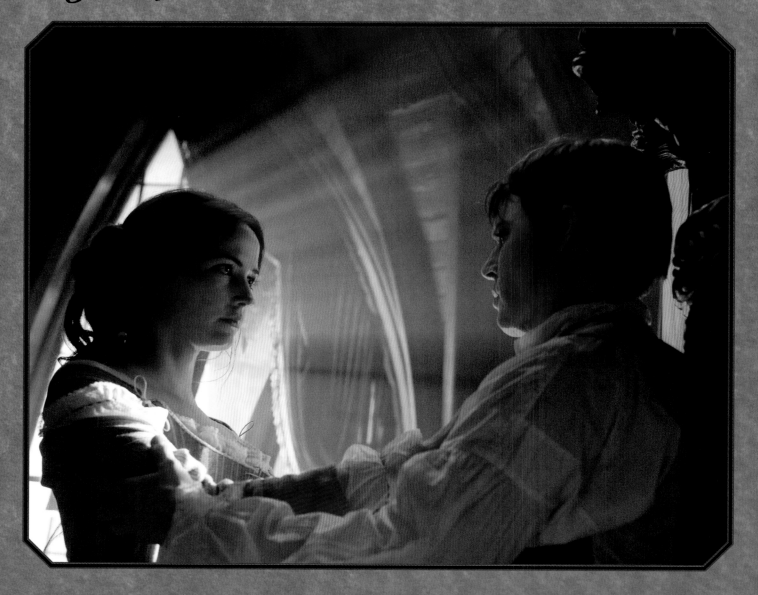

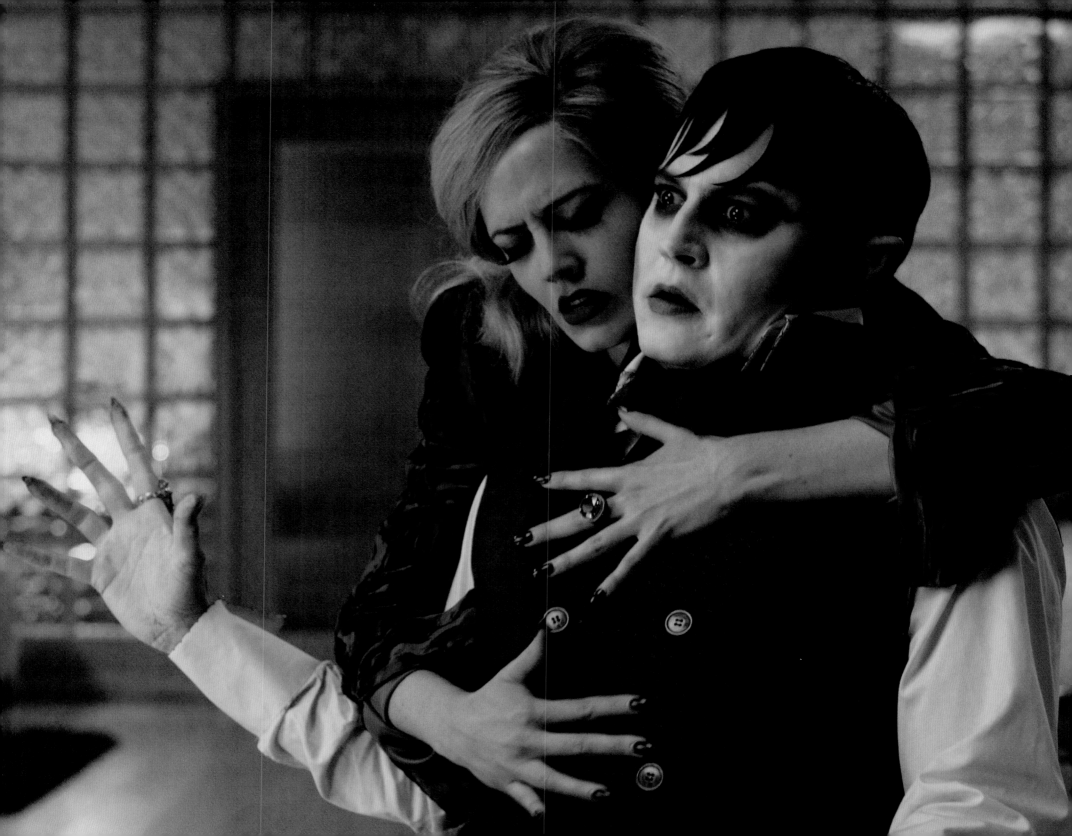

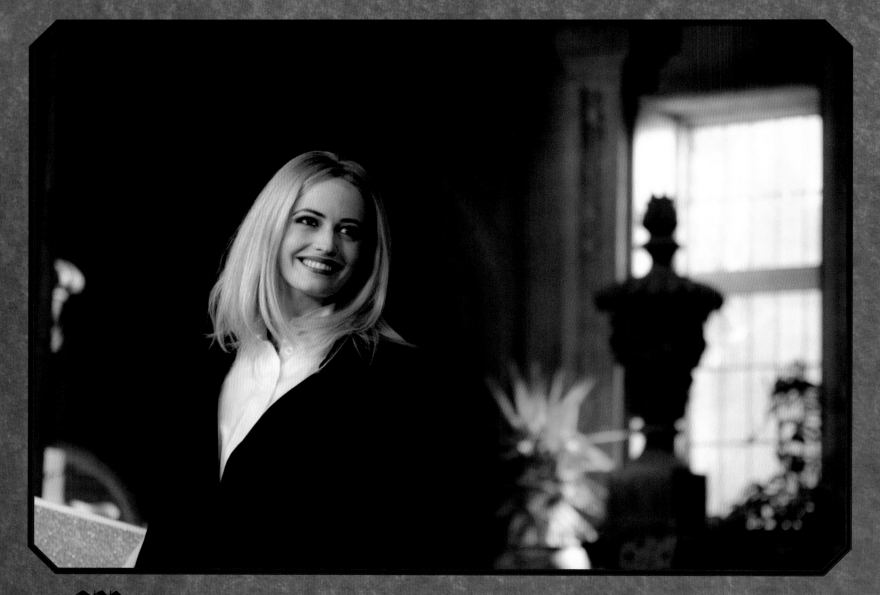

With Barnabas locked away, Angelique transforms herself from dark-haired servant to blonde, powerful businesswoman — CEO of Angel Bay Cannery. "She's adored by everybody. She's like the queen. Tim wanted her to look like the American dream. Everything about her is perfect. Too perfect. Perfect makeup, red lips, platinum hair. She's very glamorous yet sophisticated," says Green. "She rules with an iron fist and a velvet glove," explains screenwriter Seth Grahame-Smith. "On the surface she's a society lady, having tea with the other ladies of the town, and she's the most adored, loved figure in all of Collinsport. But underneath she's still the iron-fisted witch and rules through fear and intimidation, and sometimes murder. She's not afraid to do what it takes to run her business."

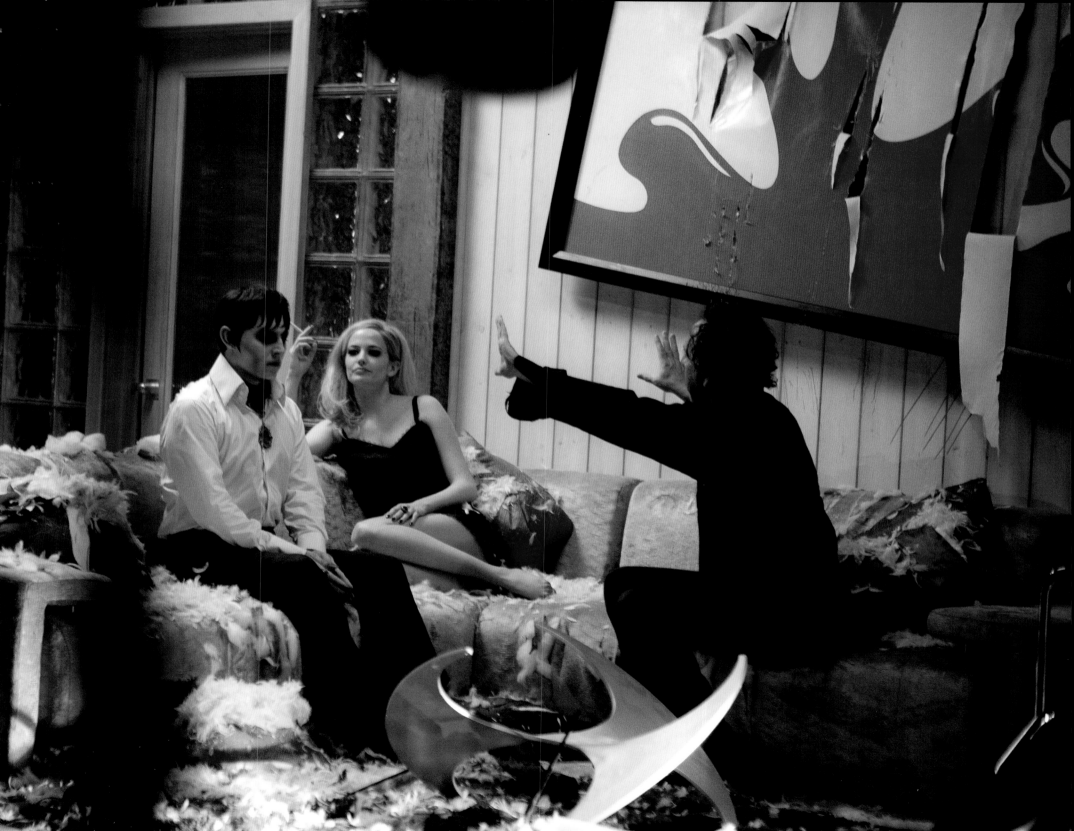

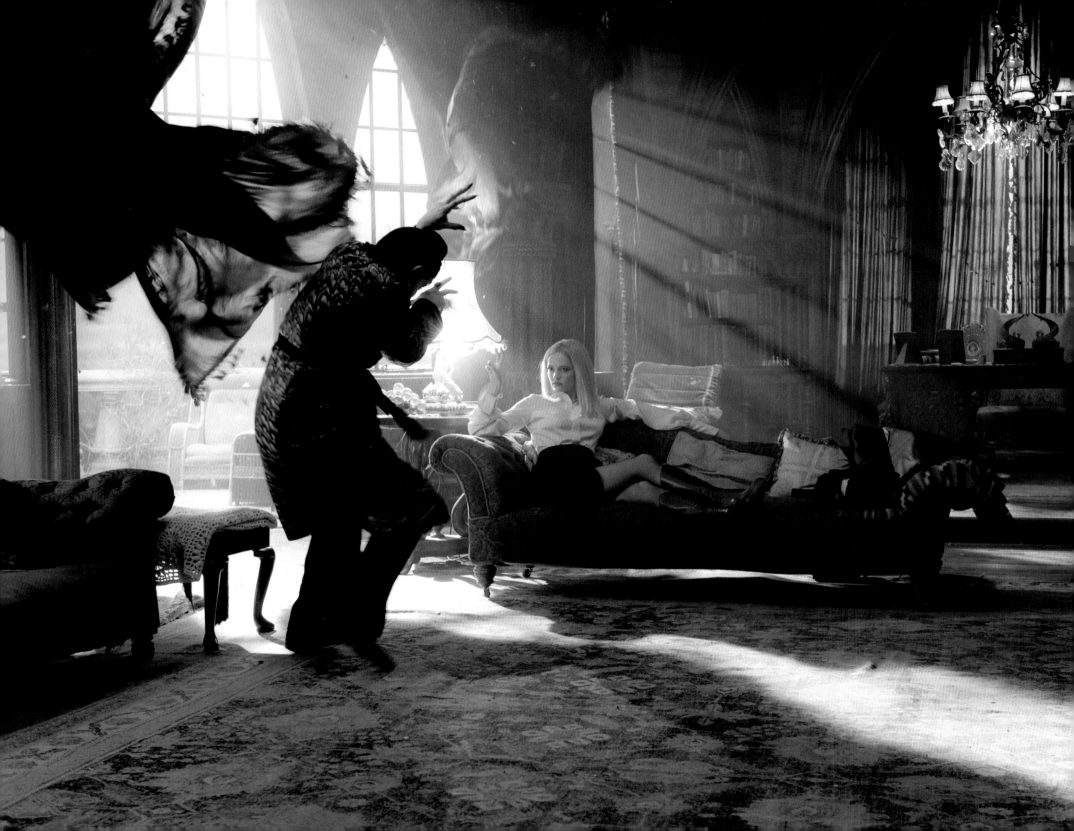

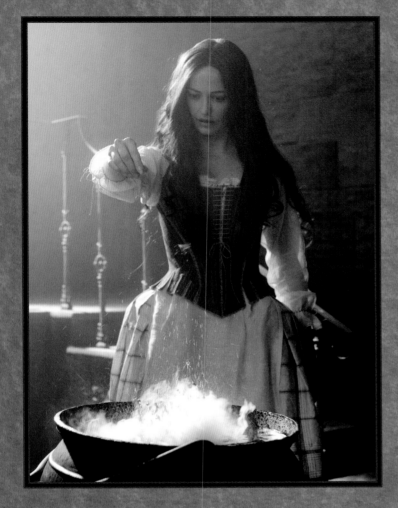

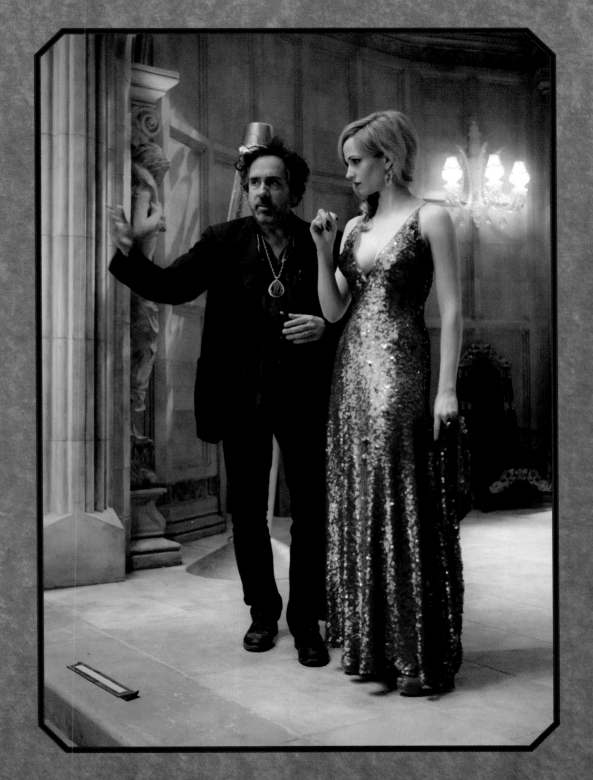

"**A**ngelique is a pretty powerful witch. She's got a lot of tricks in her bag, and, as a witch, she's a very successful one," says Burton. "I think Eva possibly is a witch. She probably doesn't want anybody to know that, but she was the first person that came to my mind for the role and I was so happy because she brought so much to it. She had great ideas, was real fun to work with and surprised me every day." Adds Depp, "That was one of the things Tim said to me early on, that [Eva], somehow, is a witch, not saying that in some horrible way, but she has this quality that is f**king supernatural. It's like she hovers off the ground a little bit."

CHLOË GRACE MORETZ AS
Carolyn Stoddard

"**M**y character is super-duper '70s," says Moretz. "She's a very eccentric child. Her relationship with her mom is weird. Deep down she loves her. But she has such a tortured secret she lets it overcome her. She wants to live in New York. She wants to be a true hippie and be who she wants to be." Since Carolyn's "secret" is that she's a werewolf, Moretz decided her character should slink around, and act a little animal-like even when she's human. "I looked at the way wolves move, and foxes. I looked at a lot of cats and foxes because we wanted to make it a very dainty werewolf, because not many women are werewolves. So I did these weird and dainty but scary head movements. Also sniffing people and acting like a freak. I did this snarl, too, which was kind of fun."

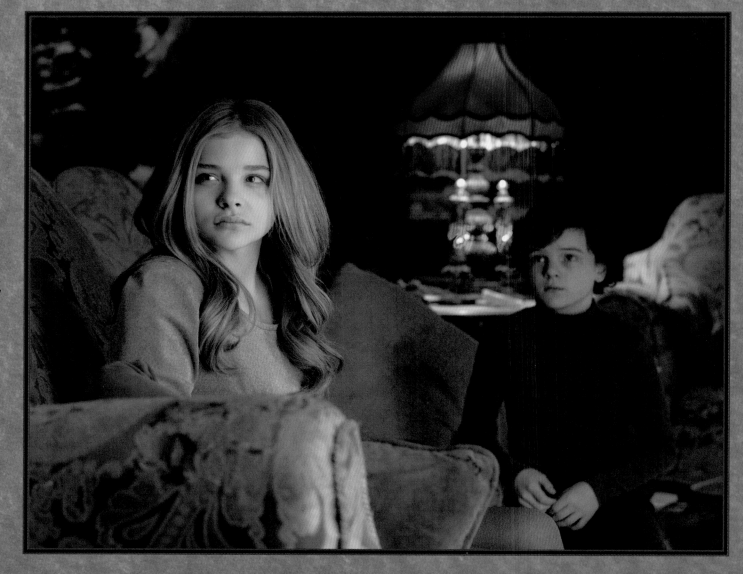

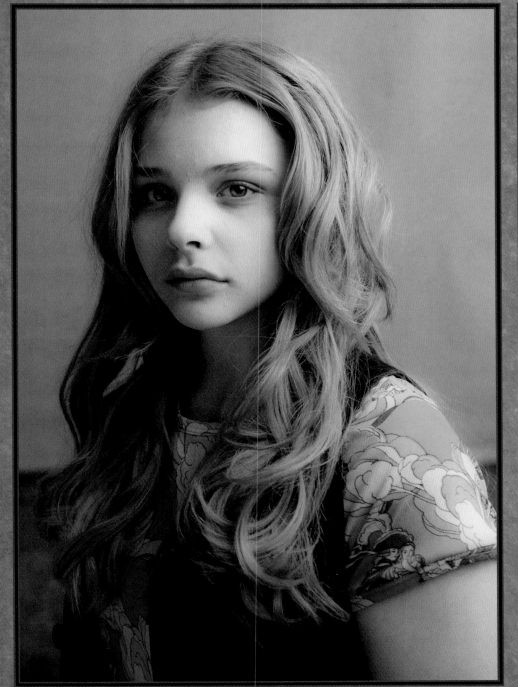
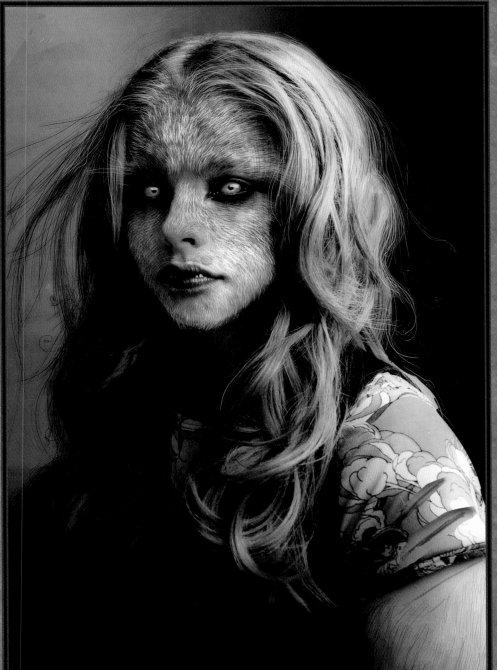

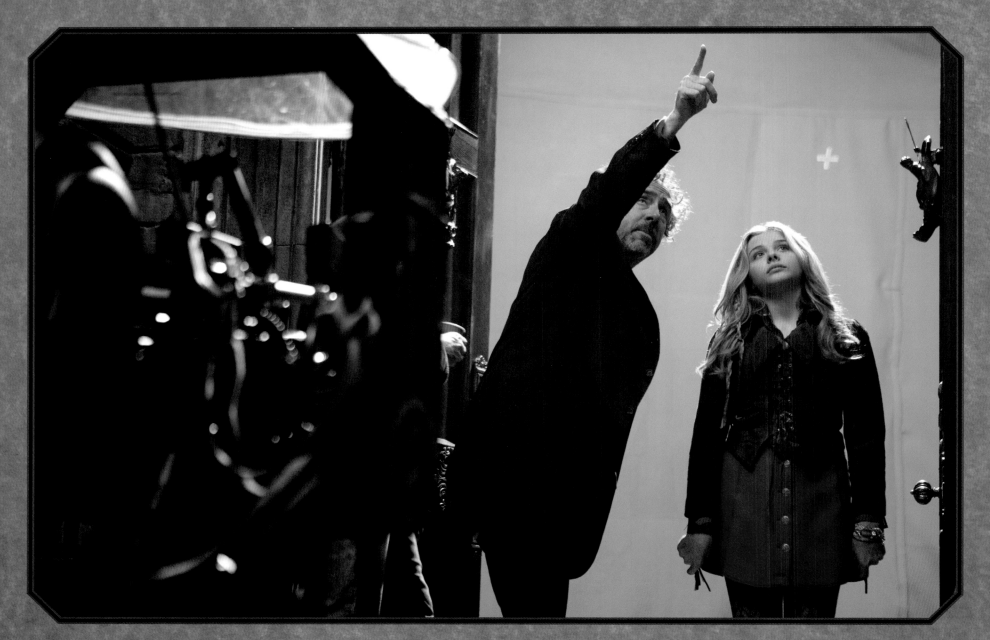

"Chloë's startlingly self-possessed," says Helena Bonham Carter. "Tim always has such a great eye for casting. And he really found a mini-Michelle. They could be mother and daughter. She's adorable and great." Declares Burton, "She tapped into that troubled teenager thing. Anybody who's been a troubled youth, like myself, you're looking for those things that speak reality and she latched onto that internal anger and feeling like you're alone and isolated, that weird transitory time when you're changing from a kid to something else."

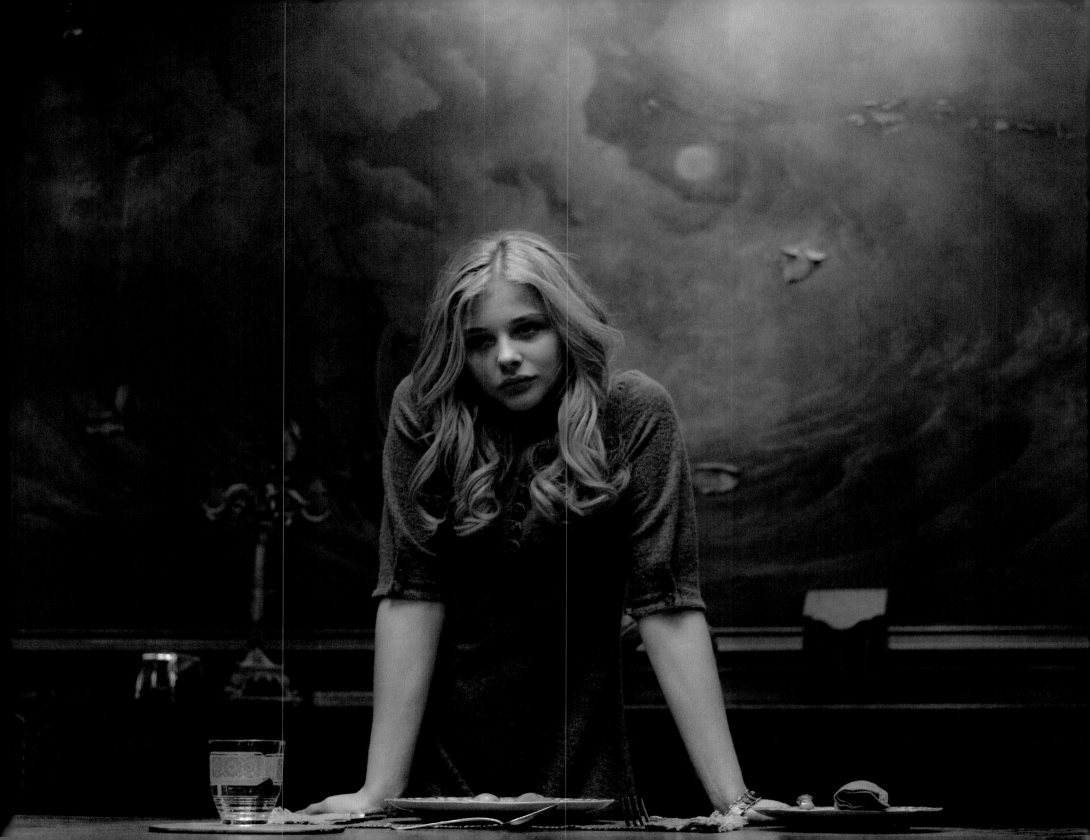

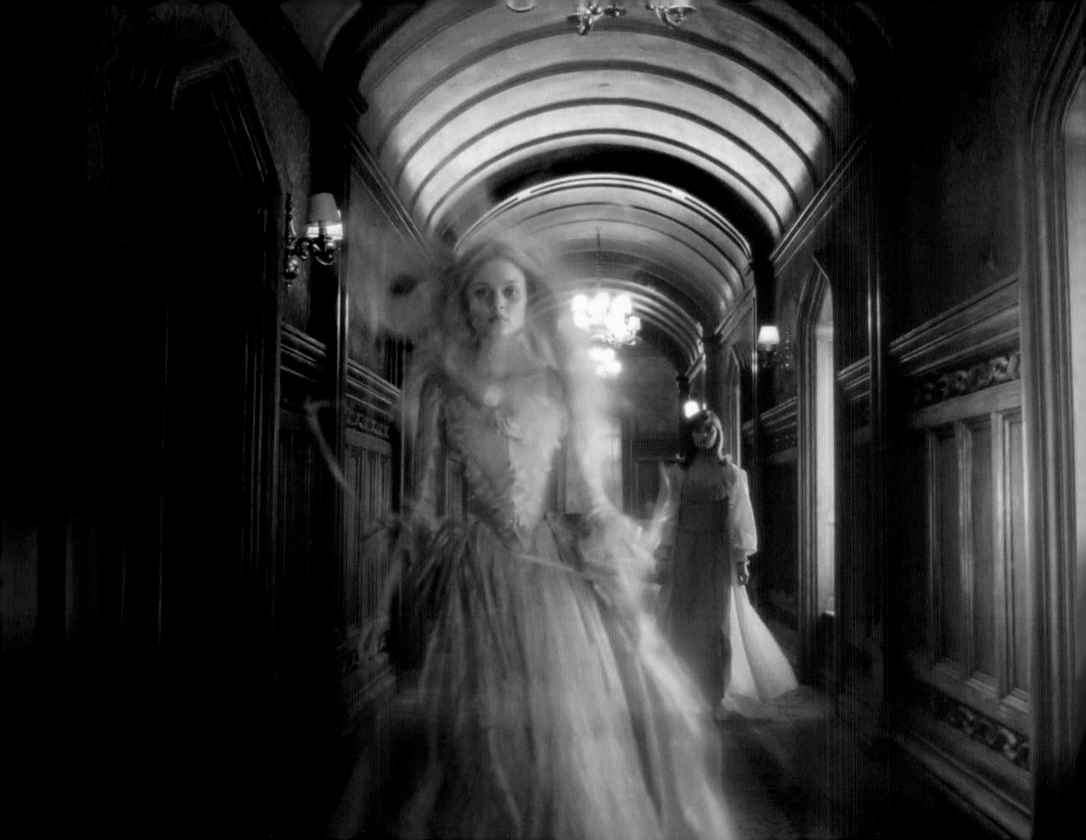

BELLA HEATHCOTE AS
Victoria Winters & Josette DuPres

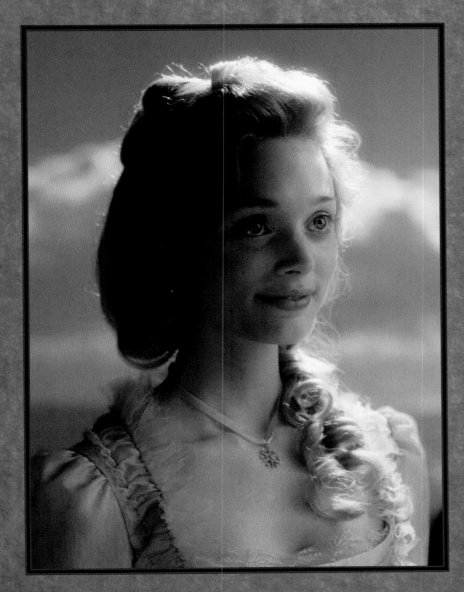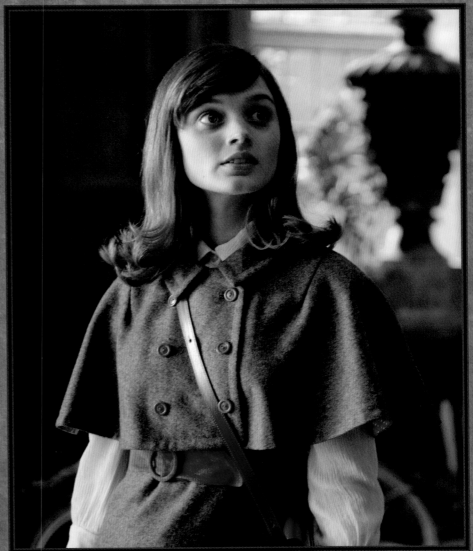

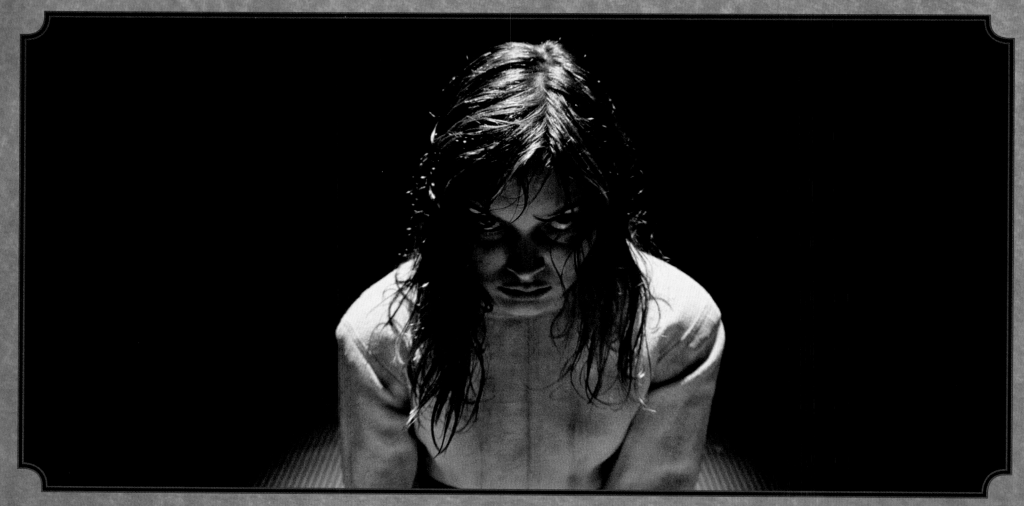

When Victoria Winters arrives in Collinsport for the job of Collins family governess, we sense she's fleeing from something in her past. "She is definitely carrying a lot of baggage she's trying to hide," says Bella Heathcote, who was cast in the dual roles of Barnabas's 18th century lover Josette and the 20th century objection of his affections. "She's quite protective of herself and isn't as ready to give her heart as willingly as we see Josette do. She's far more closed off in all aspects of her life, and we learn she has reason to be." Heathcote hadn't seen any of the TV show before being cast. "I watched some just to get a general idea who the characters all were," notes the young Australian. "The opening of each episode, with the voiceover, gave me a really clear image of Victoria. But I think this Victoria is a bit more damaged and a bit more disturbed than the original. She had that great haunted voice but was almost childlike and naïve. There's an element of that in this Victoria, but she's seen more. She's come through the asylum, she's been haunted her whole life. The fact she's overcome her past is extraordinary." Adds Burton, "Victoria has secrets of her own and Bella's got that look about her. She looks like a person who's been reincarnated. There's a mystery about her. A quality that suited the character."

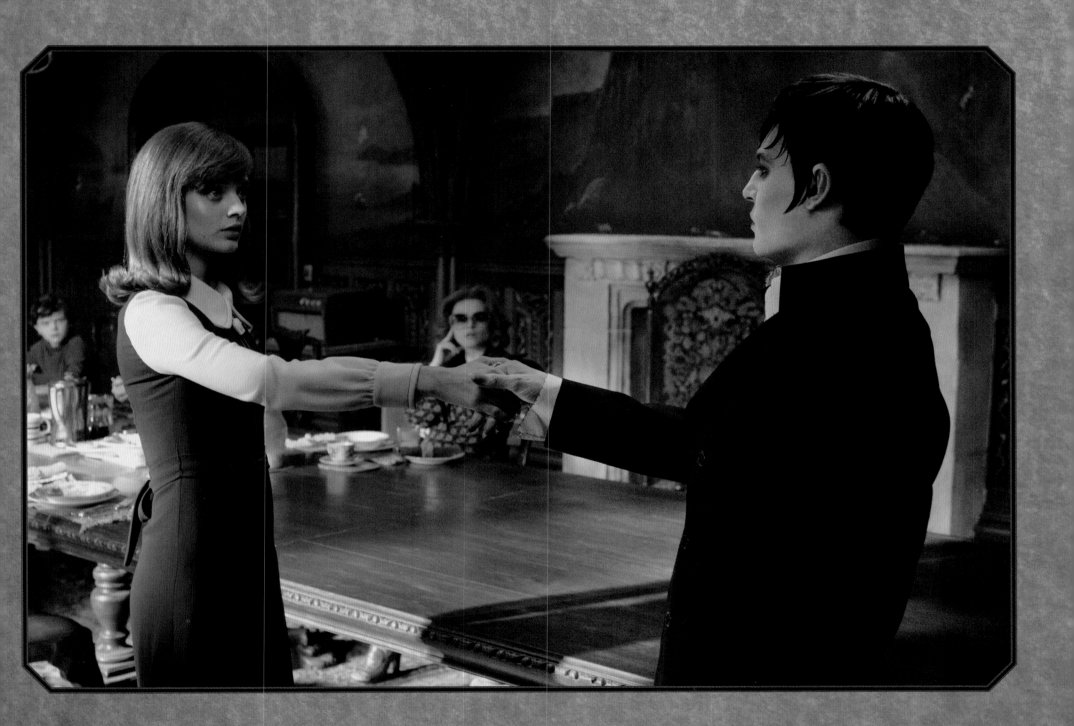

JACKIE EARLE HALEY AS
Willie Loomis

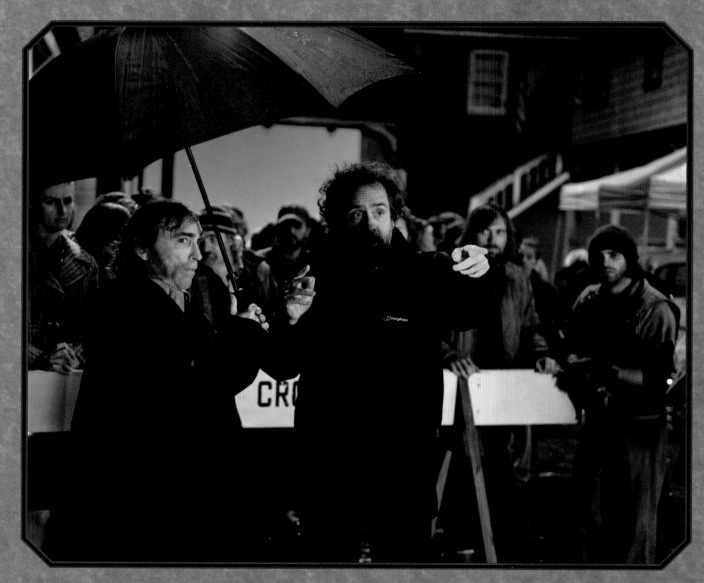

Despite their financial predicament, the Collins family still retain two live-in servants, one of whom, Willie Loomis, is the Collinwood caretaker — servant, butler, chauffeur, cook, and gardener. And drinker. "He is kind of a curmudgeon, could care less about anything," says Haley. "In an odd way, Willie enjoys the dysfunction that is the Collins family. They live in this gorgeous old, decrepit mansion, and pretend to be rich nobility. They bicker about everything. Willie is more than happy to pretend to be their servant. As long as he gets a cot and a few squares a day and a safe place to drink, he's a happy guy. But when Barnabas shows up, he gets hypnotized and becomes his servant. It's a cool dynamic." Notes Burton, "I had always wanted to work with Jackie, and this was the perfect opportunity. He is so funny, and just felt very much like a part of the *Dark Shadows* world."

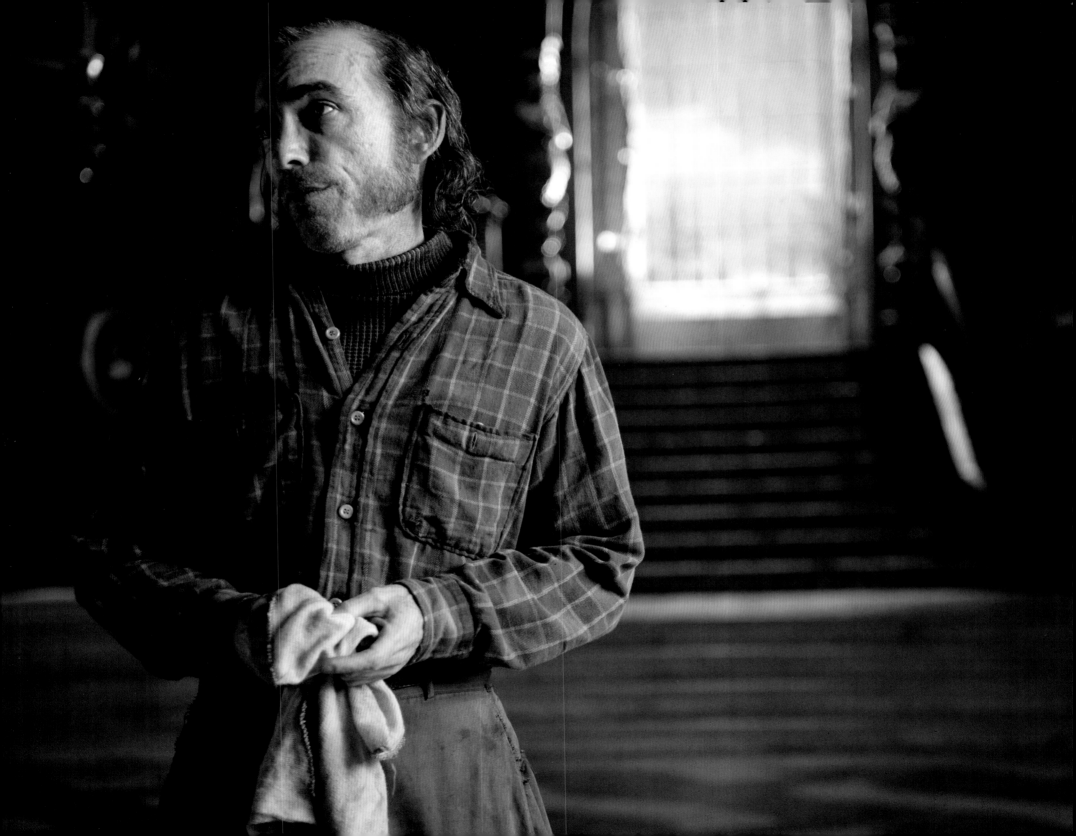

JONNY LEE MILLER AS
Roger Collins

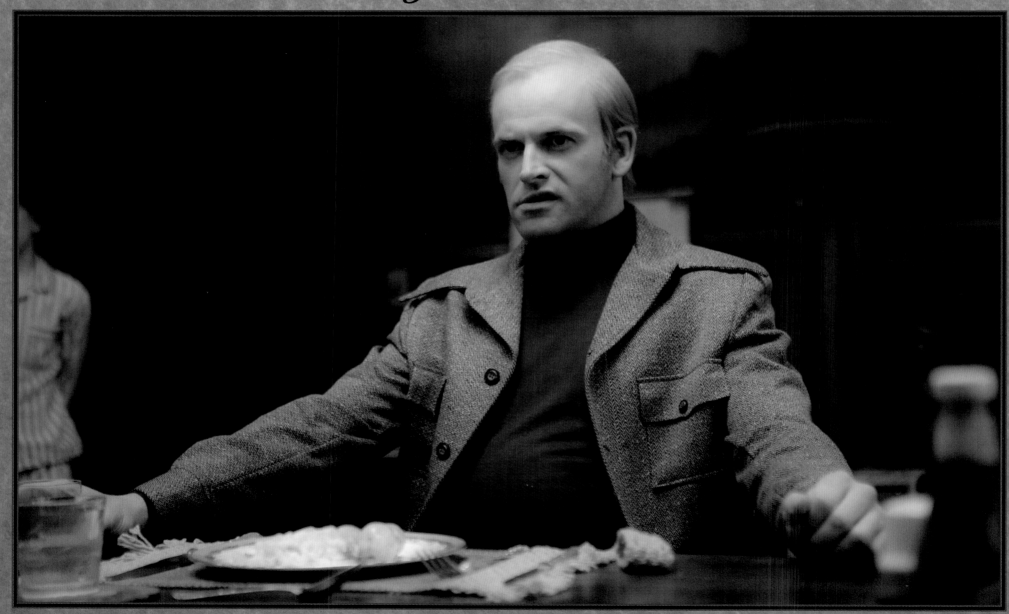

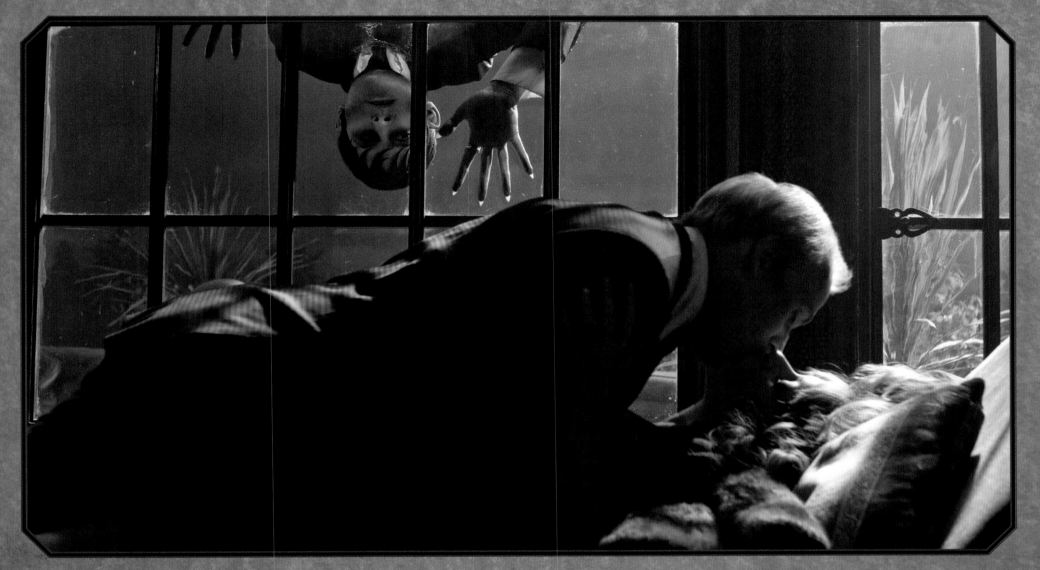

rother of Pfeiffer's Elizabeth and David's absent, thieving father, Roger is the black sheep of the Collins family. "His backstory is a bit of tragedy, losing his wife and his son sees ghosts. But he's a bit of a sleaze ball. He's got that swingin' '70s thing going on pretty good. The fashion. The Van Heusen look. The wide lapels. Reads *Playboy*. He's that guy," explains Burton. "He's quite a vacuous human being," confirms Miller of his character. "There's not a lot going on in his head. I think he used to be a much warmer human being, but his wife passed away, and since then, he's never really been the same person. He's not a very nice piece of work. But there's plenty of scope for playing that. It's nice to play someone who's a bit of an idiot." While Burton wasn't overly concerned with casting actors who looked like those in the TV series, in Miller's case it was a fortuitous coincidence. "There was something about him that captured that strange quality of the original Roger," says Burton. "I don't think he knew the series at all, but he clicked into the tone right away."

GULLIVER McGRATH AS
David Collins

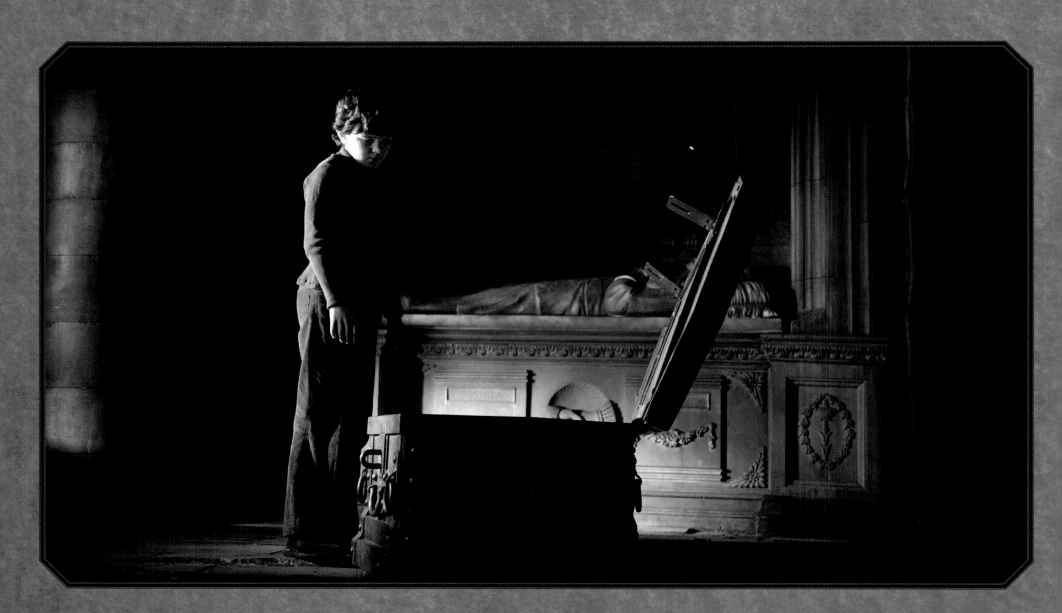

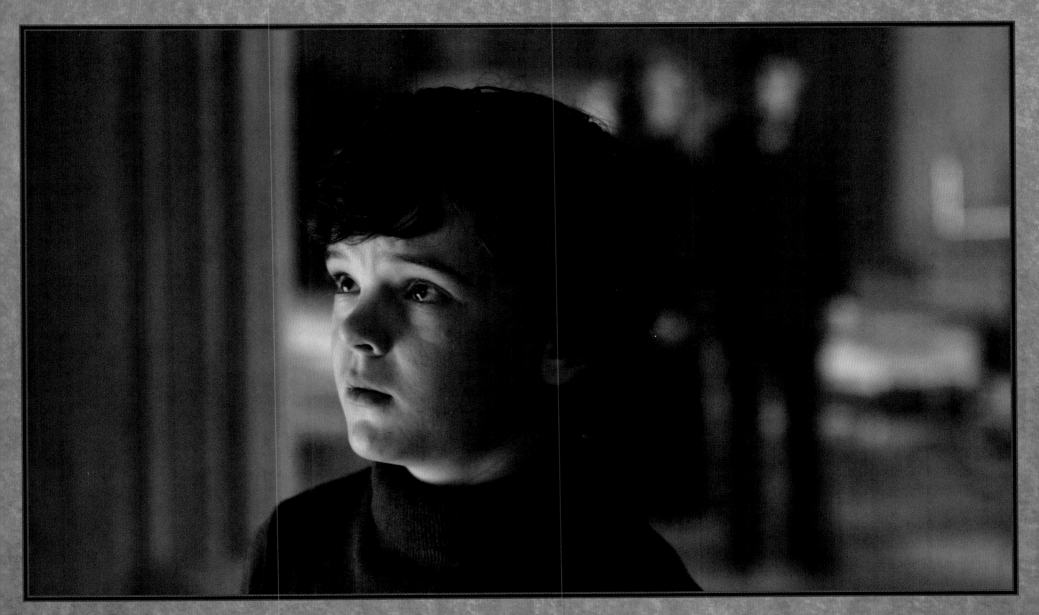

The youngest member of the Collins family is Roger's son, David, who sees his mother's ghost (Josephine Butler). "He's quite a sad character," says McGrath. "He's always felt like he was alone, because everybody's treated him like he's crazy, so he usually represses his feelings. There's like a psychic connection between him and his mother's ghost. They talk to each other, even though she's dead. She's been watching over him." Observes Burton, "Gully looks like a kid who looks like he sees ghosts. In fact, on the set, he'd be looking at something, and I'd look over and wonder, 'What are you looking at? Are you seeing a ghost or something?' Because he's got that kind of vibe. That's not something you can tell an actor; it's something they just need to have in their being."

RAY SHIRLEY AS
Mrs. Johnson

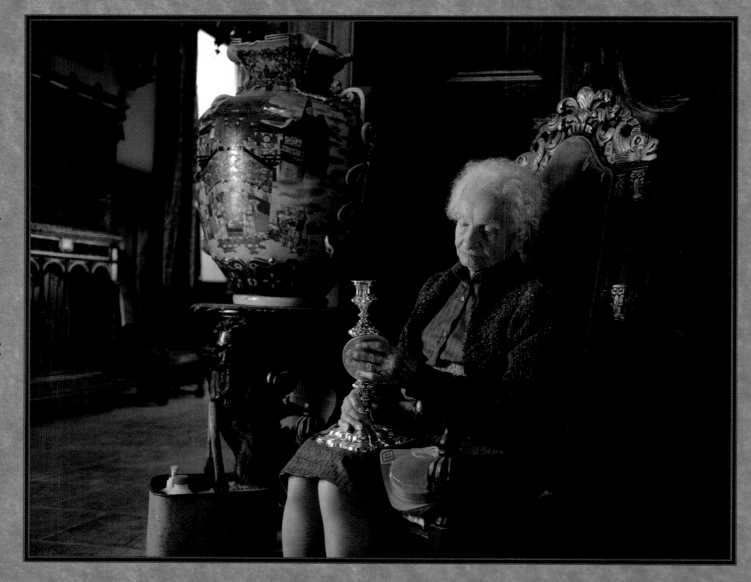

"**I** asked for an old person and she's like 90 or something," says Burton of Shirley who plays the Collins family's elderly, deaf housekeeper. "At the end of the interview I said, 'You look too young,' so she thought she didn't get the job because she didn't look old enough — which she didn't. We ended up making her look older than she looks. She's got such a great spirit and was really, really sweet, but every day she was a bit surprised and bemused by the whole thing because there was nothing really scripted. I would just throw things at her. I'd say, 'Ok, clean vomit off of Johnny's face.' 'Clean the candlestick with a piece of baloney.' 'Get on this lawnmower,' this power lawnmower which I think she was terrified of. But she was great. I love her. She was game to do anything. She turned into a favorite and I was always looking for little bits for her to do."

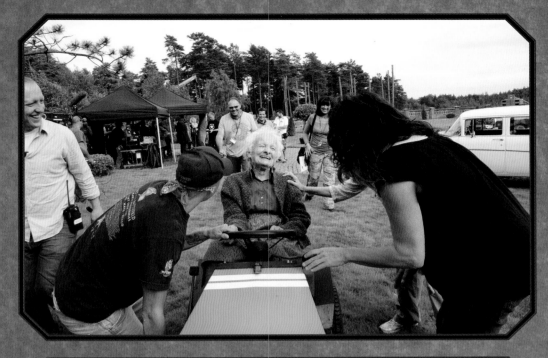

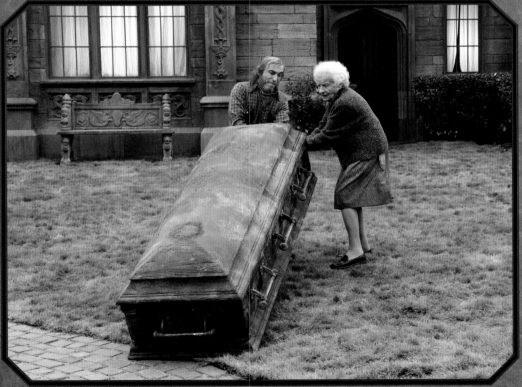

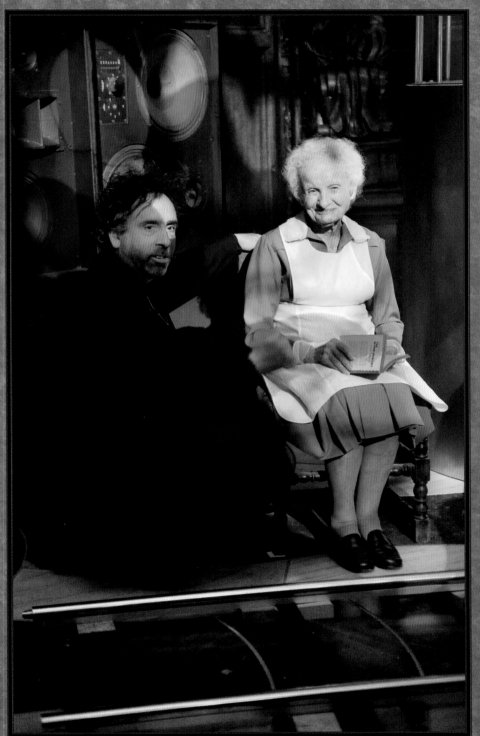

CHRISTOPHER LEE AS
Silas Clarney

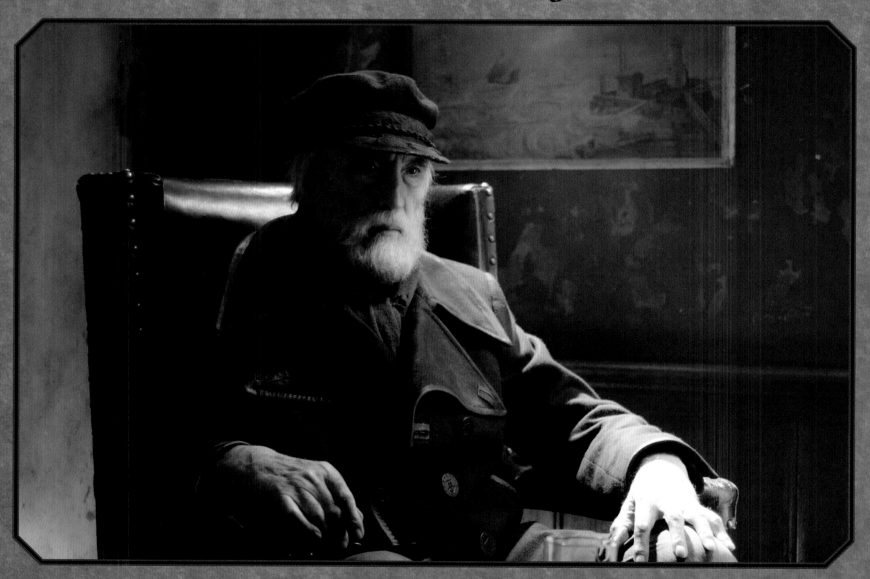

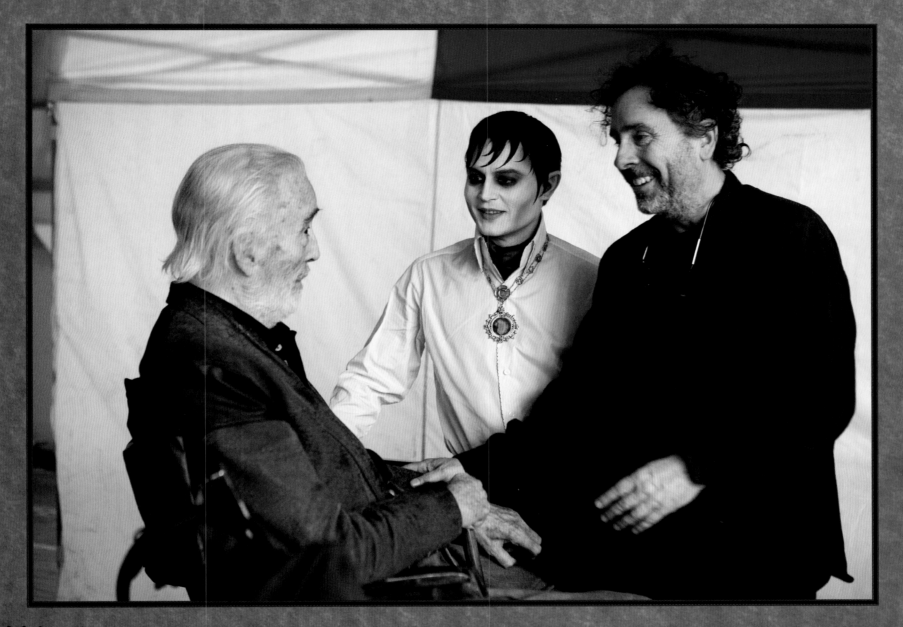

aking his fourth appearance for Burton, the former Count Dracula cameos as Silas Clarney, "Godfather of the Grand Banks." "He's tough and rather grim. We don't really know much about him, except that he obviously is not a very honest man and probably smuggles things and does all sorts of things he shouldn't do," says Lee of Clarney, who's on the receiving end of Barnabas's trippy stare and magical fingers when he tries to convince the fisherman to leave Angel Bay and join the Collins fleet. "I got to hypnotize Dracula," laughs Depp. "I got to hypnotize Christopher Lee, who is not only one of my great, great, great heroes, he's also someone I consider a great, great friend and a great, great mentor. He's played a wide range of characters but there was something about his Dracula, about his eyes, about his approach to the character, about what he did and how he did it, it was so much more sexual."

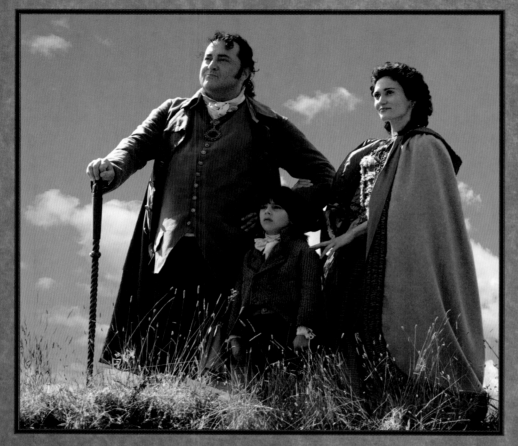

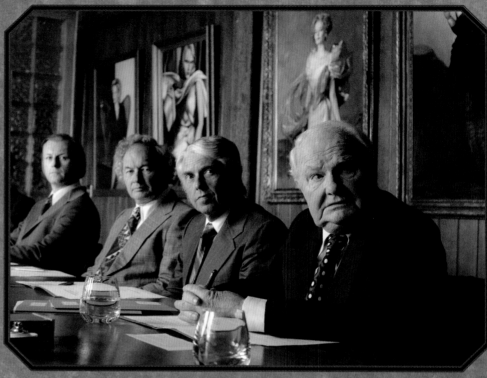

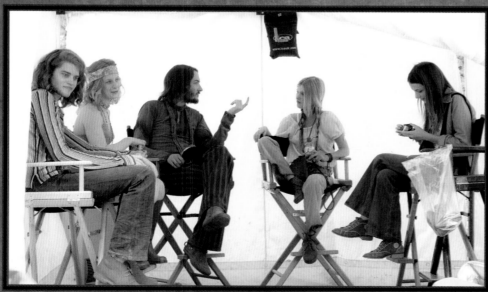

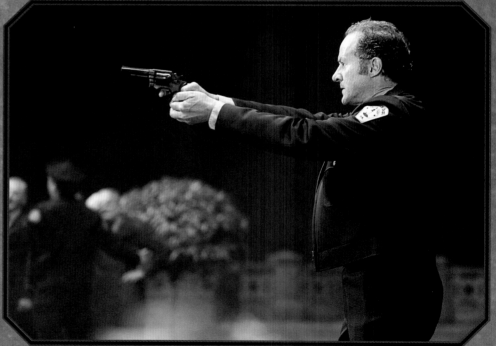

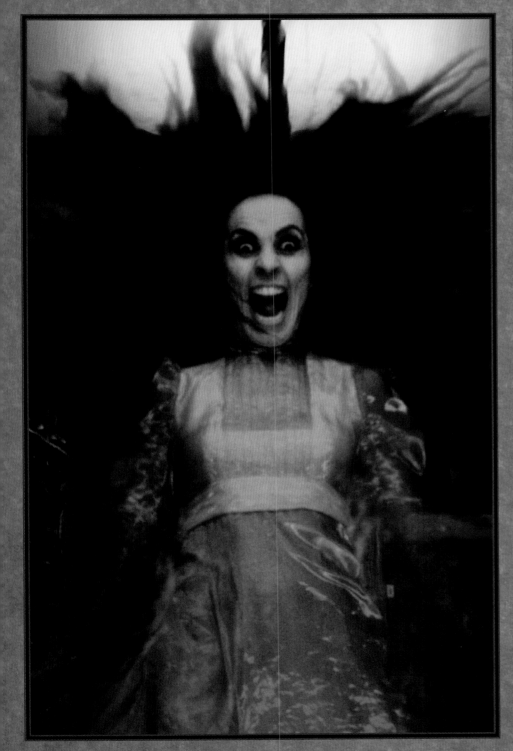

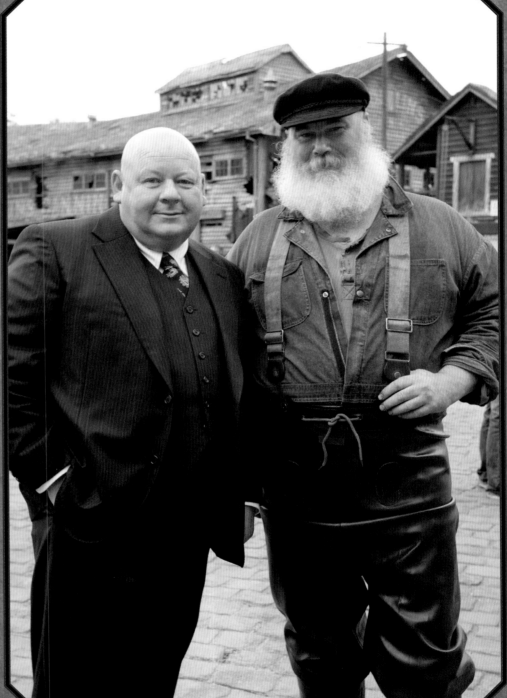

·67·

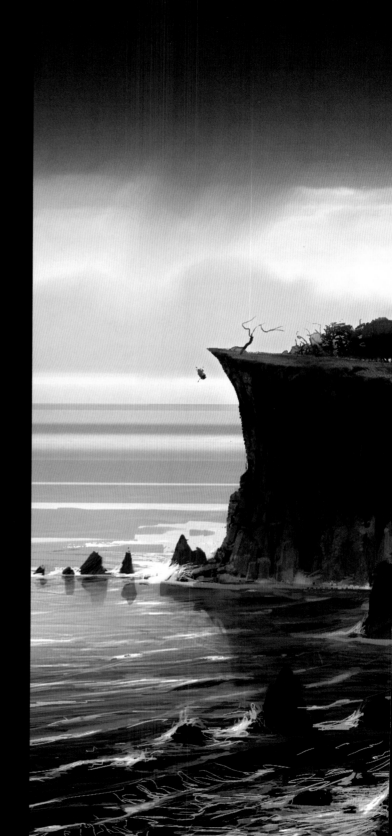

CHAPTER 2

THE SETS

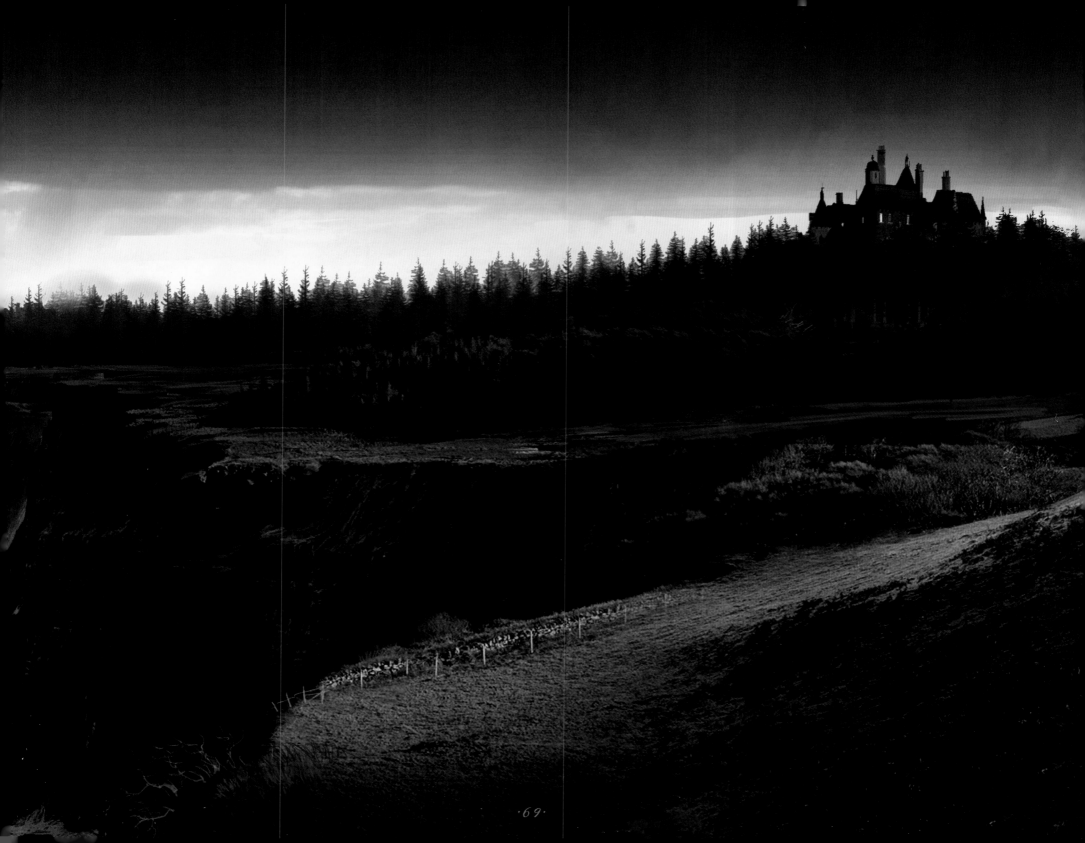

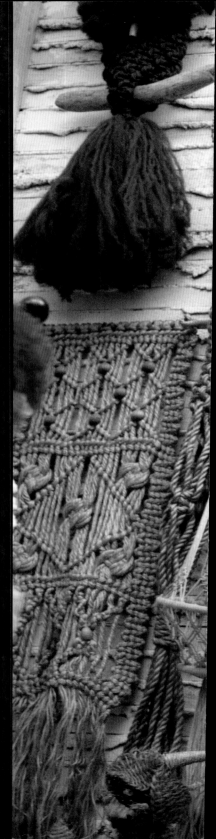

"Dark Shadows is a movie about layering aesthetics on top of each other," says production designer Rick Heinrichs. "One of the most important is the layering of the culture of 1972 on top of this Gothic horror tale. A lot of the inherent humor comes from seeing those two things together. You're looking at a culture that, to our eyes, seems a little bizarre, a little alien. Imagine what it would be like for Barnabas Collins to be introduced to that. What's lovely is the way Barnabas embraces the culture and seems very comfortable within it."

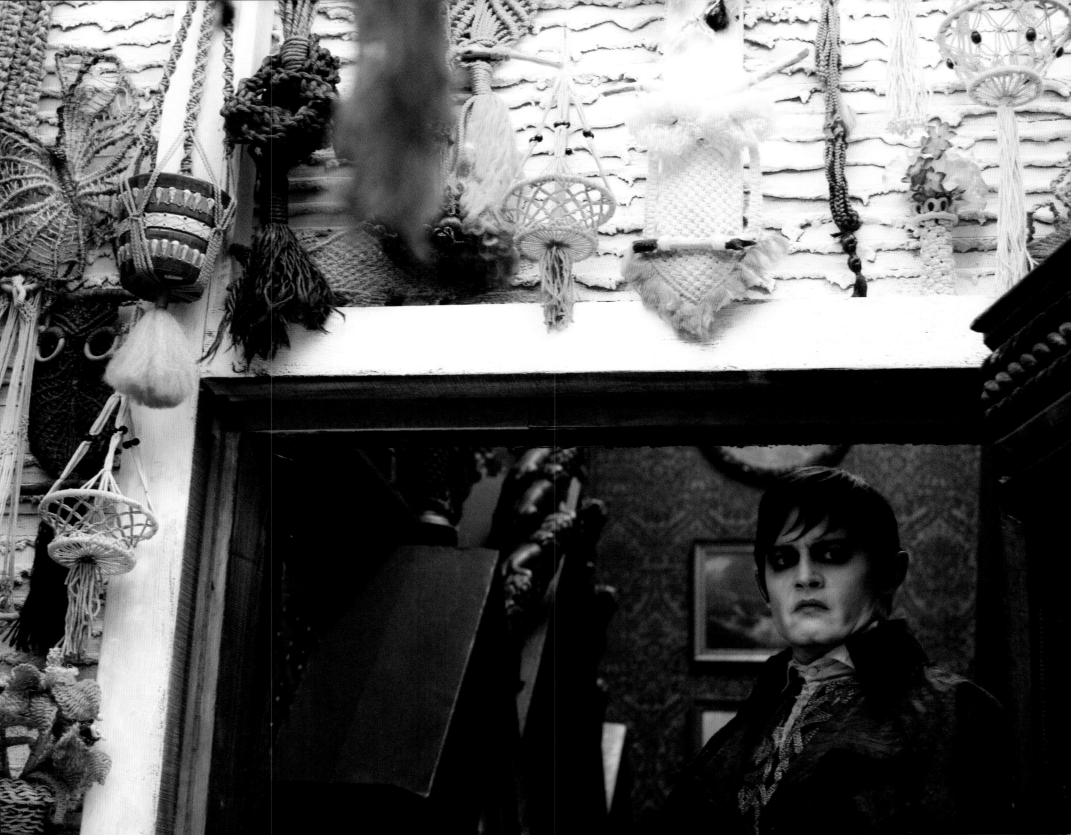

Described in the script as "a dragon curled in sleep", Barnabas's ancestral home sits high on a hill overlooking Collinsport and, as with the town, had to go through a variety of looks and time periods during the course of the film. "We see it at the height of its early years. We see it in a state of decay two centuries later. And we see Barnabas bring it back to life as well," says Heinrichs who took inspiration from the one used in the TV show, which was a real house in Newport, Rhode Island. "We tried different looks but always ended up going back to a certain vibe that house had. Ours is grander but plays out like a dream from the original series," says Burton. "Fans of the show will notice certain nods to the architecture, and some of the details of the original," explains Heinrichs, "in particular the central turret. As a character, the house had to express all of the elements of creepiness and old world charm and faded glory. We wanted the exterior to not feel stylized as an exterior on stage, but feel like it was really outside."

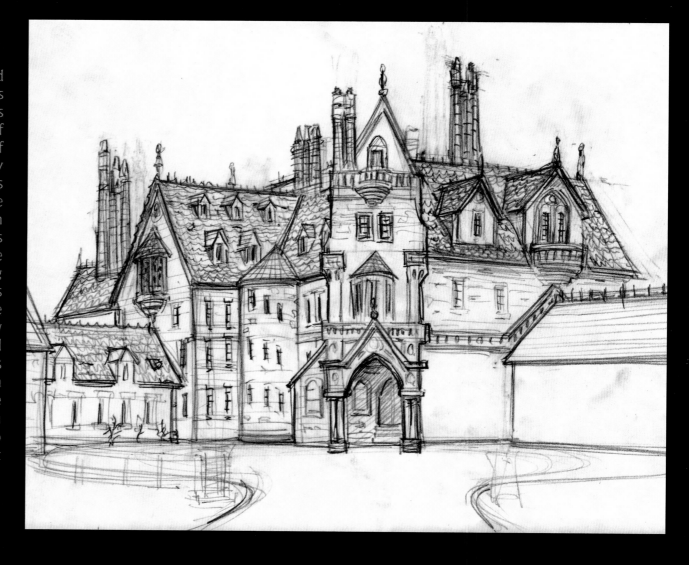

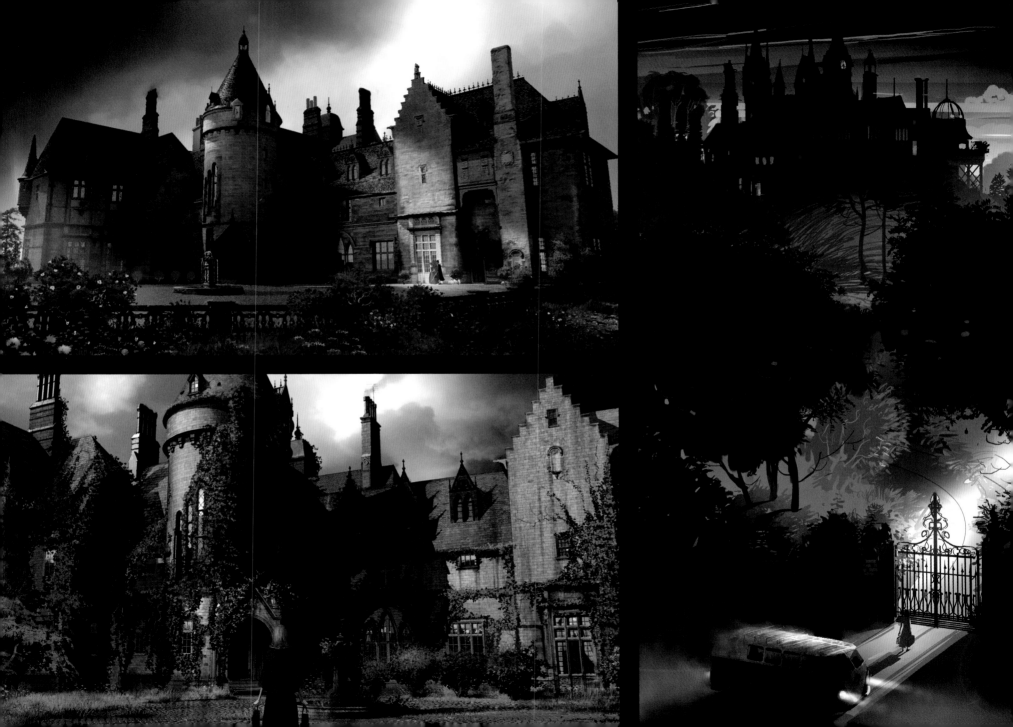

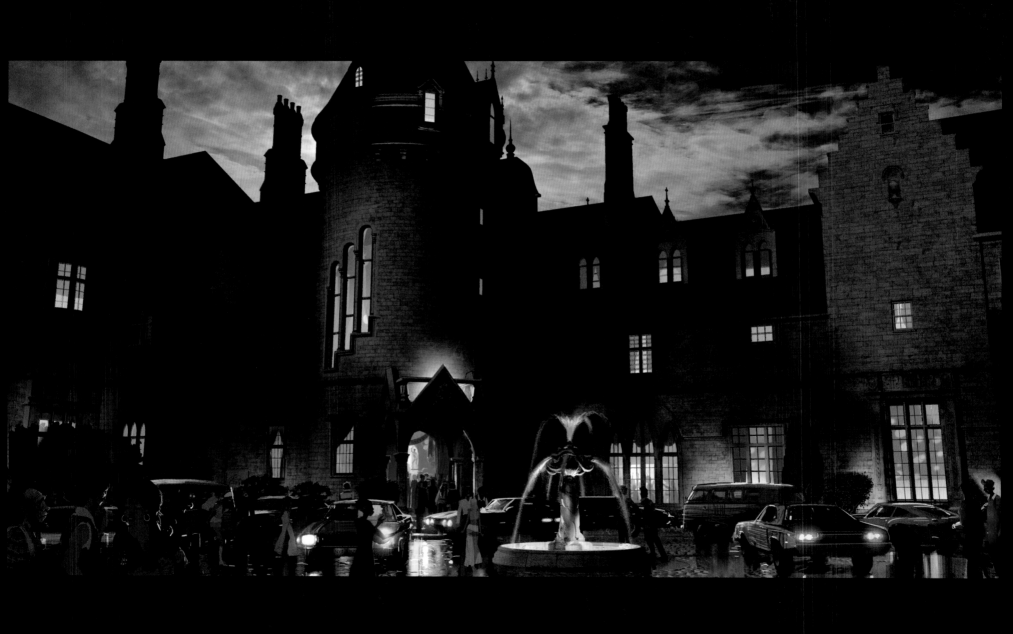

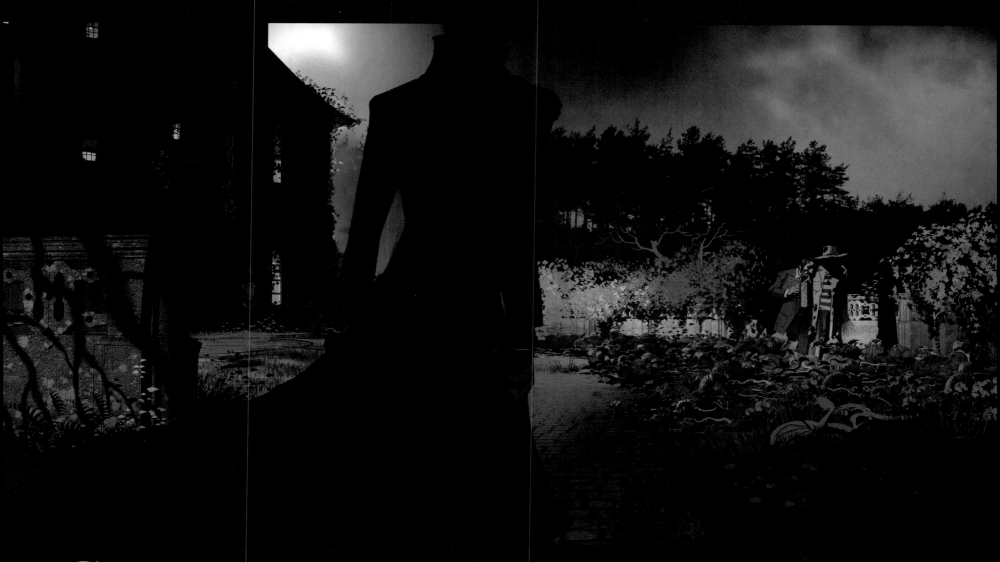

A 20-foot high, single-story facade of Collinwood Manor was built in a pine forest in Bourne Woods, Surrey, complete with courtyard and fountain, as well as a 300-foot long exterior wall. The remainder of the manor was added digitally. "We wanted the kind of scope you get by shooting it on the location," reveals Heinrichs. "The advantage of doing that set is that verisimilitude of being outside, namely the real world elements of weather. It allowed us to get a lot of wonderful pines that you would get in Maine. It was a bit of a challenge, but well worth it, given the fact we were able to show such a vast amount of set. It allowed us to shoot people in front of the walls and yet not have to build the entire thing. It was a wonderful environment. It felt real. There was a pumpkin patch as part of the lawn. And pumpkins and Halloween are all very thematic to Tim and his world."

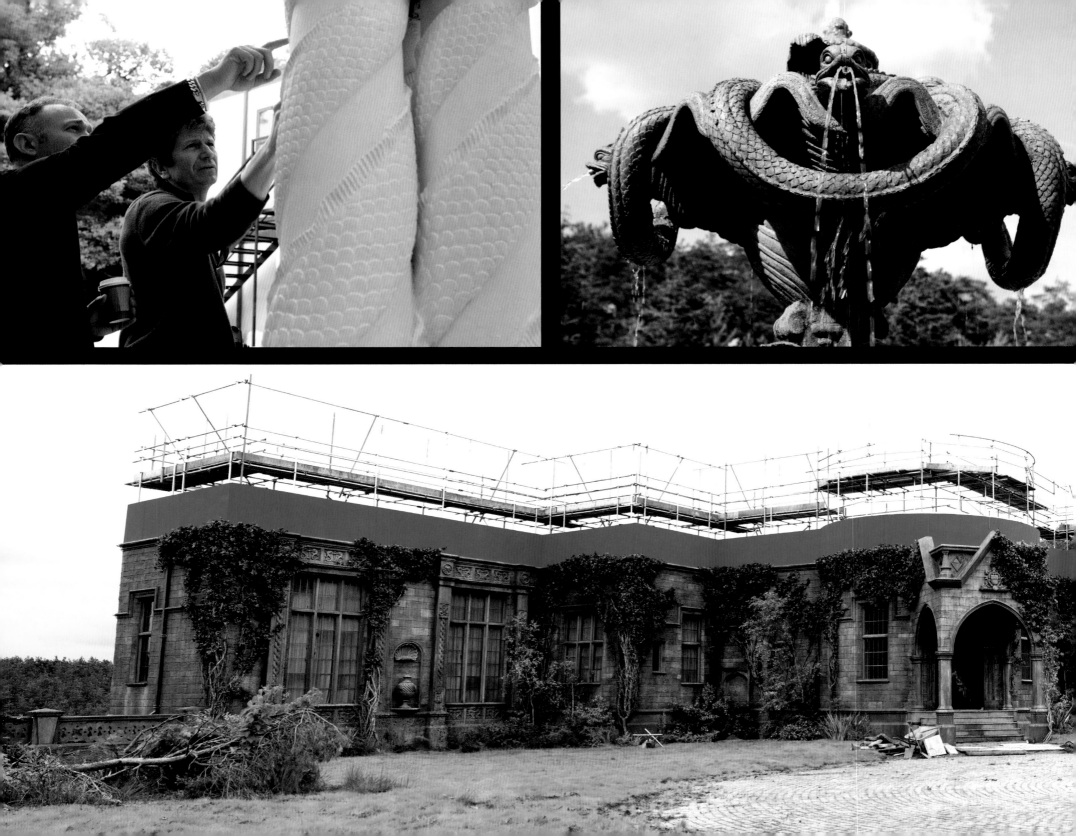

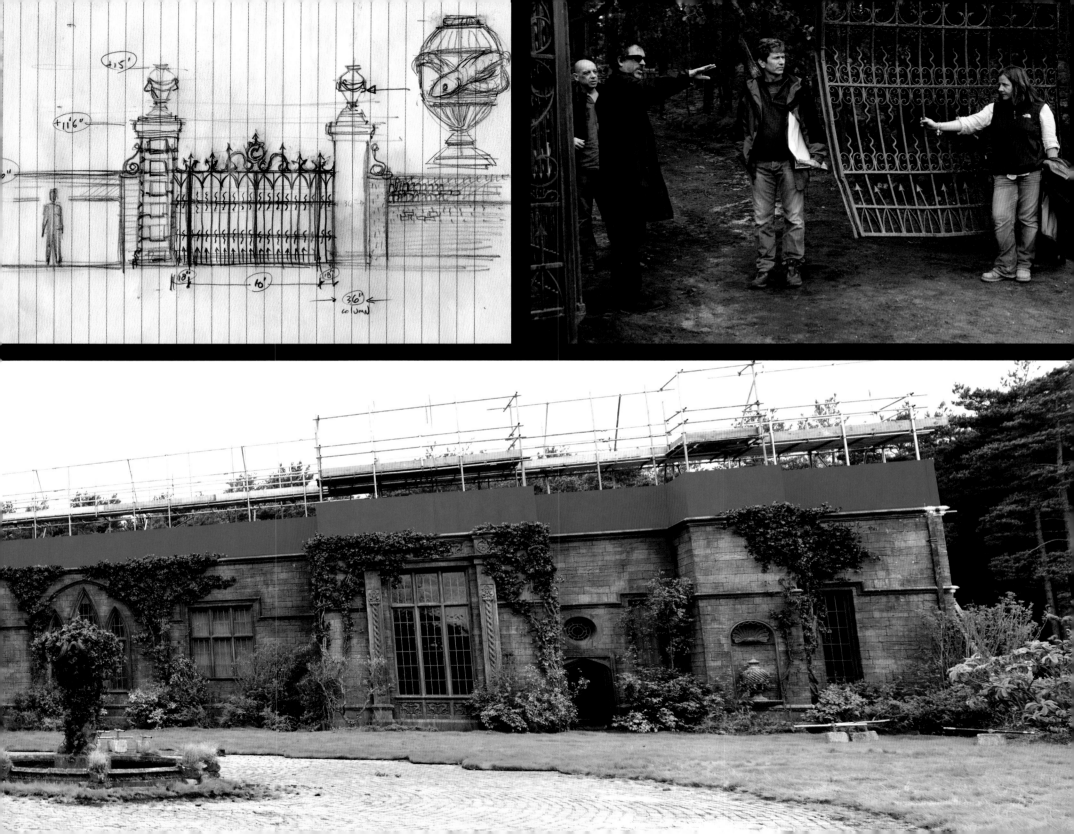

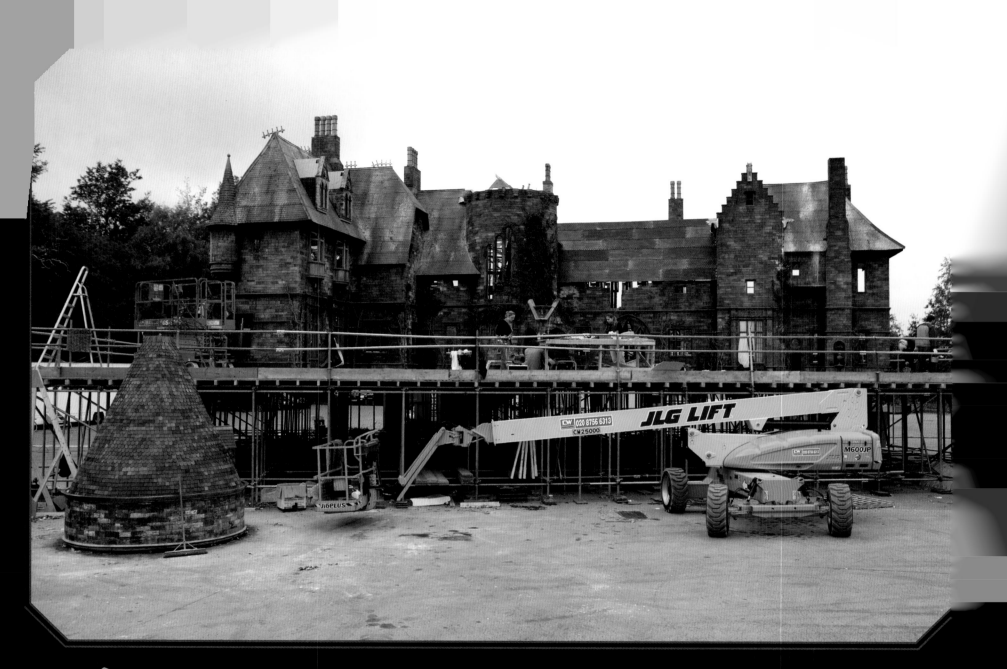

In addition to the one-story high "full-size" Collinwood, a complete Manor was constructed as a one-third scale model measuring 33 feet tall. "Tim and I like miniatures," says visual effects supervisor Angus Bickerton, "and the reason for doing it at such a big scale was not only for believable detail, but because it had to burn at the end, and flames are always tricky in miniatures. But you can get a good effect at the one-third scale,

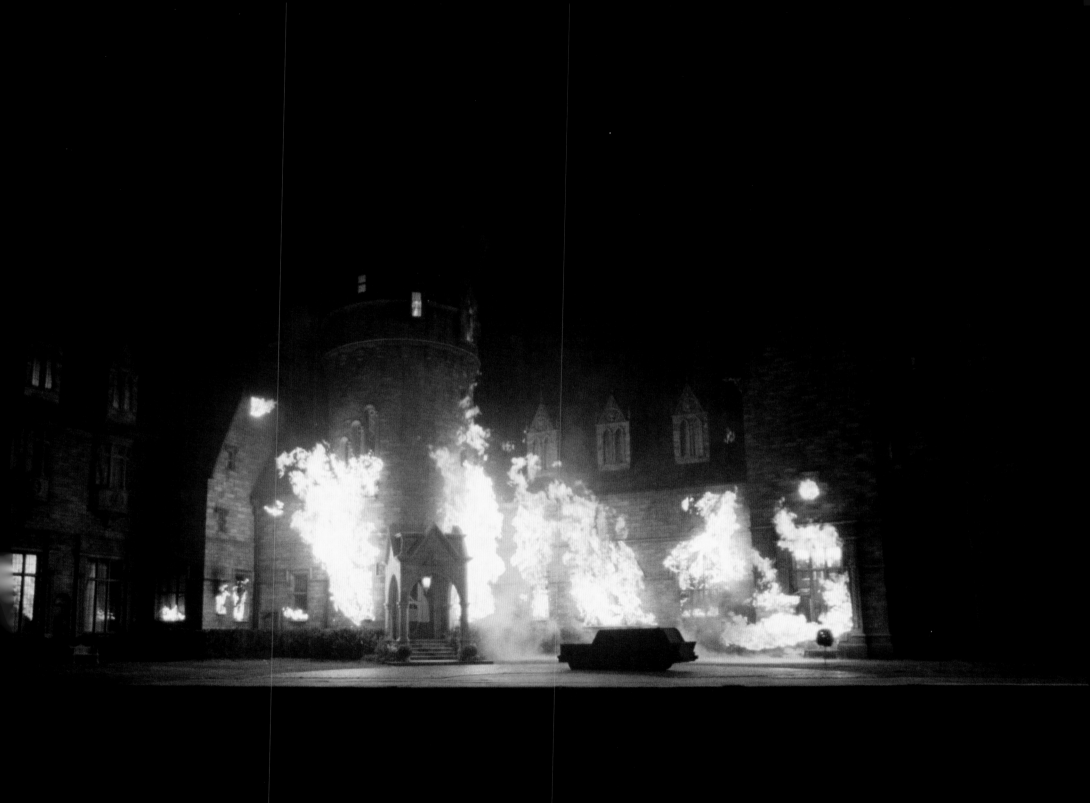

Grand Foyer

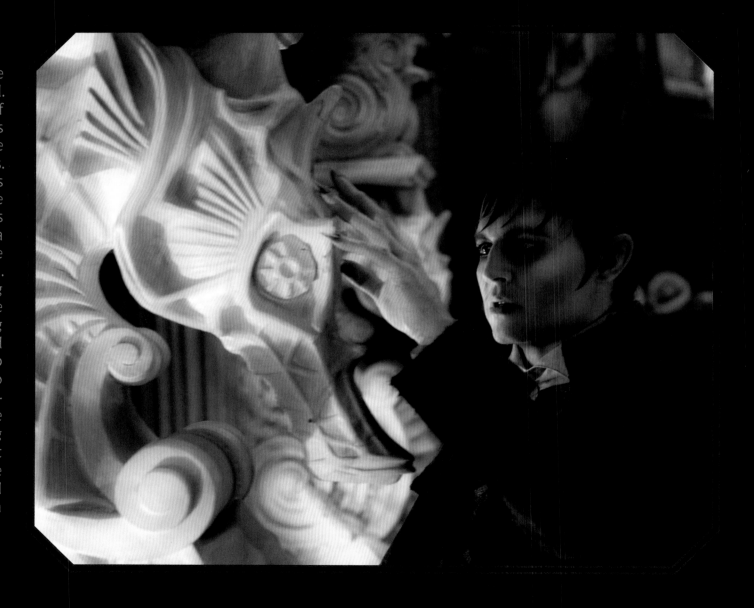

All of Collinwood's interiors were built on soundstages at Pinewood. 'When you entered the house, one of the things we wanted it to feel like was faded glory; that this is a grand house fallen on hard times," explains Heinrichs. 'But beneath the dust and the cobwebs and mess was a character, an inanimate object that almost lives and breathes to a degree. To achieve that we did a great deal of detail carving within the house, to make sure it felt old world. Johnny's an actor who enjoys touching things and using his environment. The first time Barnabas enters, he's caressing the sculptures and touching things and commenting on the fine craftsmanship that went into it. For the dialogue to say we had the finest craftsmen and finest marbles and mahogany, and to have those elements be a little disappointing wasn't going to play very well. So we put a lot of effort, and spared no expense and energy in creating a very beautiful and richly detailed environment for him to operate in."

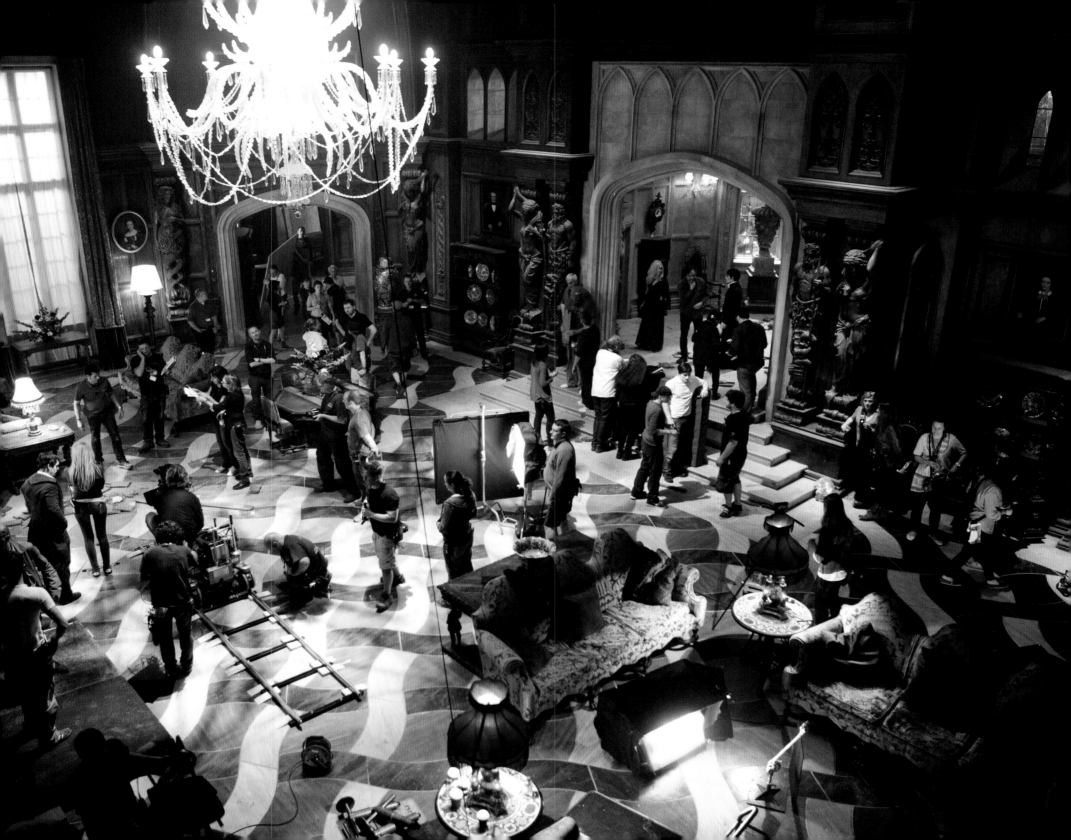

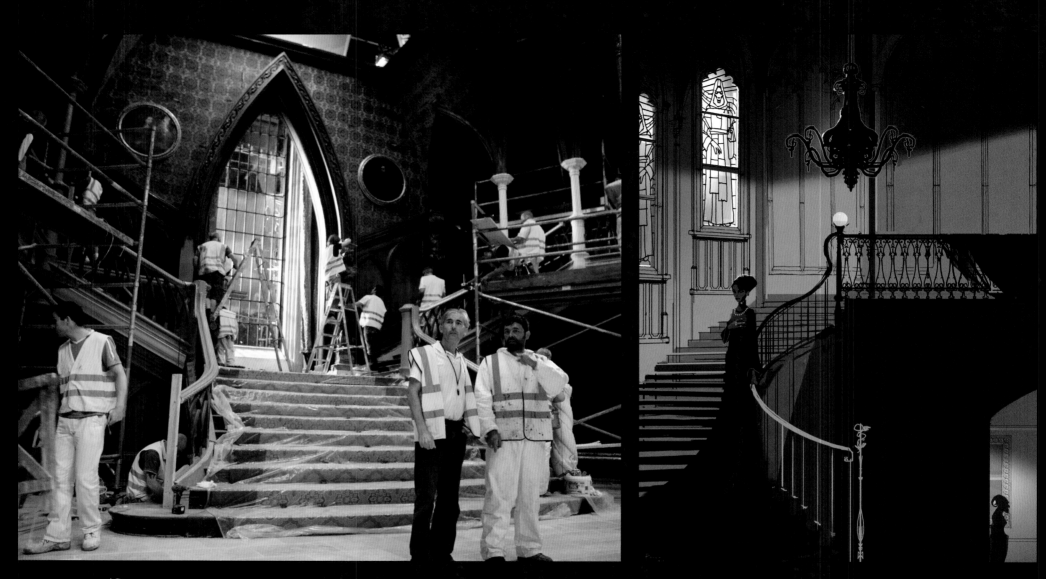

Constructed on Pinewood's E Stage, the Grand Foyer measured 64 feet by 101 feet, and was 32 feet in height, and featured a wave-like patterned tile floor, a magnificent crystal chandelier, and half-a-dozen painted portraits of the Collins family, including Barnabas, his parents and Josette. "It was doing a number of things at the same time, giving us a sense of rich detail, a sense of creepiness, a sense of drama," says Heinrichs. "When we first meet Elizabeth she appears at the top of the stairs, silhouetted by the huge window behind her. It's a very theatrical entrance, and the whole back of the set was designed around that concept of entrances and drama."

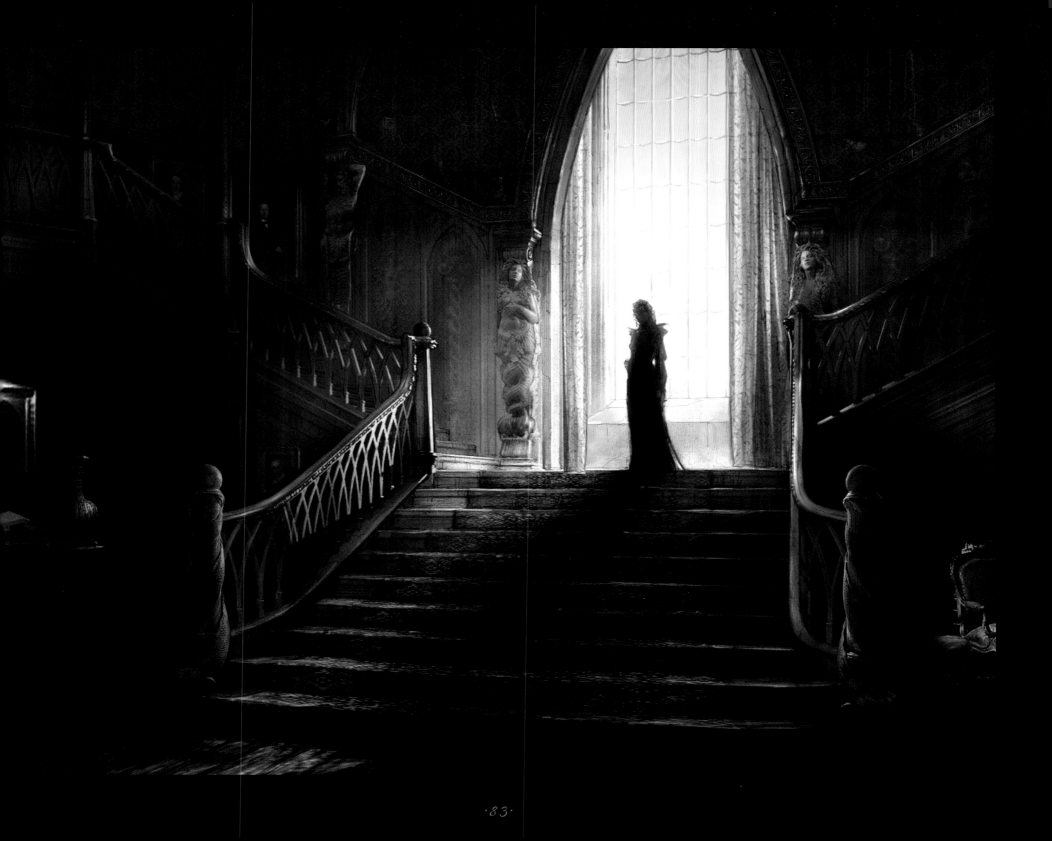

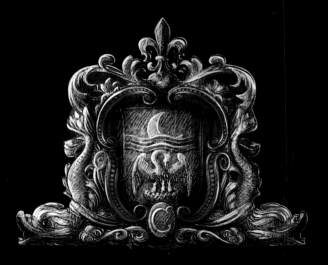

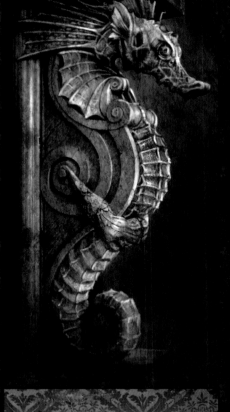

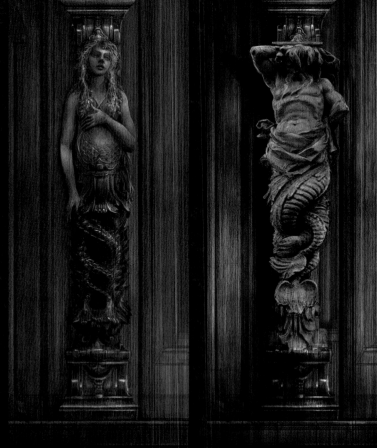

iven Collinwood's proximity to the sea and the Collins family's background in fishing, Heinrichs designed the Manor's exterior and interior to reflect that maritime heritage, with fish, mermaids, and ocean motifs present throughout the house and its furnishings, including seahorses in the fireplace and statues of Neptune. A lobster clock imported from Paris was a particular favorite of Burton's. "We did a great deal of figurative carving," says Heinrichs. "Within it there are a lot of caryatids and mermaid characters. There's a feeling of a cross between the sea and the land that lent it this creepy feeling and gave a sense of otherworldliness to the Manor. Seeing Barnabas in his makeup, within this environment, felt wonderfully creepy."

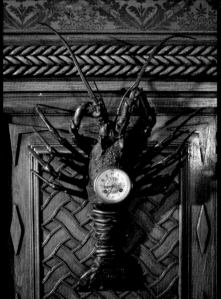

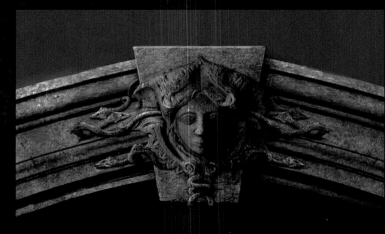

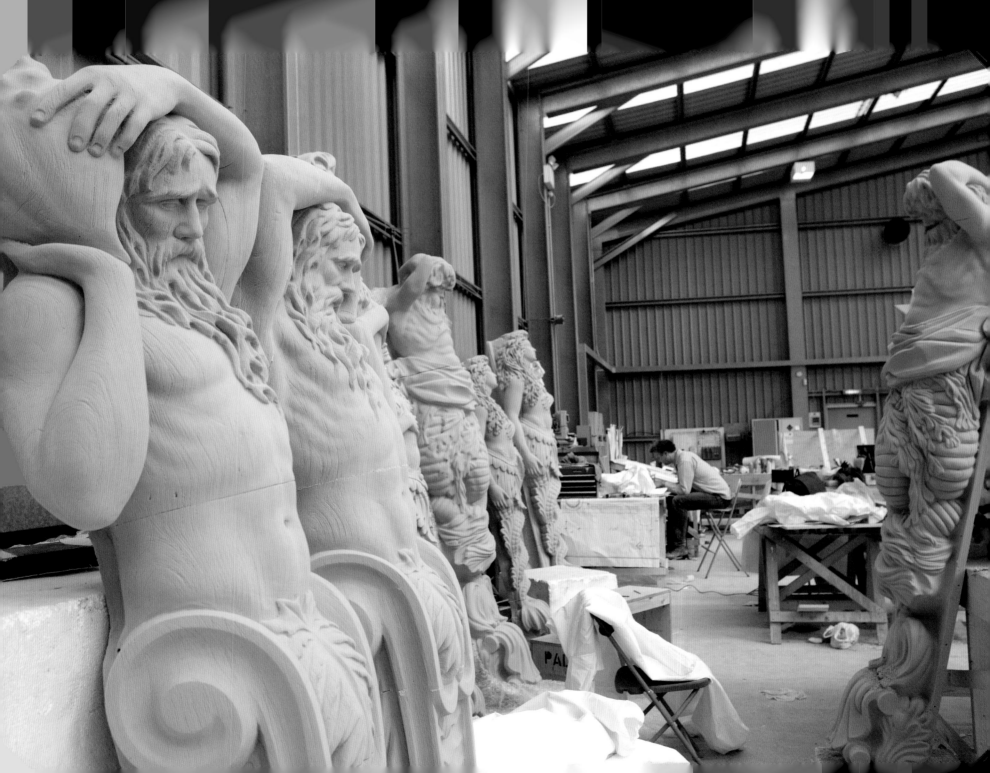

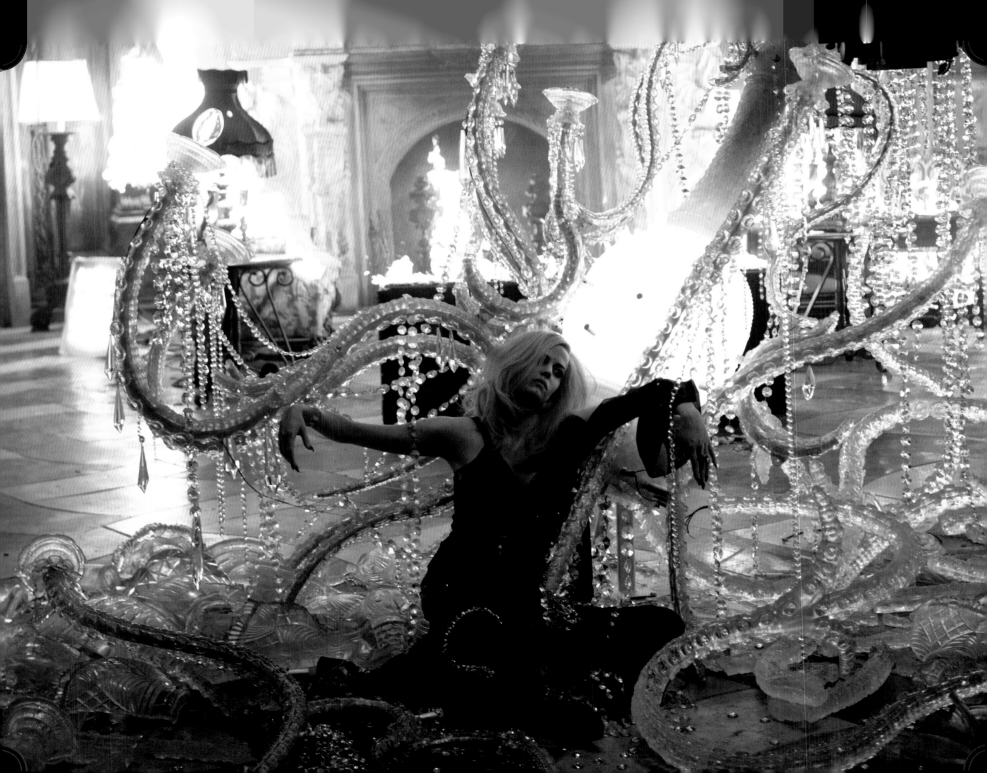

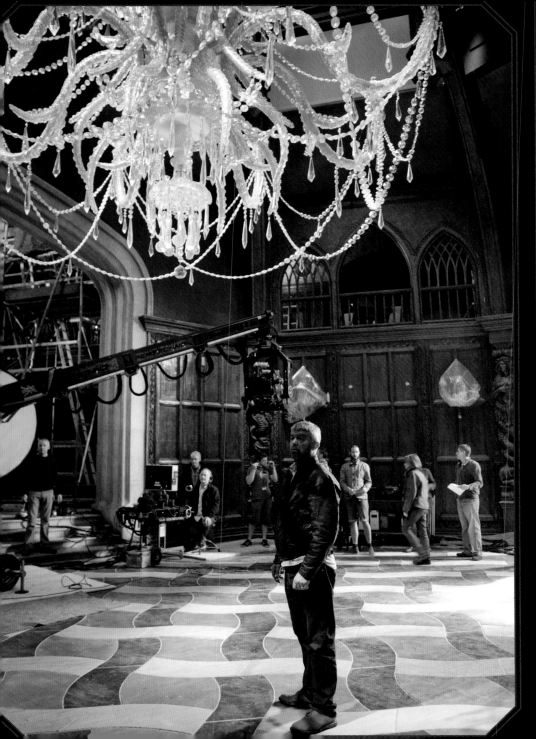

The centerpiece of Collinwood's Grand Foyer was the crystal chandelier built by David Balfour's team of sculptors and prop makers, based on a design from Rick Heinrichs' art department. "That was probably one of the biggest challenges we've had on any film for a long time," reflects Balfour. "The material we used was quite a challenge, a clear resin, which made it quite unforgiving for any slight flaws. Again there was an element of the sea in the design. We had sculptors sculpt all the arms and pieces and then mold it. It was a very complicated and tricky job. We made it in five weeks."

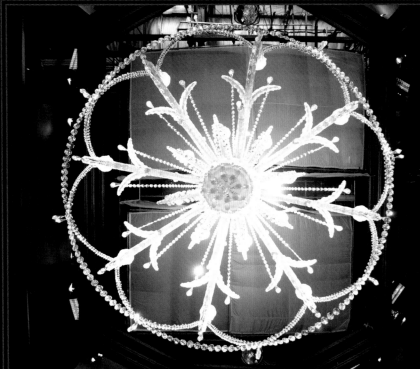

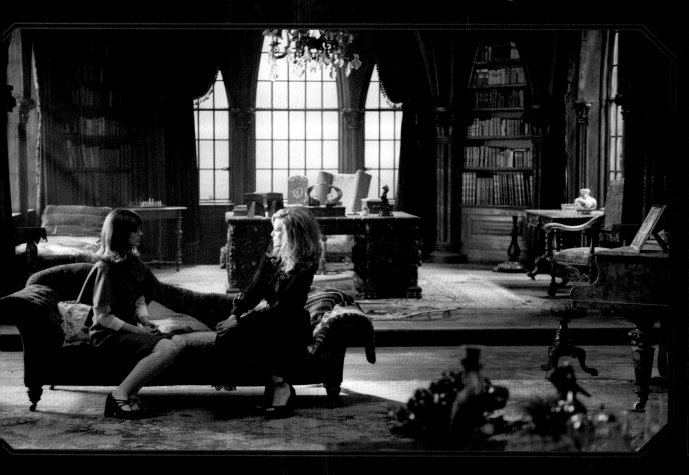

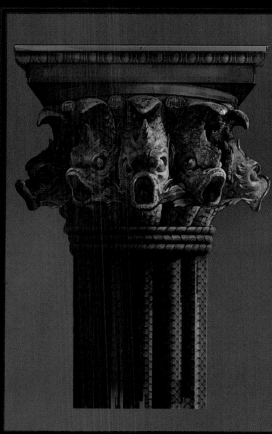

"The drawing room is a bit of a refuge from the rest of the house," says Heinrichs, who designed its panelling based on a motif from a 12th century Bulgarian church. "It's where the more private conversations happen in which Elizabeth grills Barnabas on his appearance and shares her disbelief that he is who he is, and it ties into the hidden vault where all of the family wealth has been stored away, that Elizabeth was unaware existed."

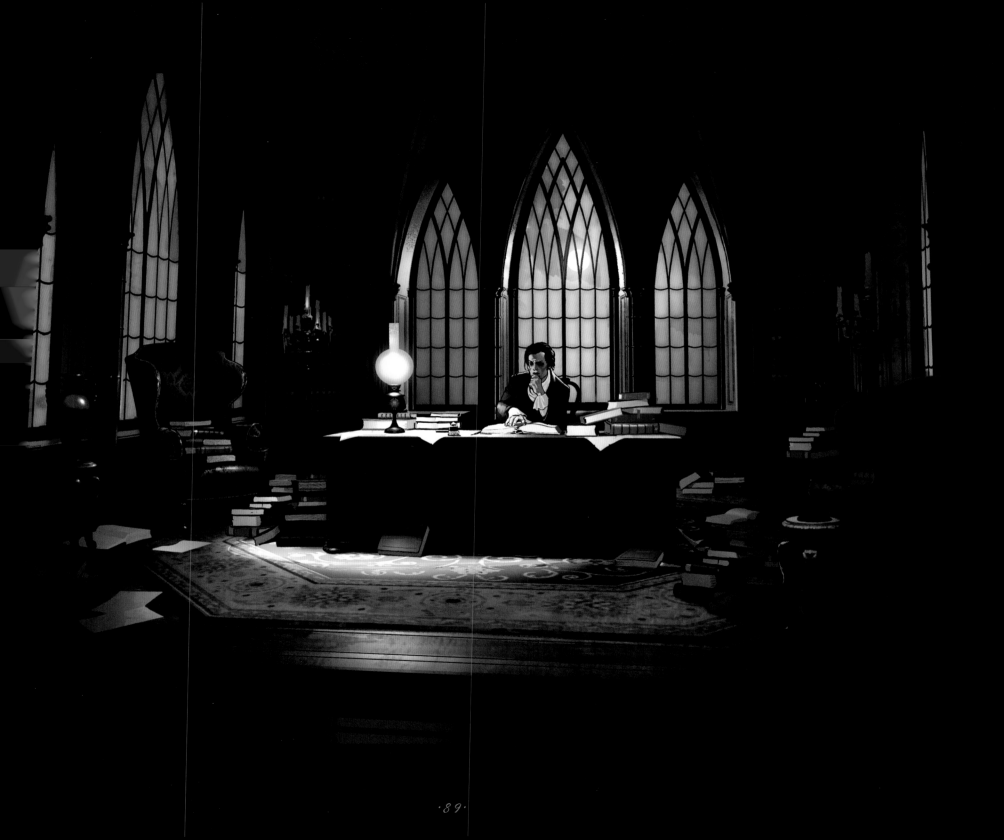

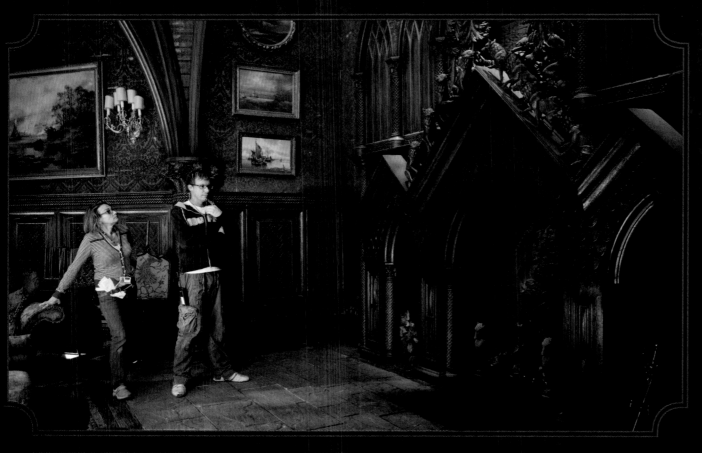

Known only to Barnabas, the treasure vault is accessible via a secret entrance hidden behind the fireplace in the drawing room, which was a fully working, mechanical set. "It allowed us the opportunity to come up with a clever way to do the entrance and stairway down into the vault," says Heinrichs. "I mean, nobody walks into a fireplace, because there's a fire there, usually. So what we did was come up with this idea that, at the push of a button, an automaton display started: waves start moving and clouds part, revealing the moon. The wolves howl, then the fireplace shifts back with much grinding of gears, and the hearth stones sink and become steps down." Notes special effects supervisor Joss Williams, "The fireplace in the study was primarily made and designed by Marc Bouilment, who did a lot of the tricky stuff on the Harry Potter films. The steps are each individually made. They're each on pneumatic rams, and as one step goes, it sets off the other step by means of micro-switches."

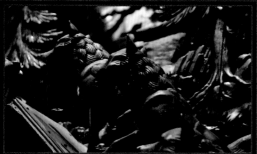

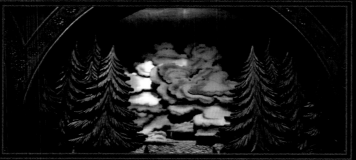

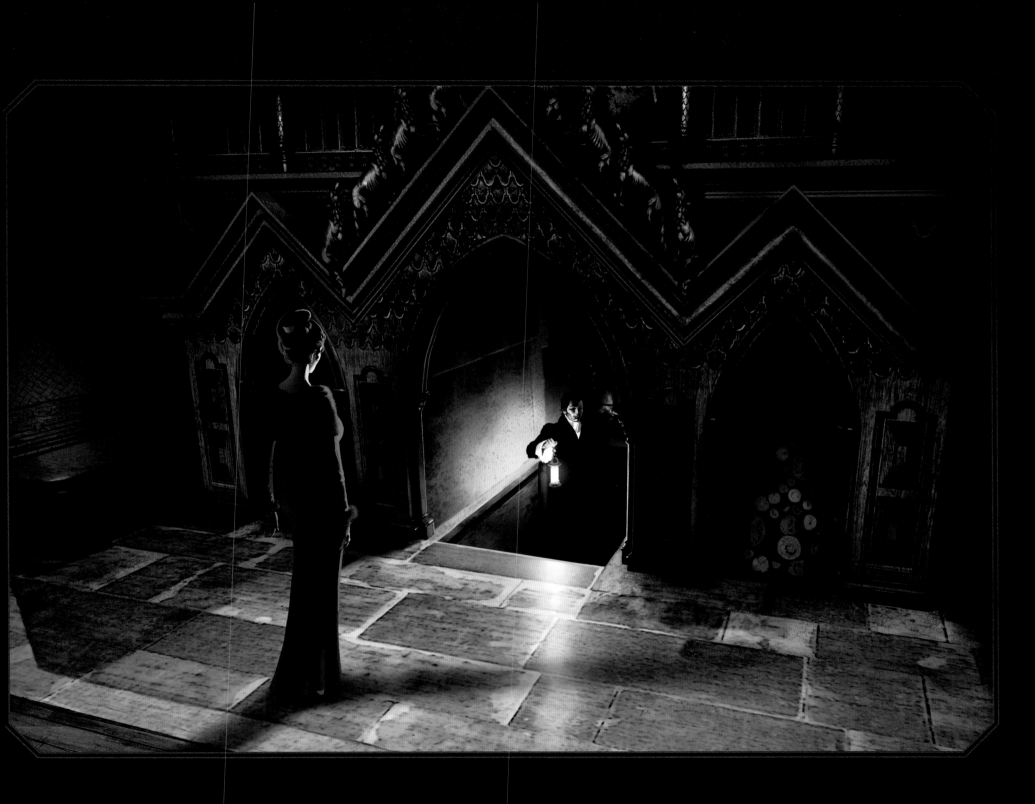

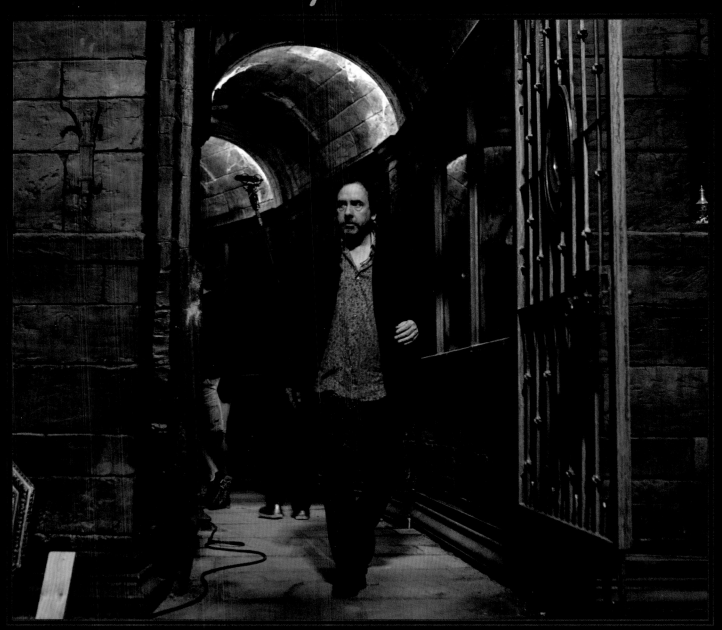

inking the hidden stairwell to the family treasure vault was a hall of mirrors. "It was an interesting set to do because vampires and mirrors don't work well with each other," says Heinrichs. "But they are old mirrors, so we were able to show them in a state of disrepair, and very dusty as well, so the realization that Barnabas doesn't have a reflection was something that dawns on Elizabeth as they are proceeding down the hallway, rather than have it be an immediately recognizable thing. And we tilted everything so there's a funhouse aspect to it. It's always fun to do dank, dark subterranean spaces."

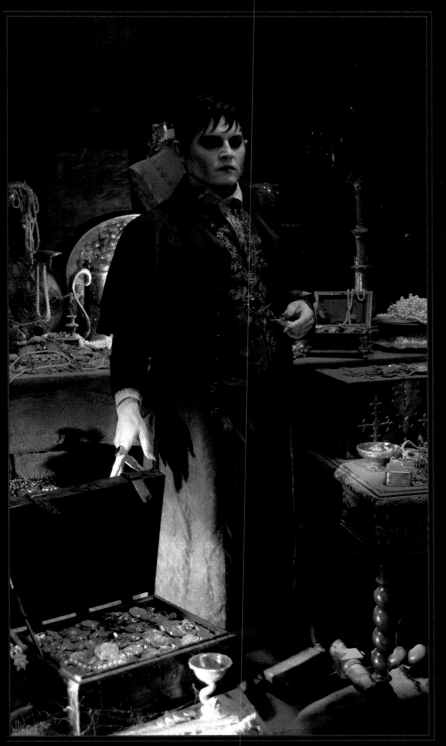

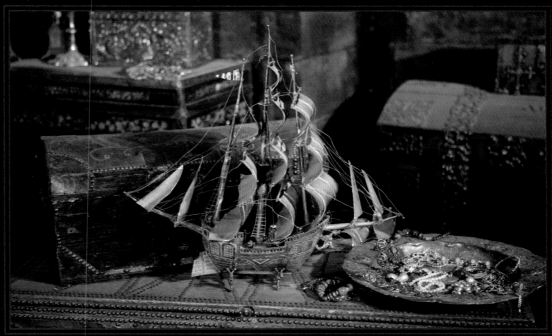

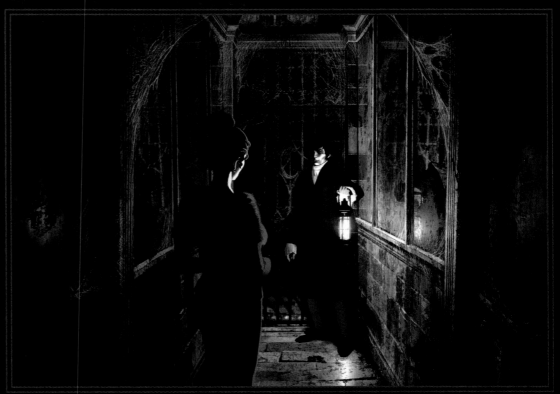

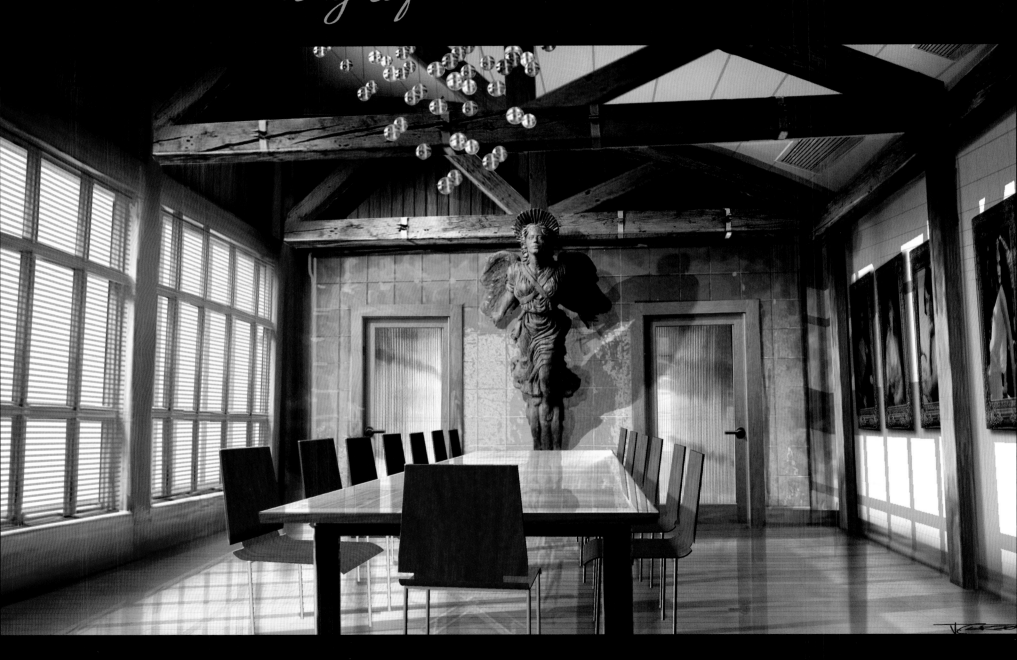

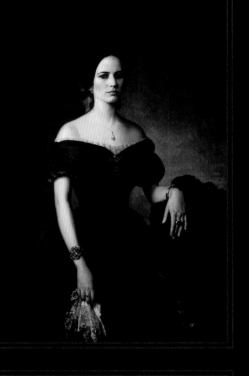
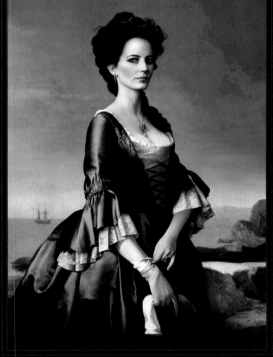
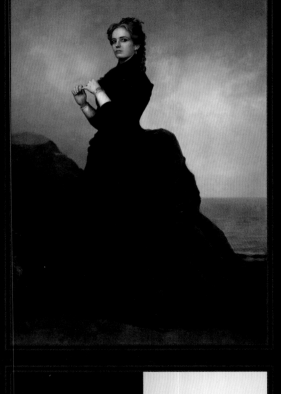
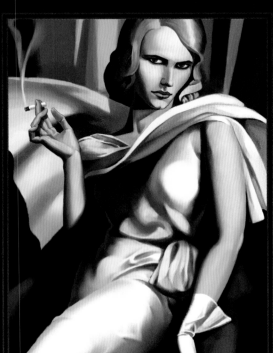
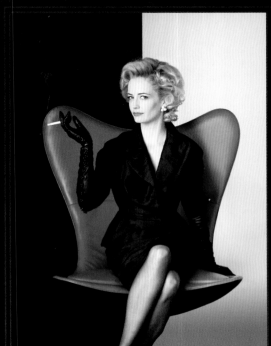

The Angel Bay board-room showcases a series of portraits of Bouchard women from the 18th century to the 1970s. All noticeably with the same likeness. "We took an iconic style of painting from each of these periods, then had a photo session with Eva Green and photographed her in the pose and with the right lighting," says Heinrichs. "The art department put them in the image we wanted, printed them out and then we painted over them." The other main element of the set was the figure-head from the HMS *Venture*, the ship that carried Angelique and the Collins family from Liverpool at the start of the film.

Dining Room

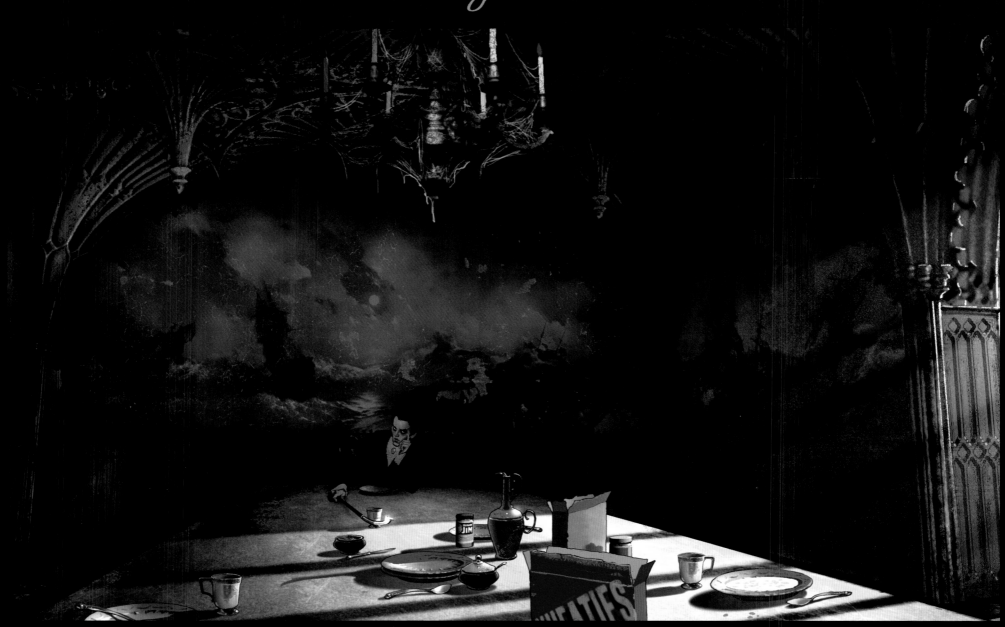

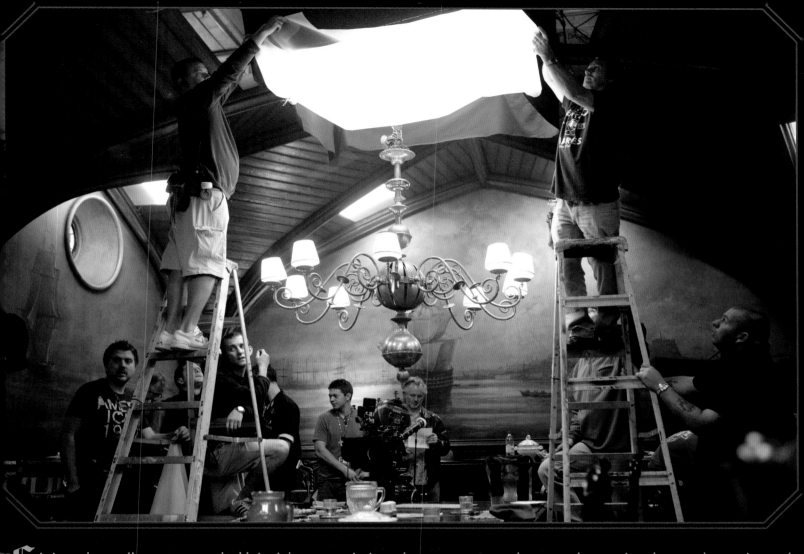

Lining the walls were murals Heinrichs commissioned to comment, almost subconsciously, on the action taking place in the room. "The family was occupying one side of this very long table, and Barnabas the other somewhat in the shade, so the sun wouldn't touch him," explains the production designer. "We depicted it in such a way there was a clear demarcation there. On the mural behind Barnabas we painted a stormy sea with ships in distress and a moon above his head. Behind the family was a much calmer day scene, so there was a transition around the room. Now, it could have been the other way. It's a very dysfunctional family, and perhaps we could have put the stormy seas behind them, but it wasn't so much a literal comment as it was a feeling for the confrontation and interaction that was happening between the characters in that room."

"Johnny had to do these dinner and breakfast scenes round a table where the whole family's there," remembers Jonny Lee Miller of working with Depp. "They take ages to shoot because there are so many angles. You take two days to shoot maybe a two-page scene. Johnny had a lot of dialogue and he's sitting there with all this makeup on and had to do the same speeches for two days. He's off-camera and a total professional. He gave it everything for two days. It was brilliant to see. I guess when you've got people like that around, that filters down to the rest of the crew and all the other actors."

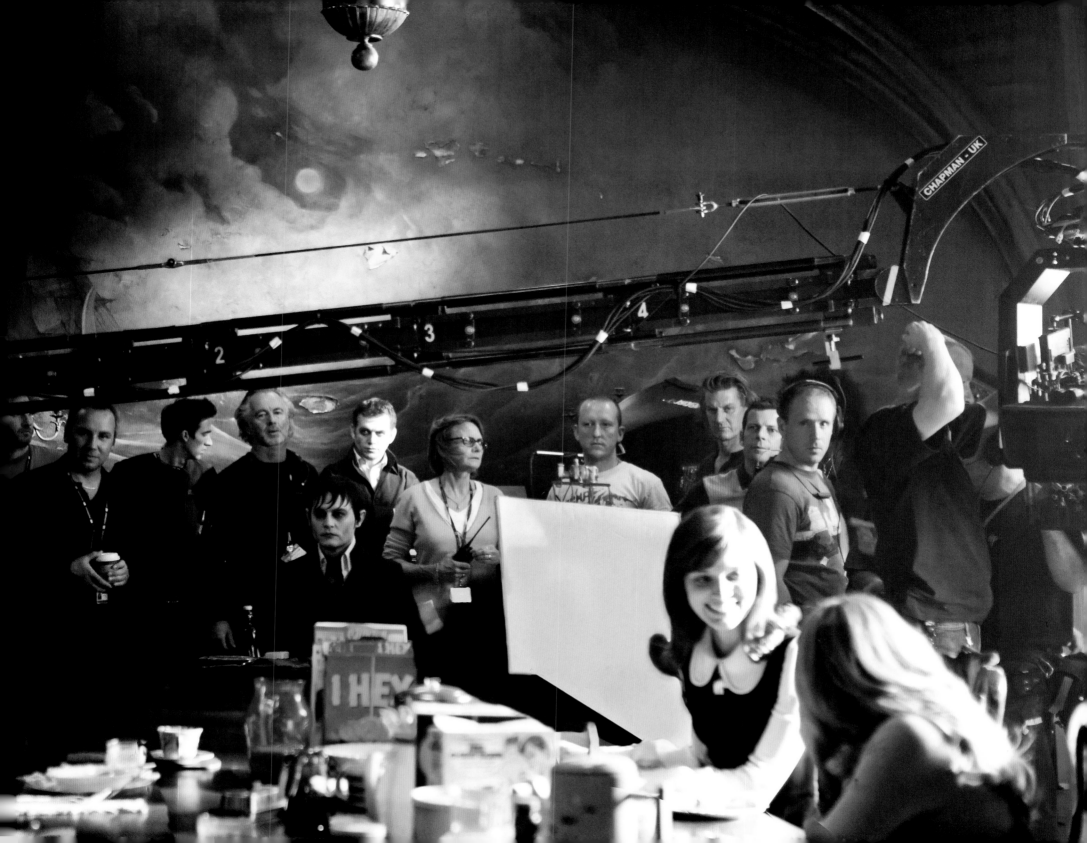

Dr. Hoffman's Office

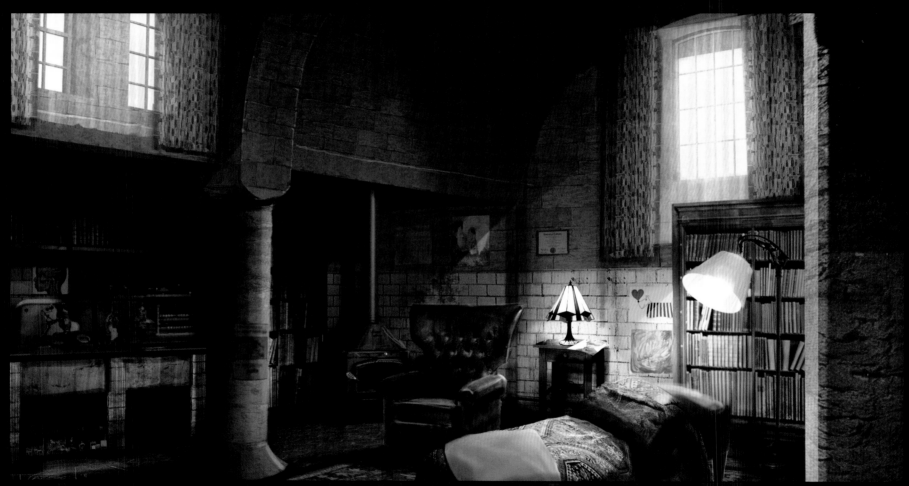

"Dr. Hoffman's office, we put down in the basement," says Heinrichs. "We wanted to make sure it felt like she's not really of the family, so we came up with this conceit that this was a space where the family used to do their laundry. A slightly subterranean room with windows, so you can see daylight coming through from above, that feels very utilitarian, cold and dungeon-like. It really reinforces the idea they put her somewhere else. It has a lot of cold surfaces in it — tile and stone — that she has tried to warm up with her psychiatrist furniture, a rug, a stove, things like that. What you get with that juxtaposition is a feeling of the uncomfortable-ness of Dr. Hoffman, who's an alcoholic and very acerbic, and the environment which really helped to reveal her character."

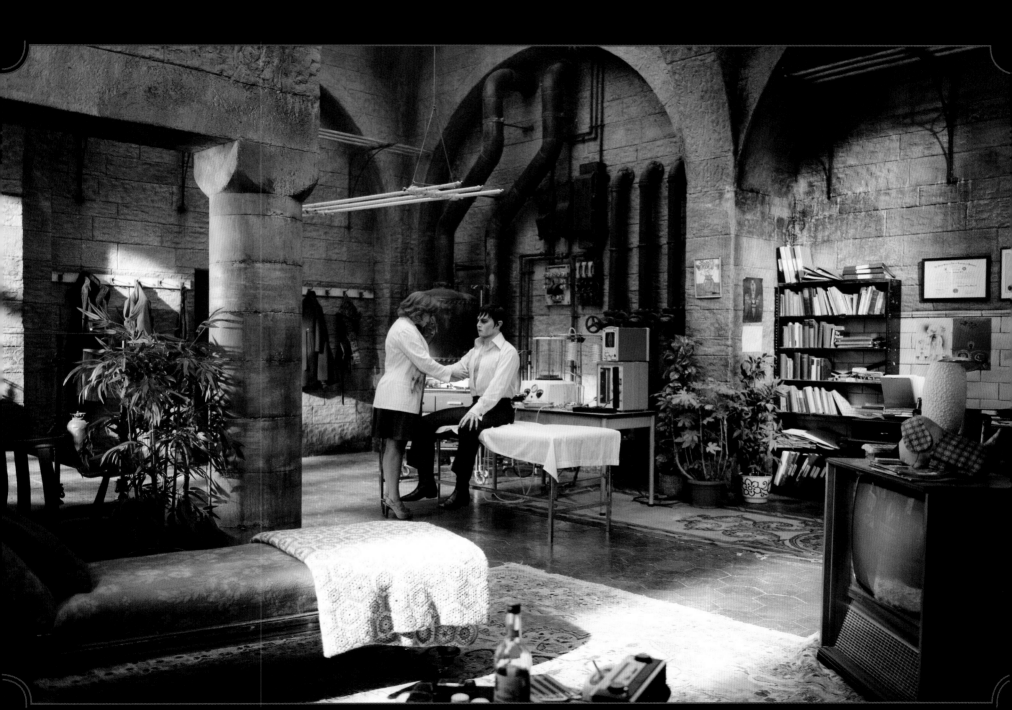

To create Collinsport, the initial thought was to find an existing fishing village, either in the UK or Maine itself, and adapt it. "We looked for different fishing villages," says Burton, "but a Maine fishing village is quite a specific looking thing and hard to find anywhere else. Even going to Maine, it's hard to find that now." Moreover, the storyline required Collinsport to go through a number of time periods — from the 18th century to 1972 — and evolutions. "We did our due diligence," explains Heinrichs. "We looked at photographs. We took a scout around the UK. But it was clear there wasn't a coastal village or a fishing village that looked like Maine, or would give us what we needed in terms of all the various stages our town was going to have to go through. All the practical concerns of night and day and tides, compounded by the fact we had to blow up a factory and have our two canneries facing each other across the water. There were so many very specific aesthetics to it, I realized that we were going to have to build it."

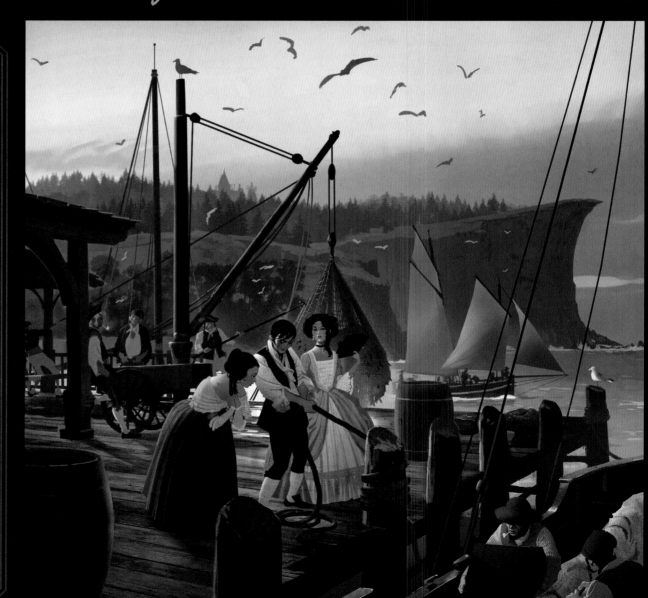

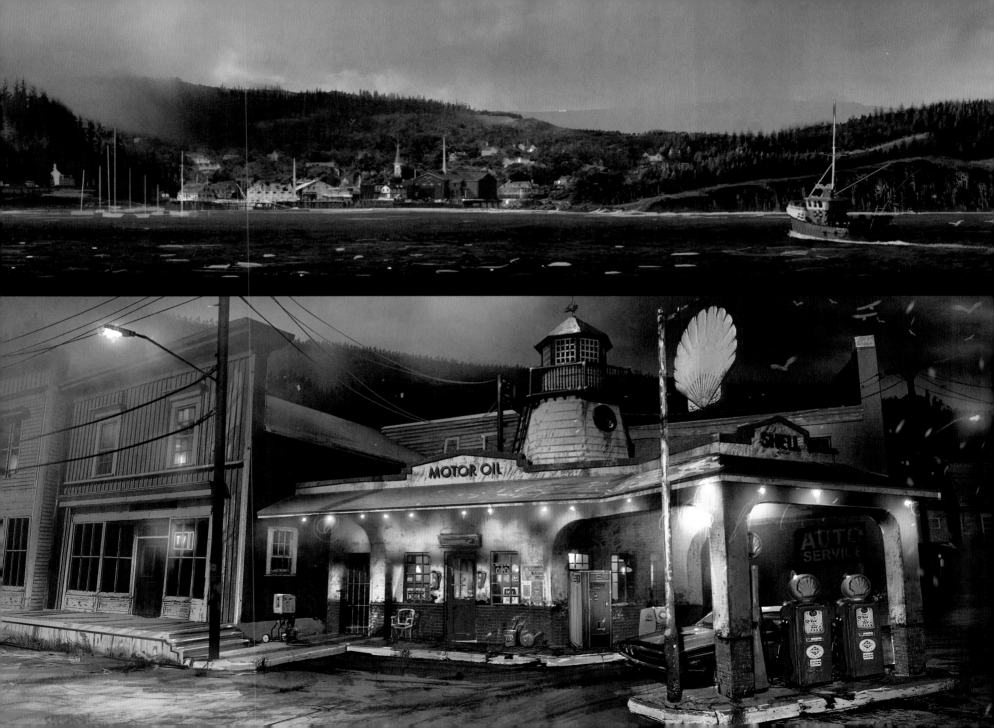

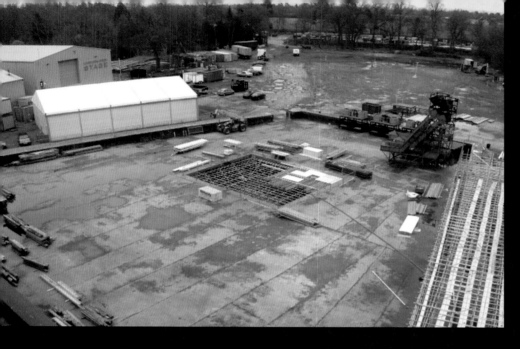
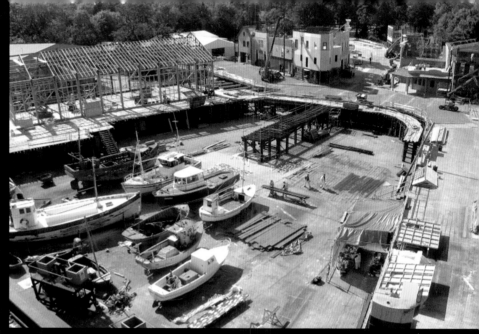
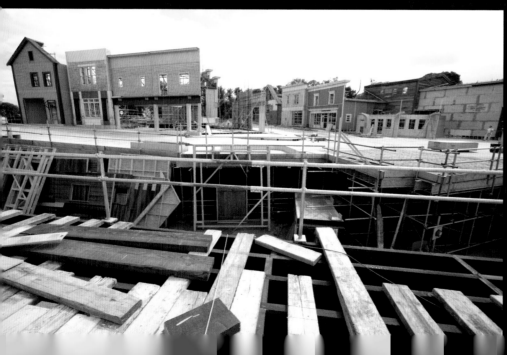
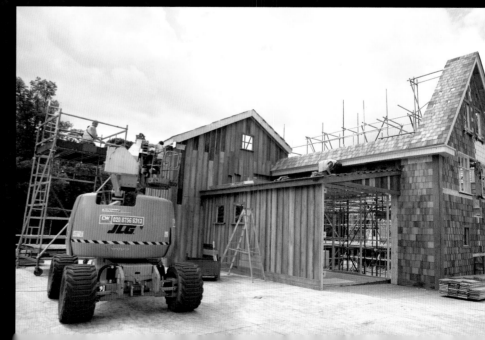

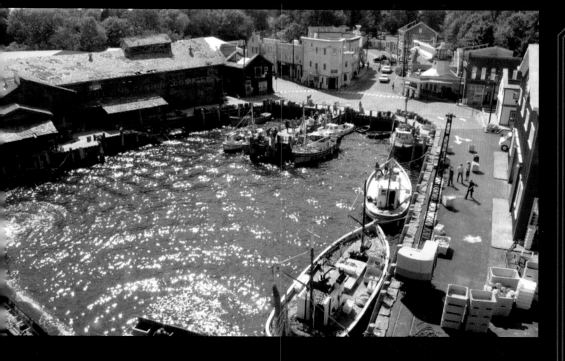

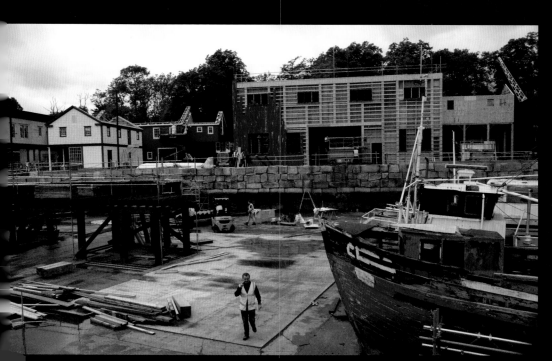

Heinrichs built Collinsport from scratch on the backlot at Pinewood, utilizing the studios' massive paddock tank and pre-existing green screen, as well as a vast area of car park. "It allowed us to have exactly what we wanted in a very controlled situation, to put fishing boats right into the water," he explains. The infrastructure took an initial six weeks of work, installing pipes and scaffolding. Since the entire set had to be built above the water line of the paddock tank, that meant a minimum of ten feet above the ground level, rising to 15 feet at the back end of the town. "You need to contour the land, so it feels part of a landscape. Fishing villages always come down to the shore and tend to merge up into hills beyond. We went to the trouble of creating a natural bowl shape to it. Those things are very subtle. They cost more money, but really make it feel real." All remaining building work took an additional 22 weeks, with the final dressed set measuring around 480 feet by 316 feet. "To see the evolution, this foreign environment appearing within the lot, was fantastic," recalls the production designer. "As it was growing, you started to realize you were no longer in a movie studio. It was such a thrilling experience, and it's one of the reasons I love doing what I do. When it was finally done, when it was lit for night, it was a very believable place to be, walking around and feeling like you were really in Maine. You had to remember not to walk off the 15 foot edge of it, and stick to the stairs." The extraordinary set was a boon for the actors. "My brain was tricked every day, I couldn't believe I wasn't on a location," says Heathcote. "It was extraordinary," concurs Pfeiffer. "You wanted to stay there for a couple of days, in a bed and breakfast. Truly, that was one of the most impressive sets I've seen."

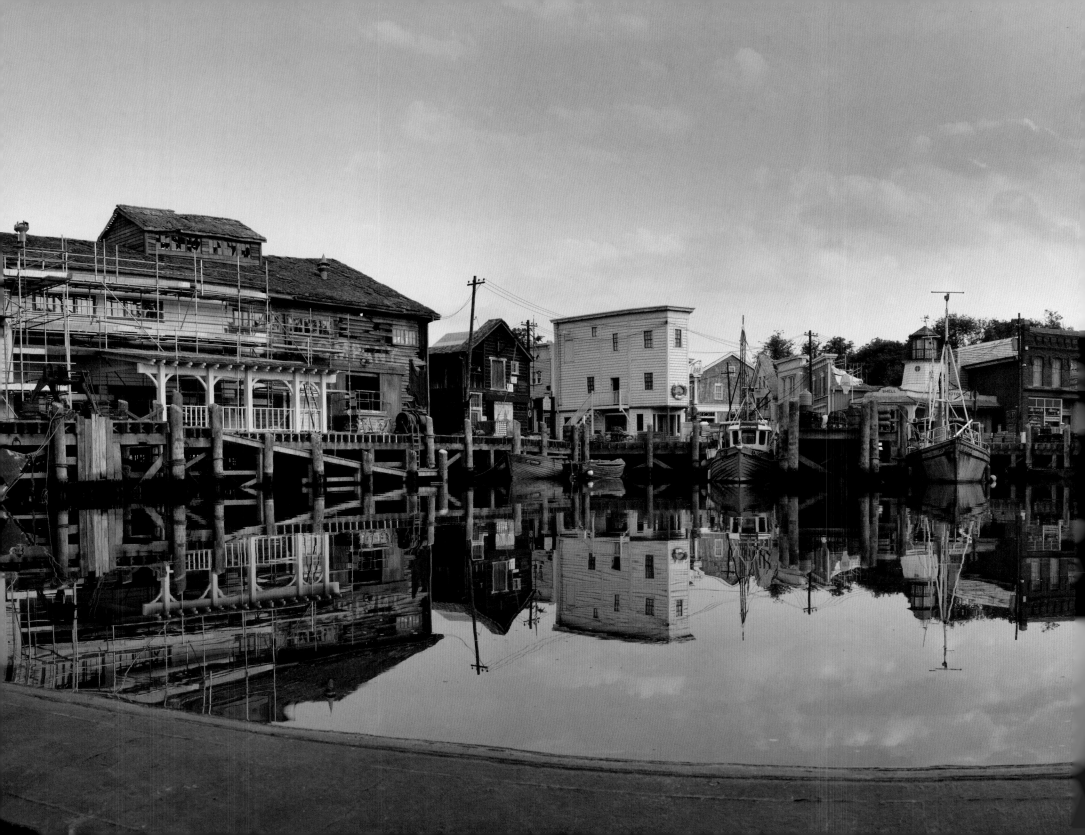

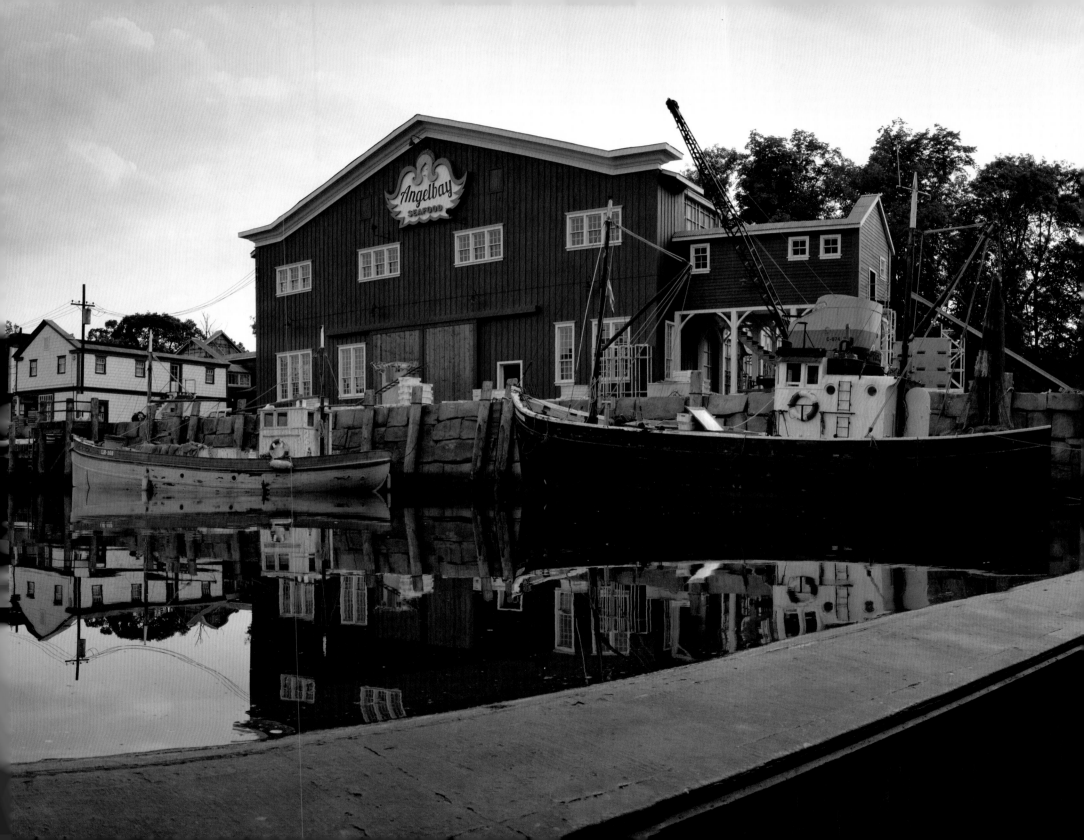

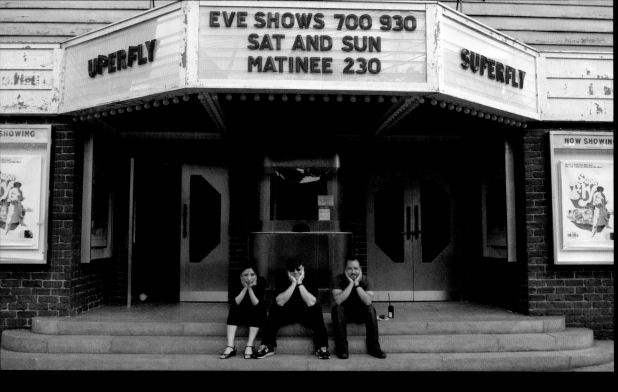

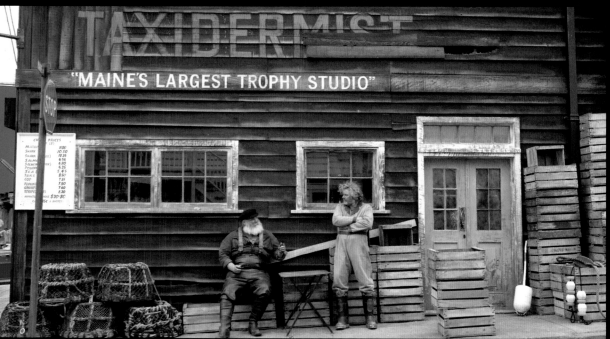

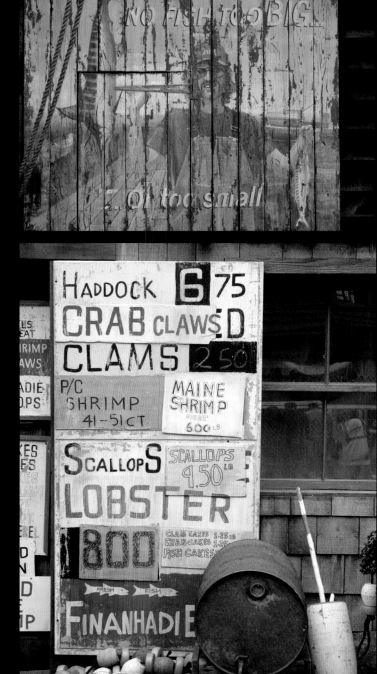

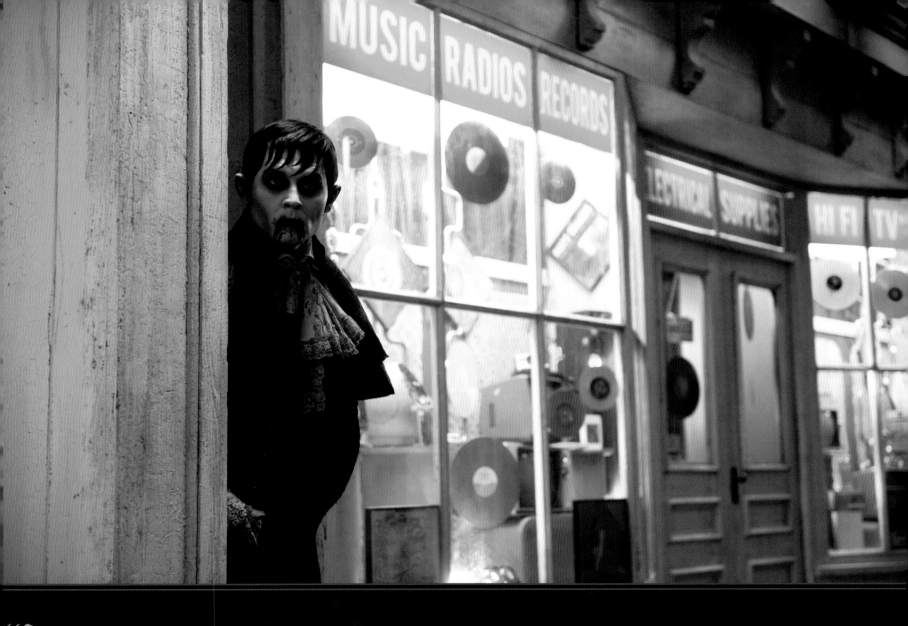

"I've worked with Rick [Heinrichs] on a number of films, and I told him, 'You've done what I thought was impossible — you've out-done yourself,'" recalls Depp. "The world he created for us to live in and act in and work in was absolute perfection, down to the tiniest detail. I just wanted to live there. I wanted to live on the set. It was so beautiful. I've never seen anything like that on any film I've ever done. It was mind boggling. We even shot interiors there, and walking through the streets at night just felt real."

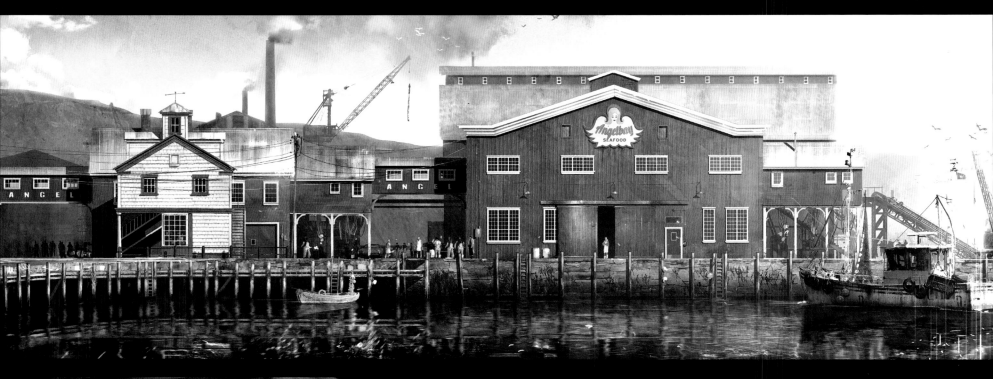

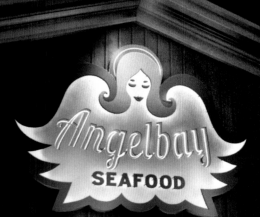

"Tim did a really quick little sketch of the Angel Bay logo outlining what he was hoping and we developed it and developed it, bringing it into the world of the '60s," explains Heinrichs. "It was great fun playing with the colors, and tying in images of waves and sea, angel and halo, showing Angelique as a modest, innocent, angelic creature."

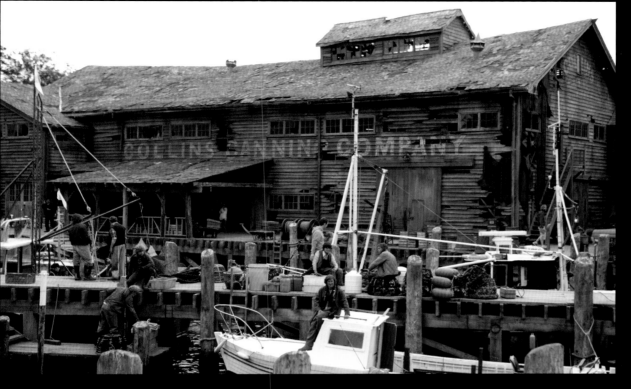

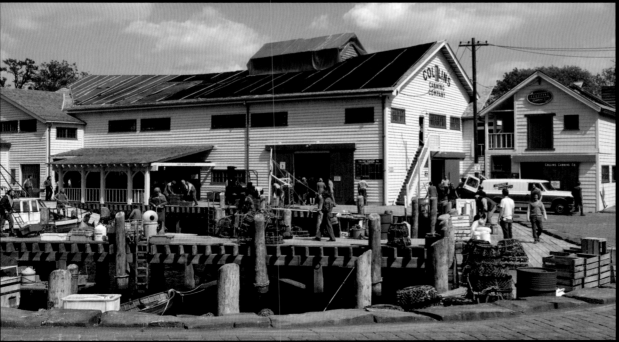

key component in the design of Collinsport was the two, opposing canneries of Angel Bay — a collection of white and red-painted wooden buildings — on one side of the harbor, directly across the water from the dilapidated Collins Cannery, which is renovated over the course of the film before it is razed during the climax. "This is a story about rivalry, about Angelique destroying the Collins family by creating this rival canning company, and bringing the inhabitants of Collinsport over to her side, and we showed this rivalry as a very graphic element, a face-off between these two large structures, built out onto the jetties that go out into the ocean," says Heinrichs. "But they were a challenge. Tracking the Collins Cannery through its evolution from nothing at the beginning, to a thriving place, to a down-and-out structure, one of the things we did was age the structure way down, put a huge swale in the ridgeline and paint it so it looks like it's about ready to fall apart."

ngel Bay wasn't simply a wooden facade. Inside there was working equipment and real fish. "When we started we weren't quite sure how much cannery we were going to be able to show," explains Heinrichs. "But we discovered a number of canning companies were going out of business, so we were able to get a great deal of equipment from them. We did a great amount with conveyor belts, to make things much more visually interesting, with fish ferried through various stages, conveyed off the boats, having them knobbed, which means having their heads cut off, then stuffing them into the cans, labelling and shipping them out."

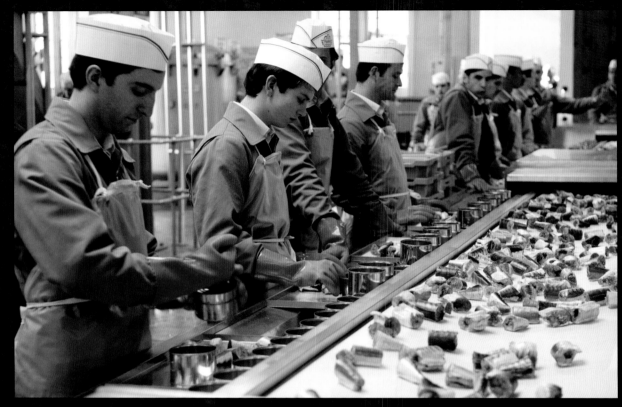

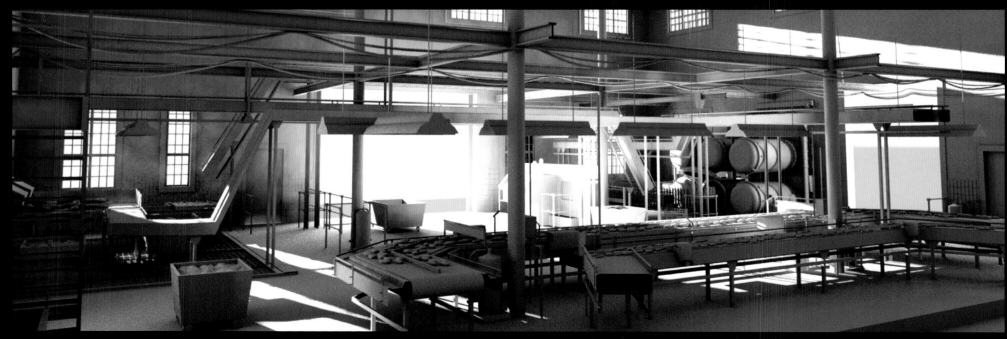

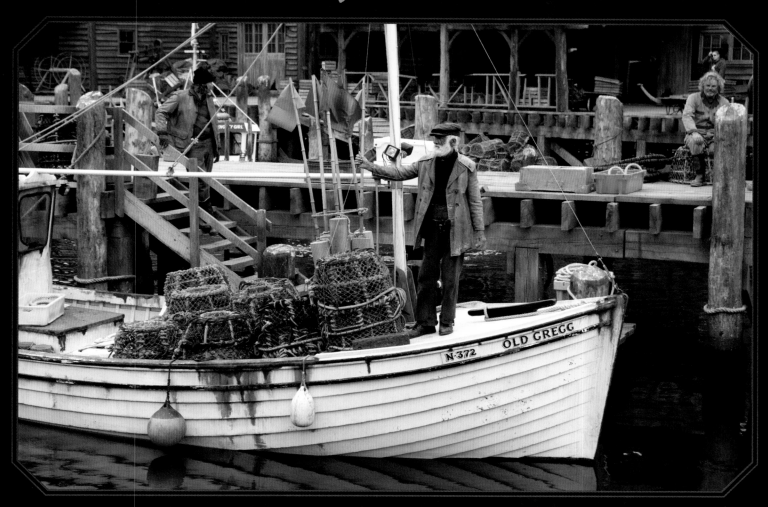

Collinsport Harbor was filled with boats of every size — from small rowers to a fishing vessel measuring 52 feet — and sourced from all over the UK. "We were searching for wooden boats, specifically, to fit the period, so we could set the harbor in different sizes and raise the type of fishing that was happening during the '70s," explains marine co-ordinator Ian Creed. But since Pinewood's paddock tank was only three-and-a-half feet deep, many of the boats had to have parts of their hulls removed in order to sit naturally below the waterline. "It was very tricky on a couple of them," says Creed, "but we managed to do it in the end."

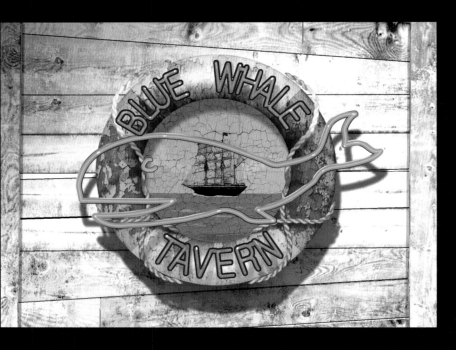

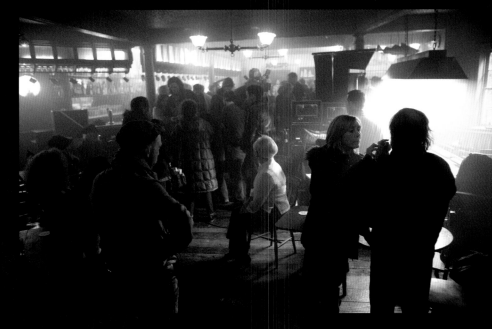

avored watering hole of the Collinsport fishing fleet, the Blue Whale Tavern dates back to the 1750s and the creation of the town itself. "We made sure the basic structure looked authentic to the colonial era," says Heinrichs who also took inspiration for the drinking establishment's color and character from The Pig's Nose in East Prawle, Devon, an English seaside pub he visited during location scouting. "The Blue Whale's architecture is out of square in response to the geography of its location; its ceilings are too low and after 200 years it has been appended with finishes and add-ons of questionable taste. You can practically smell the centuries of beer that have been burnished into the woodwork."

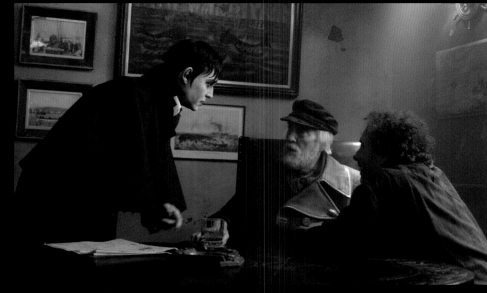

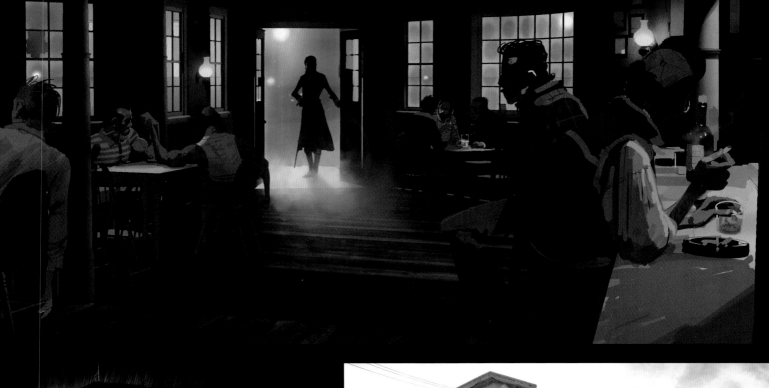

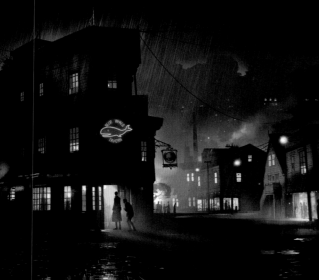

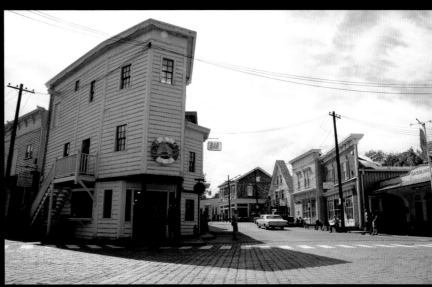

Widow's Peak

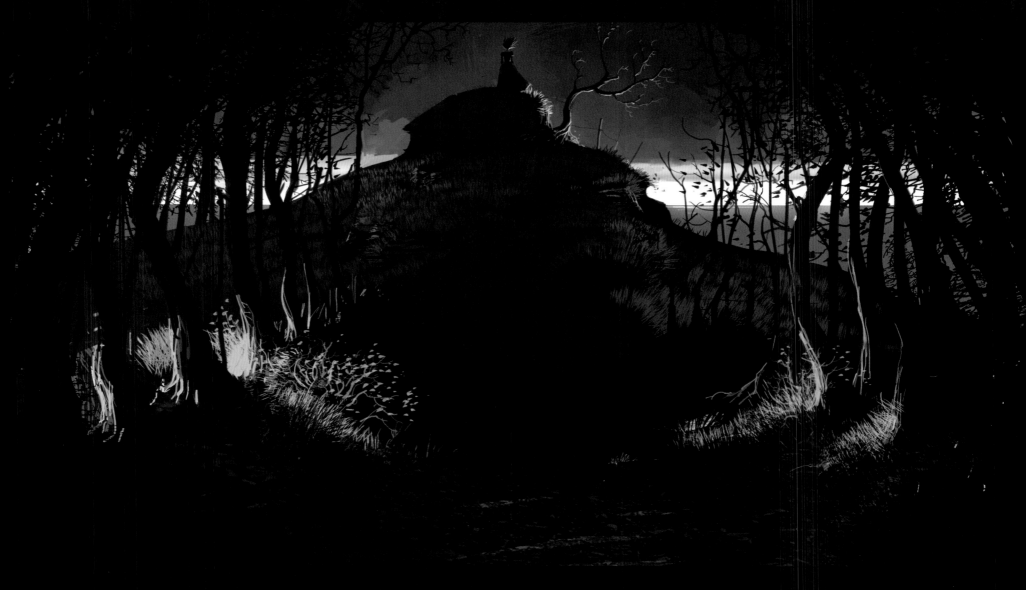

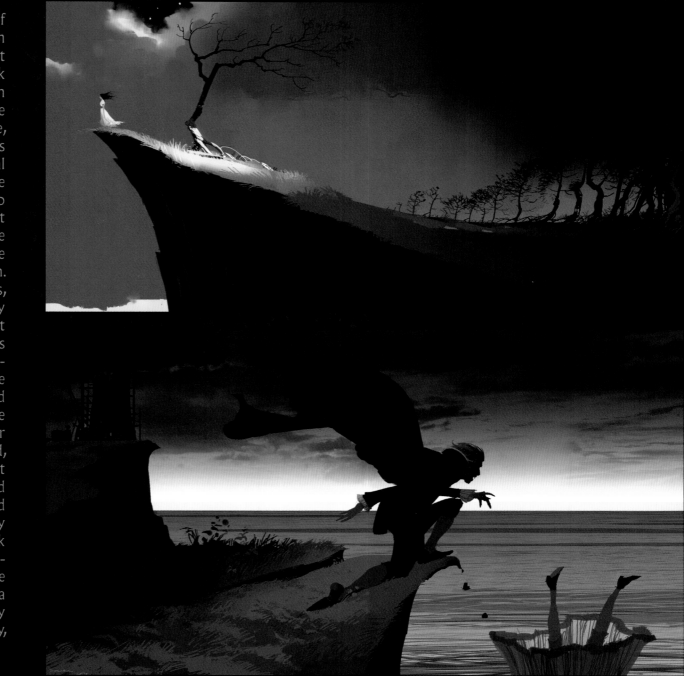

The cliff from which Josette throws herself at the start of the film and from which Victoria and Barnabas fall at the end was built in sections at Pinewood. The top, with its thick grass and various trees, was constructed on stage, while its rocky base was built outside on the backlot. "It was a fantastic cliff shore, not just a bunch of rocks piled there," says Heinrichs of the latter element. "It had a real fabulous character which not only looked like it hurts to fall on, from 100 feet, but also had a lot of great direction and shapes to it that were very opposing and uncomfortable looking." Everything else was created by the visual effects department in post-production. "Tim's brief to the locations department was, 'Find me a cliff.' But he wanted it to be fairly sheer-faced, tall, and a sort of ski-jump about it, so it would rise towards the tip," recalls visual effects supervisor Angus Bickerton. "Location scouted the length and breadth of the British Isles, and we found some pretty good places. But ultimately, nothing quite fit the bill. We liked some rocks at one particular location, and a face at another." In the end, a maquette was made by the art department which coalesced all the different elements and places that Burton liked, and was then handed over to visual effects who created a wholly realistic CG model of the cliff with real rock textures. "It's an important character, the crashing waves," says Burton. "It was part of the series, the credits. The waves were kind of a theme, part of the mystery and the family turmoil, romantic and haunting and ghosty, and part of what that original vibe was."

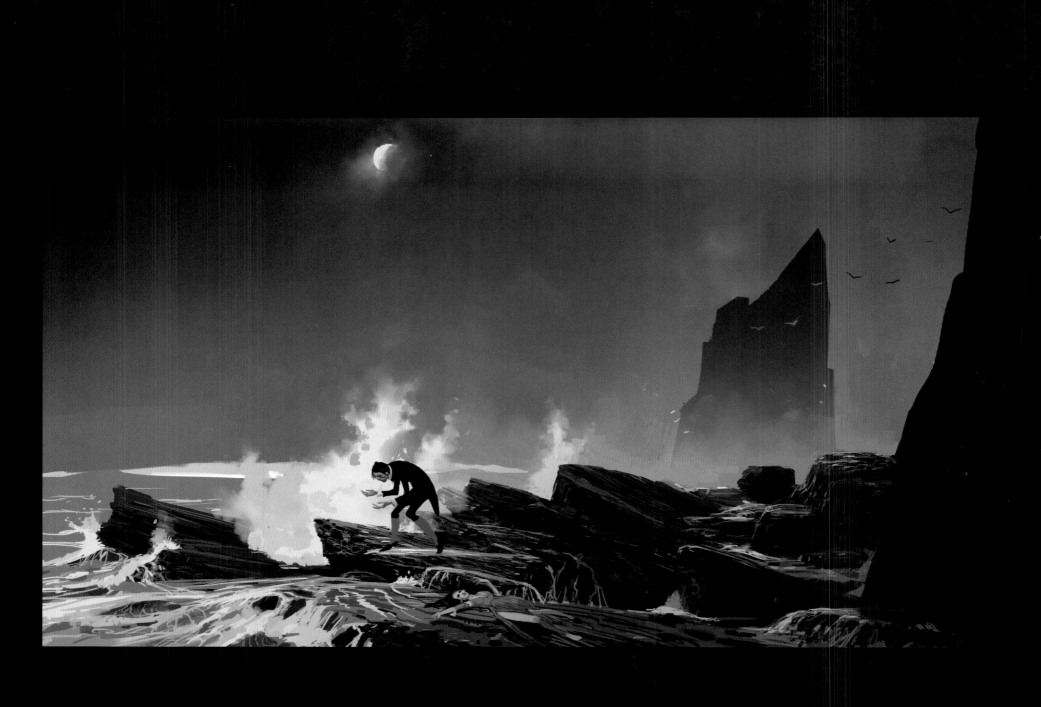

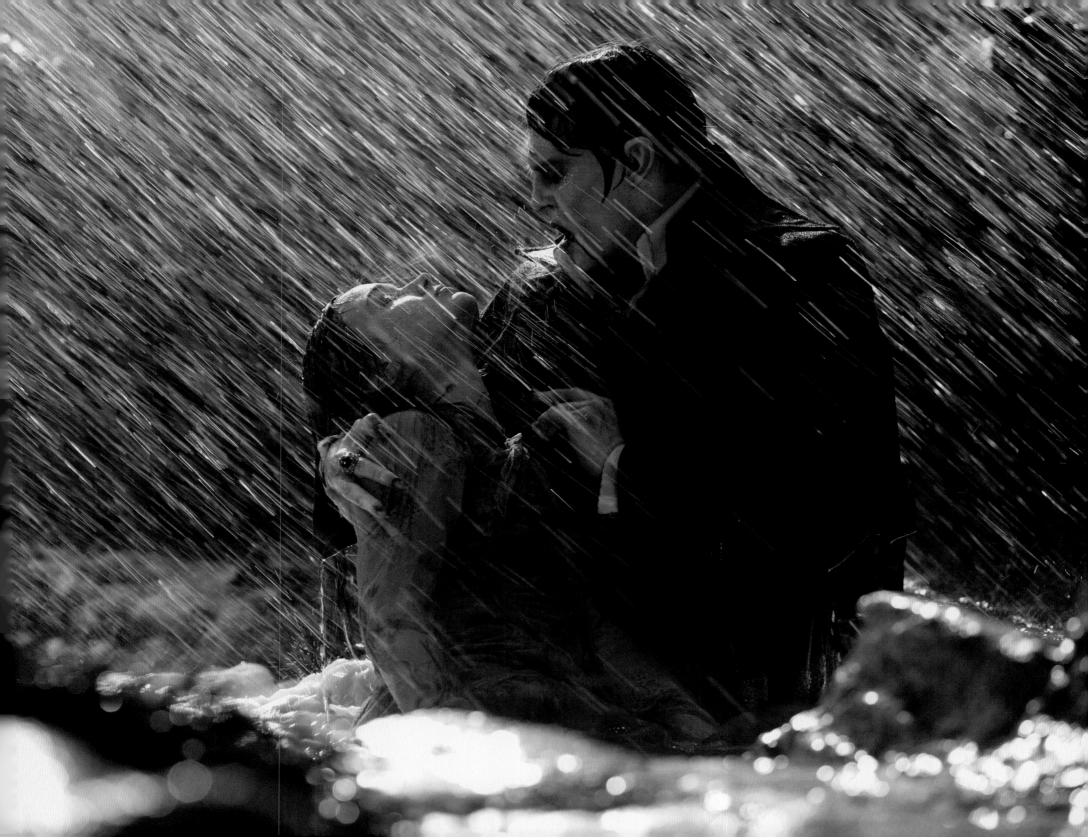

The Happening

As Barnabas's powers of persuasion begin to restore the Collins family's fortunes, he decides to celebrate with a grand ball, or rather, in the parlance of the day, a "Happening," with Collinwood's Grand Foyer transformed into a pulsating disco, complete with a mirror ball, strobe lights, cage dancers and a special musical guest — Alice Cooper (who turns out not to be the kind of "Alice" Barnabas is expecting). "This is one of those things that I'll go to my grave kind of wondering how something like this could happen," says Depp of Cooper's casting. "We were talking about the idea of the ball and then the idea of turning it into a Happening or a rock and roll concert, and for some reason it just flew out of my gob, 'It would be great to have Alice Cooper because he looks exactly the same as he did then and his style matches what we're doing in the film.' Tim said, 'That's a cool idea' and the next thing I know they contacted Alice and he said 'yes.'"

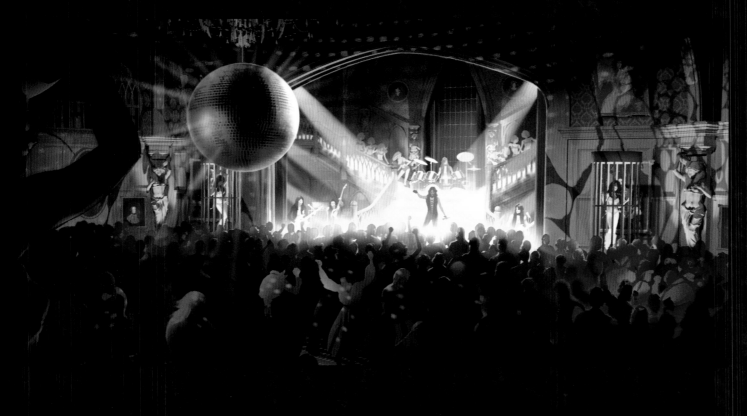

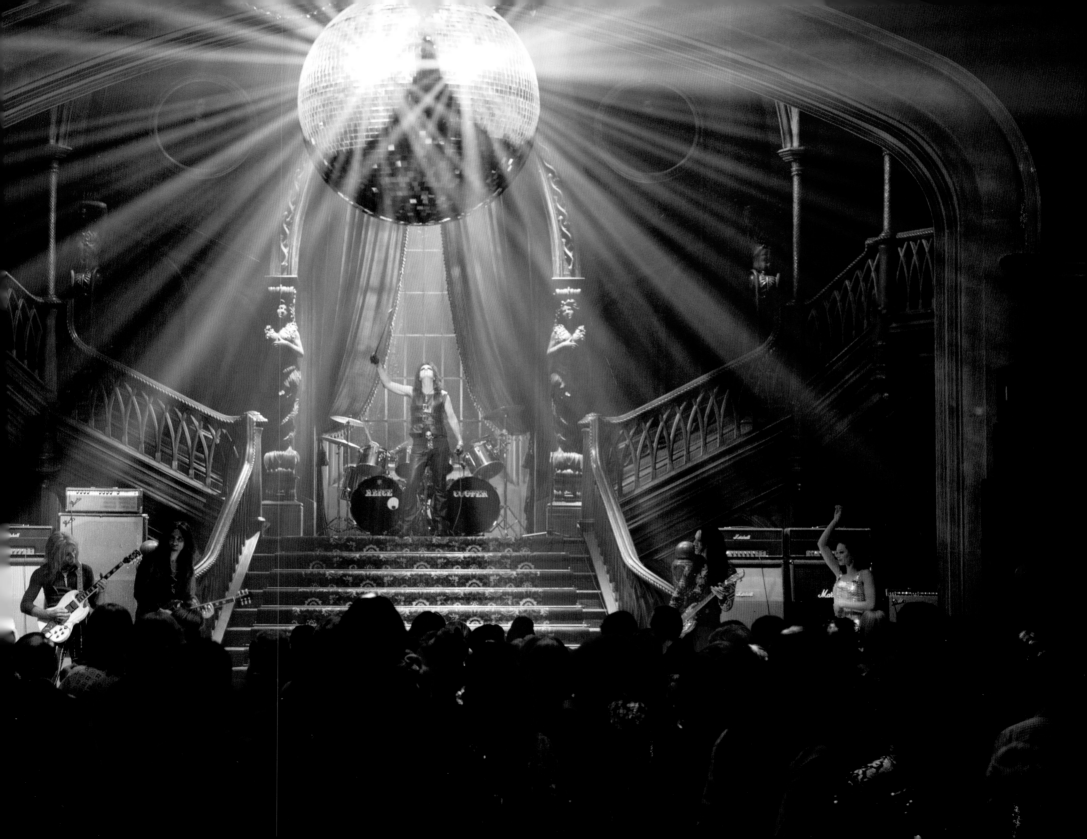

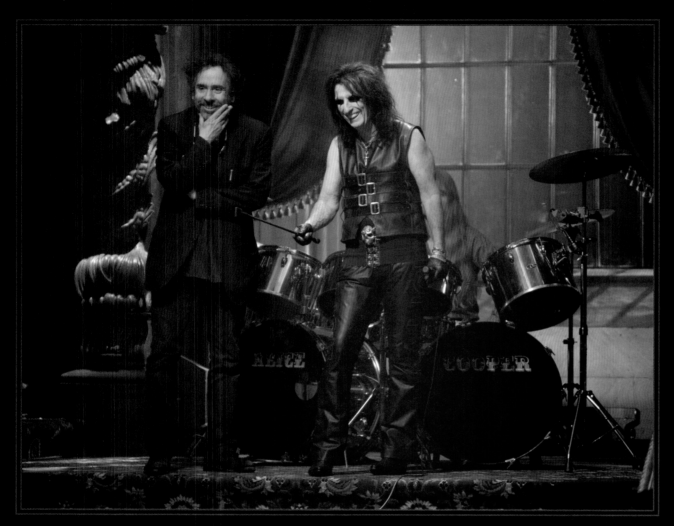

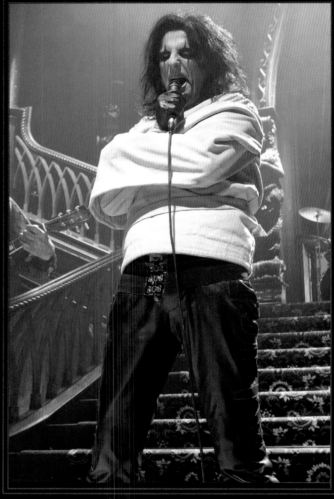

"Alice Cooper was very much of that period, and he just fit the tone of the film," says Burton. "The scary thing is, he looks exactly the same now as he did then. In fact, we had a copy of *Rolling Stone* with him on the cover from that time and I think he might actually look better now. It's really, really strange." Cooper was happy to revisit the '70s and to have the chance to work with Burton and Depp. "I've always been a fan of Tim's," he says. "He and I have kind of the same background; we enjoy all the same horror movies. And I've always admired Johnny as the man of 1,000 faces. I don't know anyone who does that as well as he does."

The entire population of Collinsport turns out for the "Happening", including four guests making a return to Collinwood Manor after a long absence: Jonathan Frid, Lara Parker, Kathryn Leigh Scott, and David Selby, all favorite cast members from the series. "It was such a kick to have them there. Everyone wanted their photo taken with them. Just to have them come bless the set, so to speak, seemed appropriate," Burton states. "Getting to meet Jonathan and the other members of the original cast was a real kick," agrees Depp. "It was nice to have their support because, ultimately, we are saluting them, we are paying tribute to something they were involved in and created 40 odd years ago."

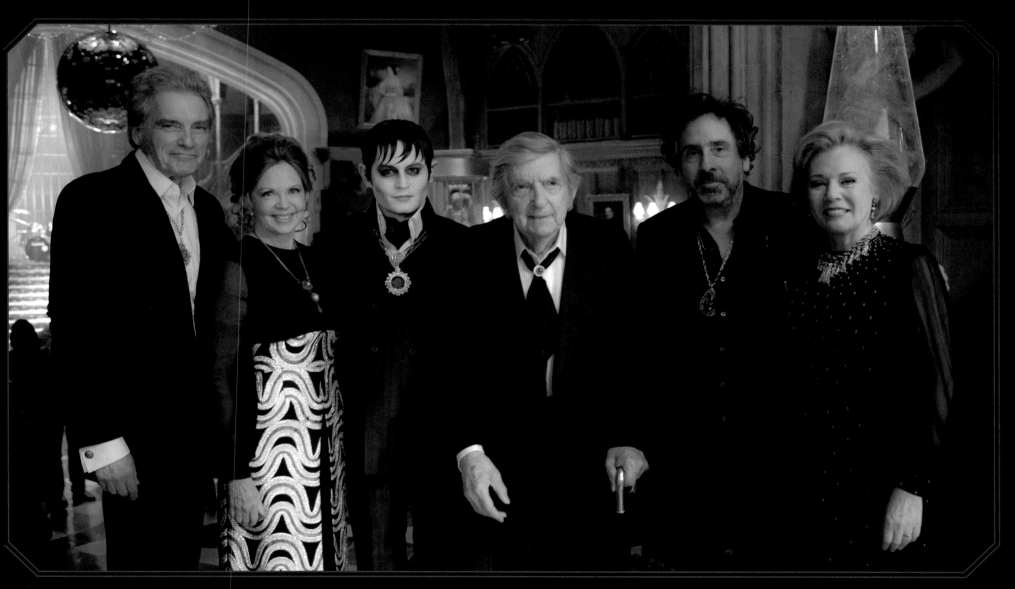

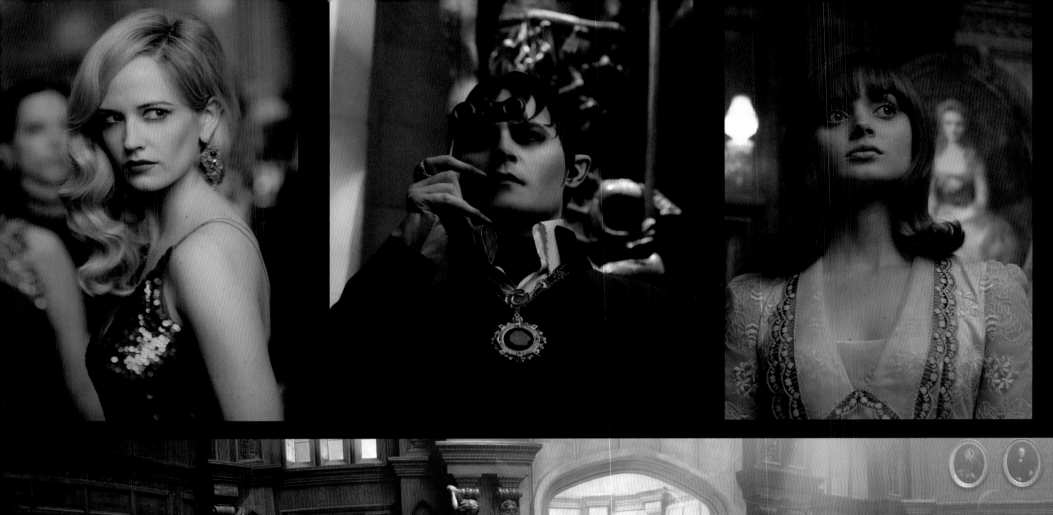
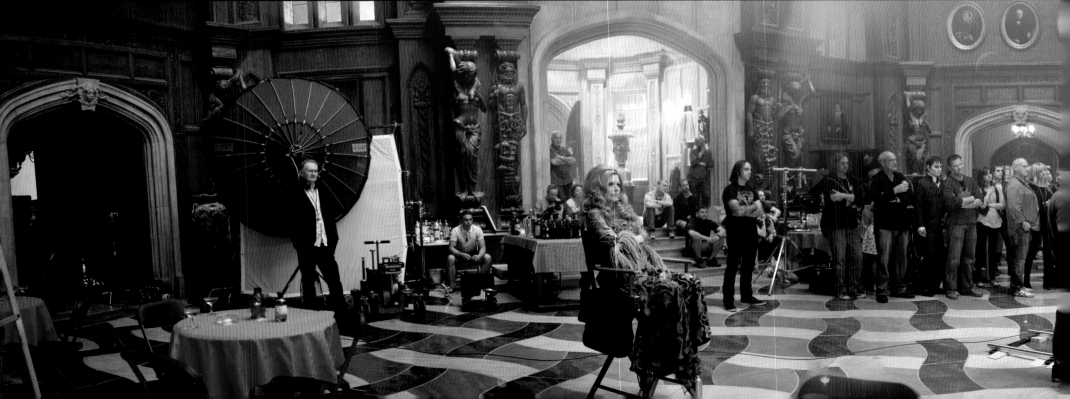

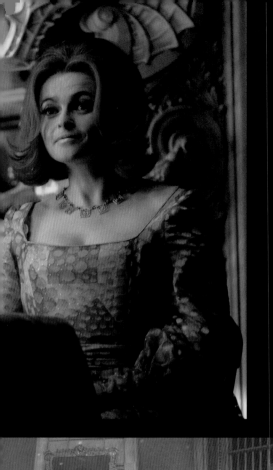
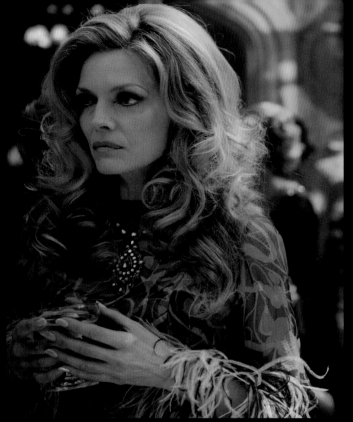
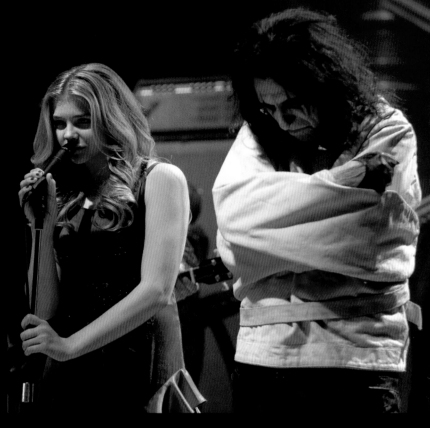
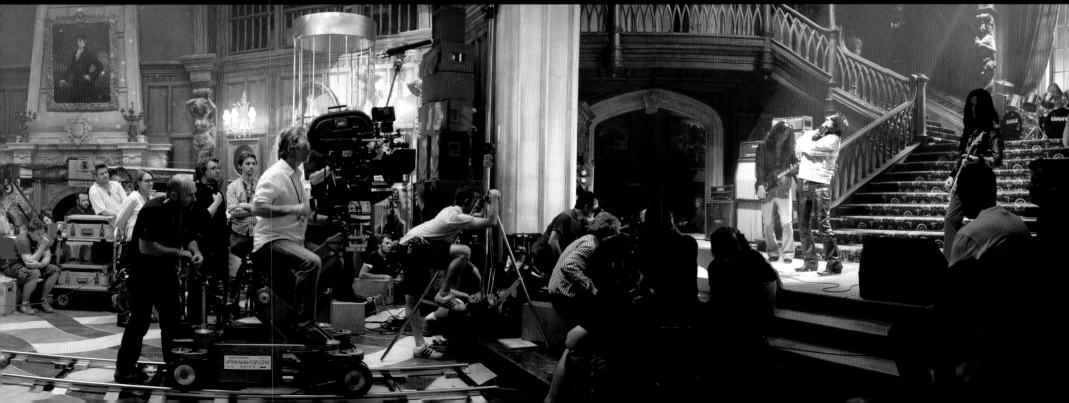

CHAPTER 3

COSTUME

HAIR & MAKEUP

PROSTHETICS

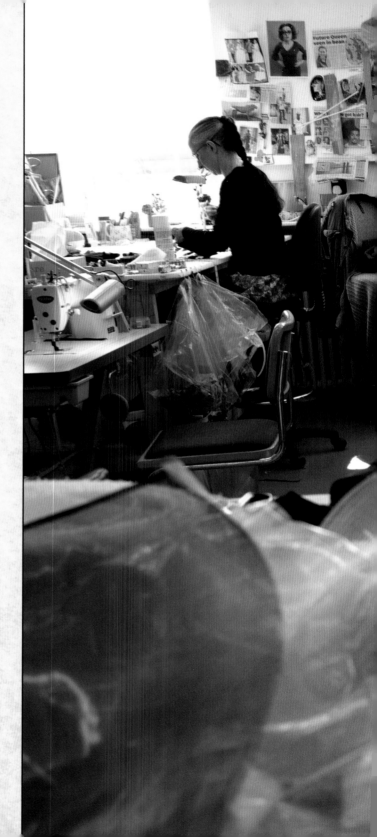

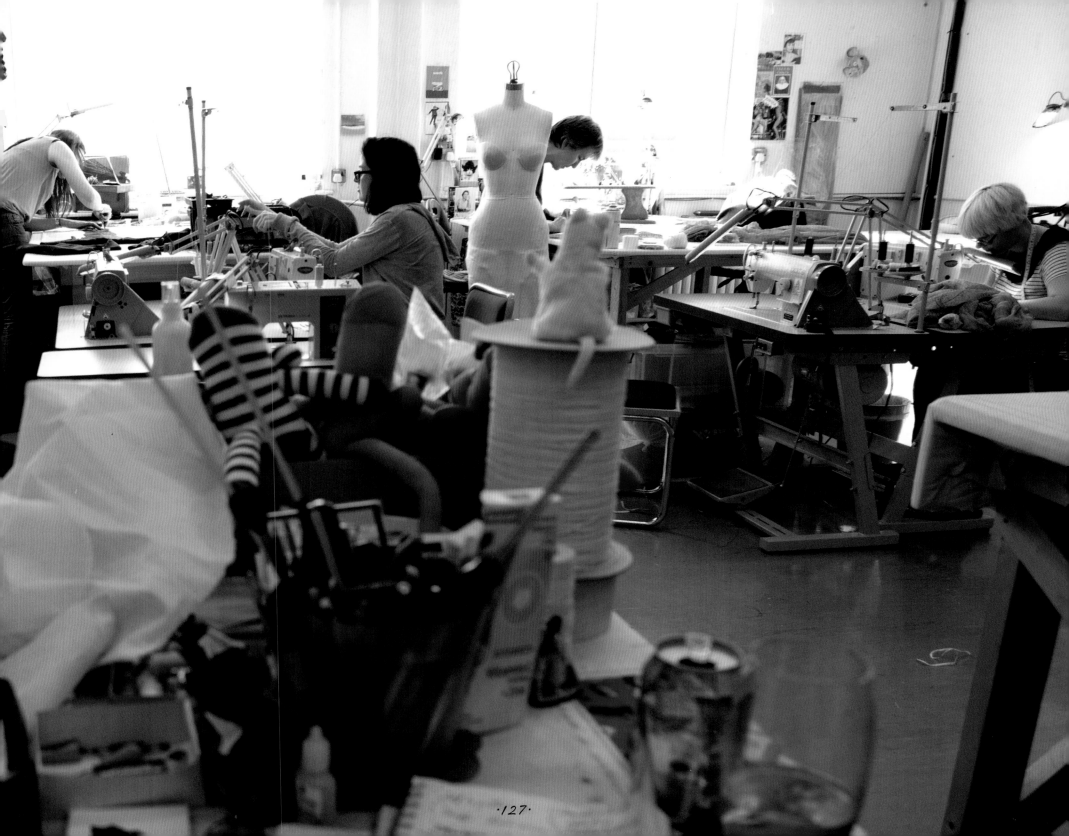

Costumes

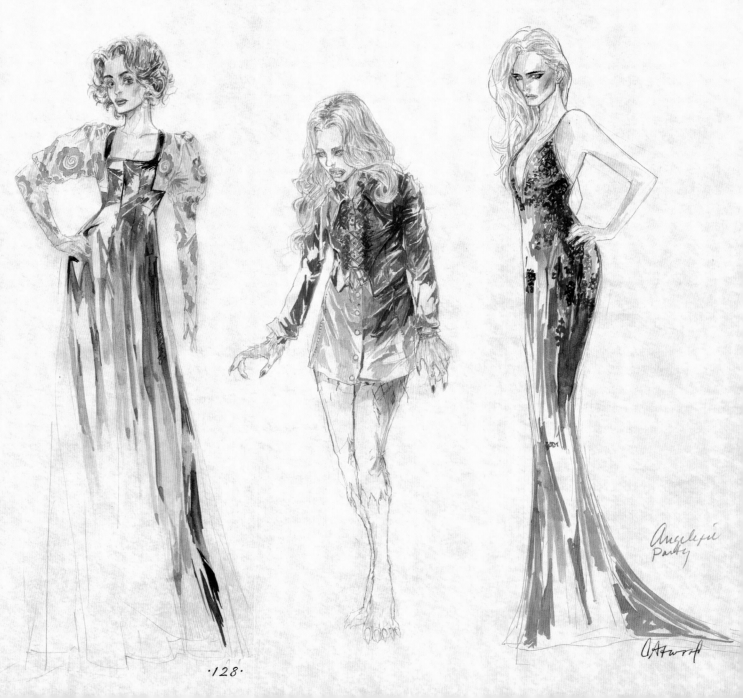

When it came to dressing and styling two centuries of fashion, Burton called upon costume designer Colleen Atwood. "I've worked with Colleen many times. For me, she is a real artist, in the sense she tries to get into the character and understand what it is, whether she's doing a complete fantasy or tapping into reality. We were trying to be true to the spirit of what the costumes were, without treating them like a joke, because the fashion is extreme. But it's texture, the same as with the texture of the house. Again, it was very important because it's all through Barnabas's eyes, and you wanted to be able to see the textures and feel the textures and get the vibe of that era as strongly as you can."

"**C**olleen never misses," states Depp. "Her taste is impeccable, her approach to every character was right on the money, and the second you put on the costume, that suit, that armor, you stand differently, you turn differently. It made me stand taller. It made me walk differently. I found the character on a whole other level once the wardrobe came into play. Colleen will ask a few questions about your character, then she goes and does her research."

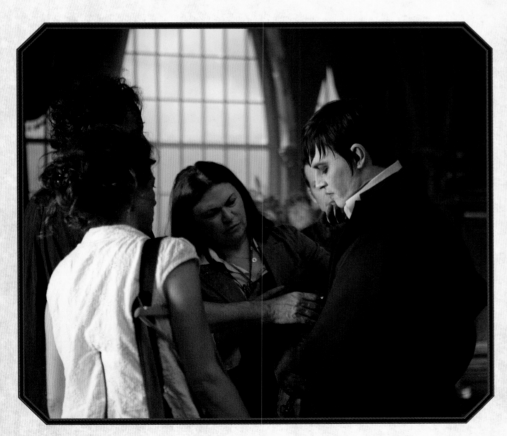

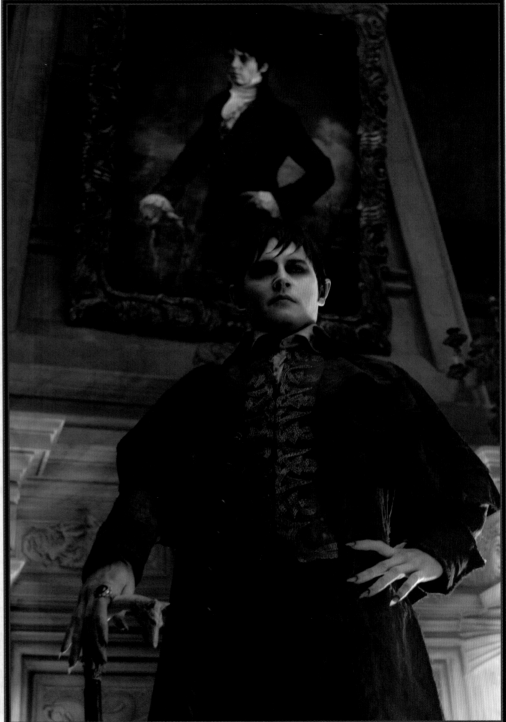

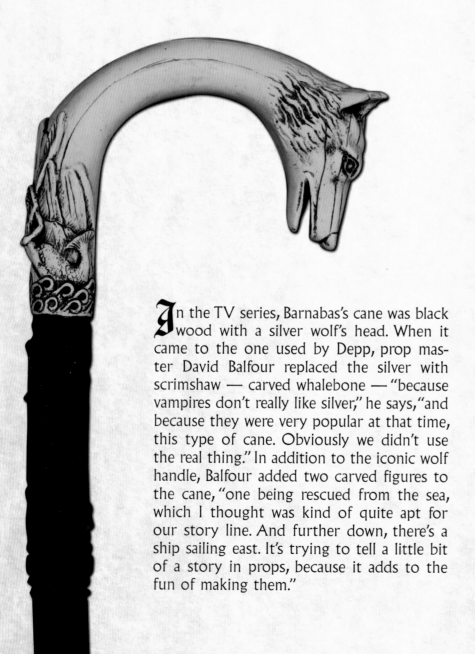

In the TV series, Barnabas's cane was black wood with a silver wolf's head. When it came to the one used by Depp, prop master David Balfour replaced the silver with scrimshaw — carved whalebone — "because vampires don't really like silver," he says, "and because they were very popular at that time, this type of cane. Obviously we didn't use the real thing." In addition to the iconic wolf handle, Balfour added two carved figures to the cane, "one being rescued from the sea, which I thought was kind of quite apt for our story line. And further down, there's a ship sailing east. It's trying to tell a little bit of a story in props, because it adds to the fun of making them."

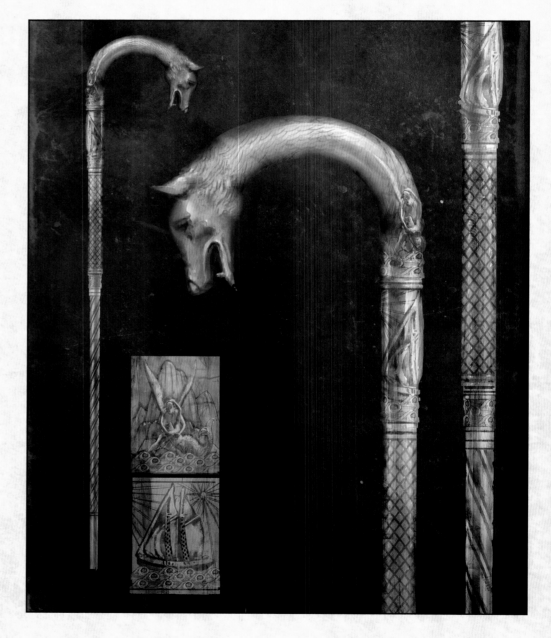

Barnabas's Ring & Pendant

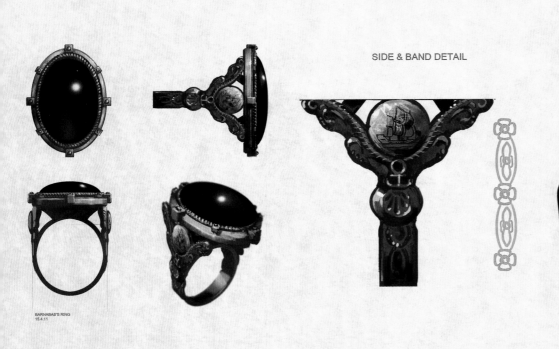

SIDE & BAND DETAIL

BARNABAS'S RING
15.4.11

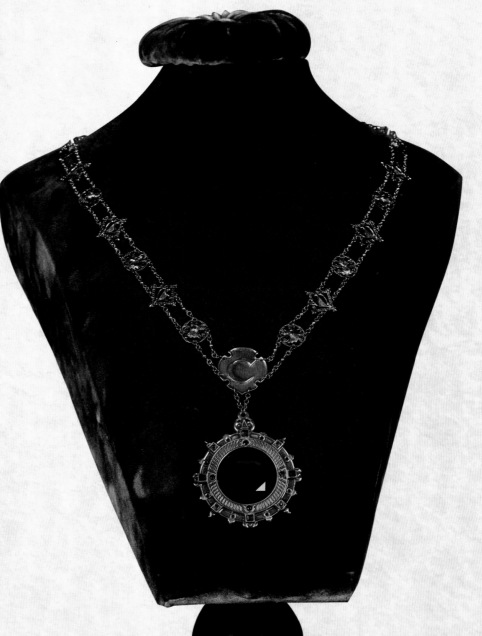

For Barnabas's ring, David Balfour was keen to create something unique and not follow the design of the one worn by Jonathan Frid, and commissioned jeweler Steven Einhorn to make it. "With something like that, that is so personal, we can make it as a prop but if you can get it made for real it makes it a bit more authentic," says Balfour. "It was all hand-made. Again we came up with a lot of nautical themes. We made it in rose gold with a black onyx stone and there's a ship carved into it. The pendant, too, was made in rose gold, to get that nice finish, because it was going to be seen quite a bit in close-up."

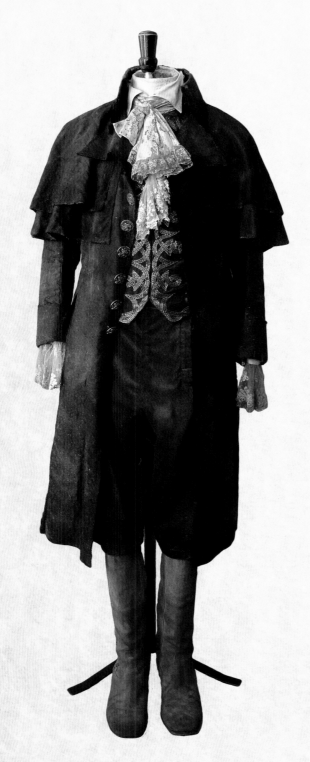

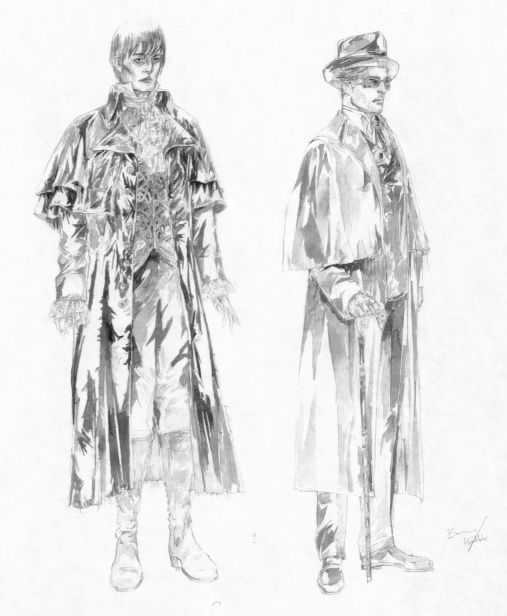

In designing Barnabas's costumes, Atwood was keen to retain the elegant, Goth feel of his 18th century attire in his '70s wardrobe, "so it wasn't the goofball kind of '70s, big lapel kind of thing, that it still had the elegance of the earlier times." While Barnabas's high collars are a nod to Karl Lagerfeld, his cape coat in 1972 is based on Jonathan Frid's coat, but "I changed it up a little bit, gave it a higher collar and more of a vampire shape. It's a little bit more elegant coat shape in general."

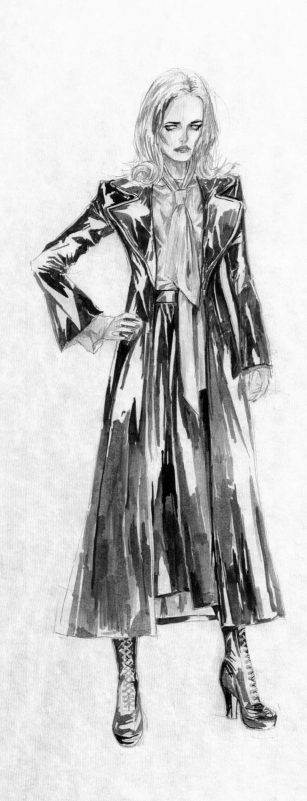

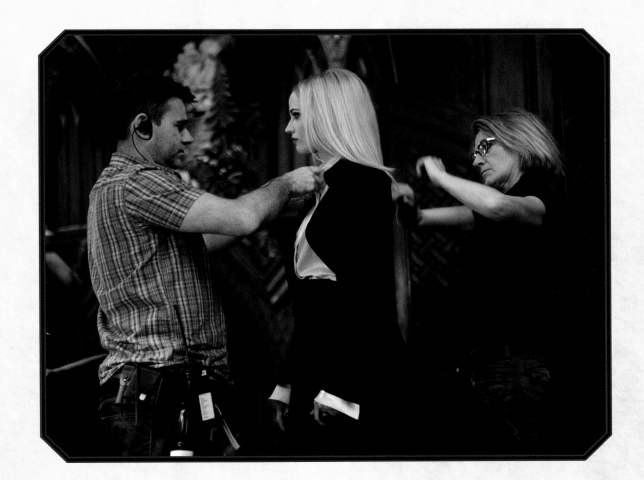

For the 20th century Angelique, Atwood wanted to reflect the strength of the character and took inspiration from a line in the script that described her as having "'stepped out of a Virginia Slims ad.' It stuck fairly close to that, a modern woman even though she was an old soul. Her clothes were very '70s, very tailored, very operable in a man's world; also very strong in shape, like armor because she's quite frail inside, this character. They're sexy but tailored sexy." Recalls Eva Green, "I wanted something a bit timeless for Angelique. It's the '70s but there's a little edge to it. It's the Burton '70s. Angelique has a very individual style. She's very cool, very much ahead of her time, while the Collins family's costumes are more old-fashioned. I remember I picked pictures of very famous actresses from the '30s, like Marlene Dietrich, Bette Davis, Gene Tierney. Colleen was amazing. She makes these amazing shapes and chooses the right fabrics, which is magic on screen."

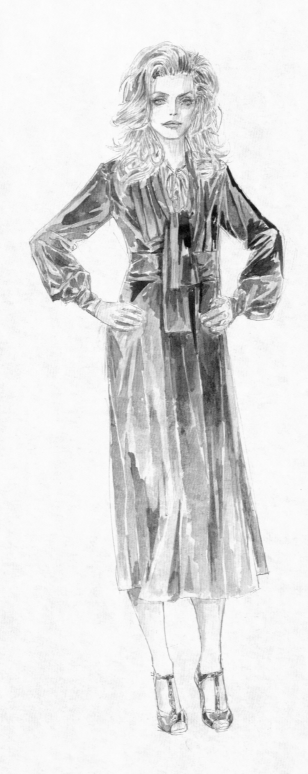

twood began by watching the original *Dark Shadows* to get a sense of "the atmosphere it had, and pulled what I could for each character," she recalls. "I didn't pull much. It was more the feeling of the series. The actual clothes were not what we had in mind, rather the sense of fun the original had. Then I looked at the fantastic set design by Rick Heinrichs, talked to Tim. I started with the 18th century research first because it takes longer to make those things and find the materials. Then I overlaid the two periods to find similarities between them so I could have a play with the neck collars and all those things from both to make it work. And then we got into the swinging '70s. I pulled a lot of great stock pieces for the crowd and we built all the principal clothes apart from a few things."

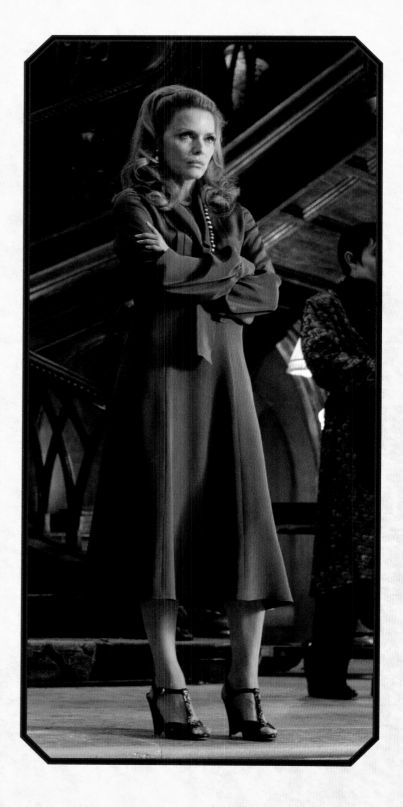

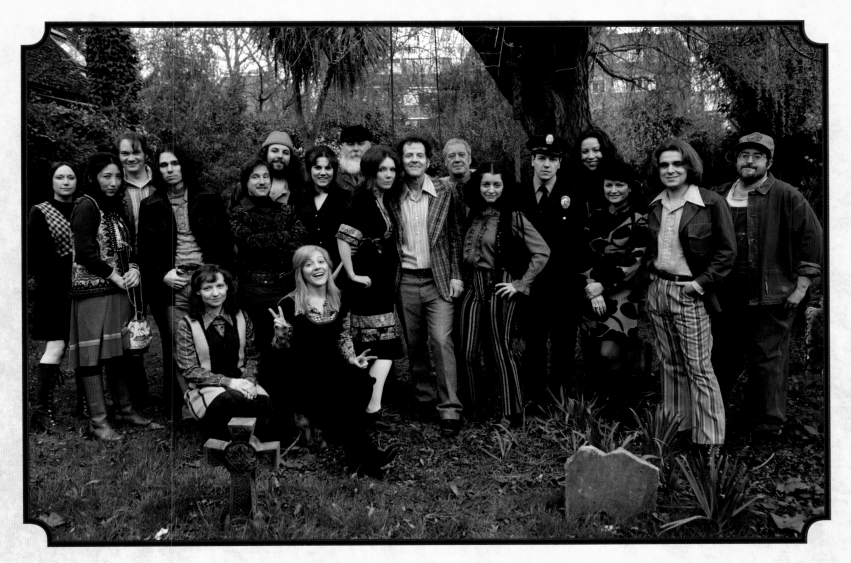

For some of the cast, the era's looks and fashions were more than fun; they meant a return to the good old days. "I grew up in the 1970s. So for me the '70s are incredibly nostalgic," says Jackie Earle Haley. "I'm all for it if everybody wants to bring bellbottoms back, especially on girls; they really look awesome on girls. I was one of those guys that hung on to bellbottoms like long after everybody else had abandoned them. I guess I wasn't paying attention." Another fan of that particular item was Pfeiffer. "I will always love bellbottoms," she insists. "I'm just a hippie at heart, I guess. I was a little bit too young for the whole kind of late '60s happening and that kind of groovy mod kind of thing, but I got to do it in this movie."

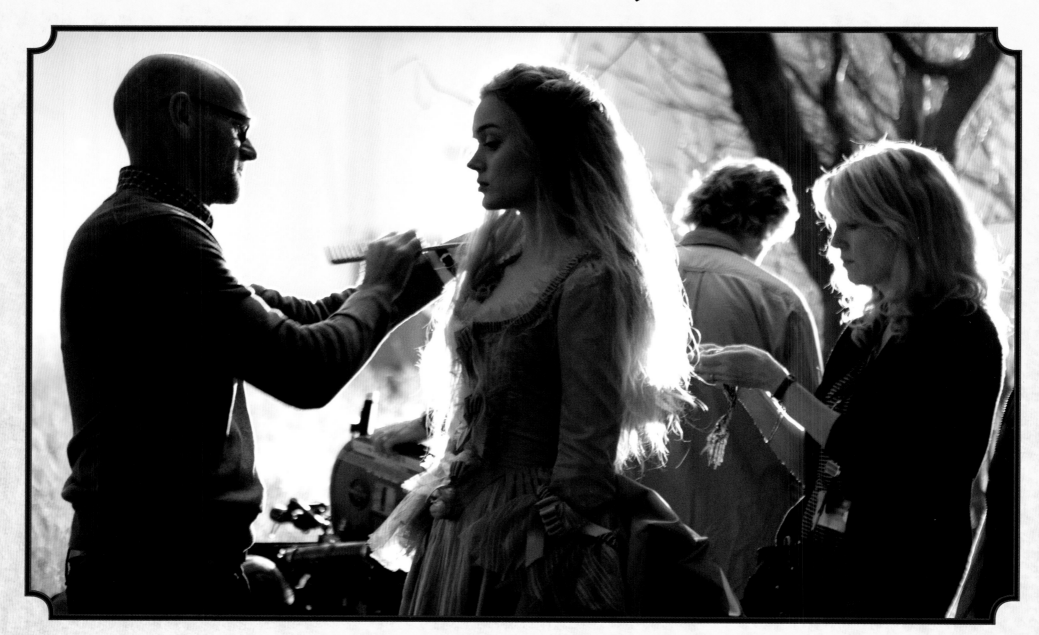

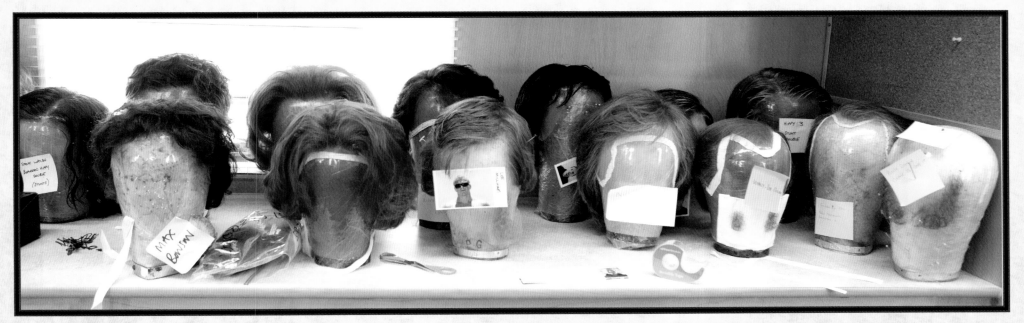

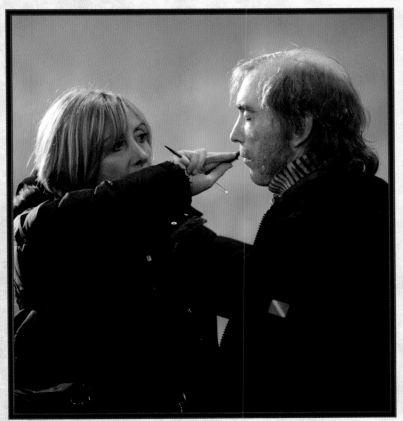

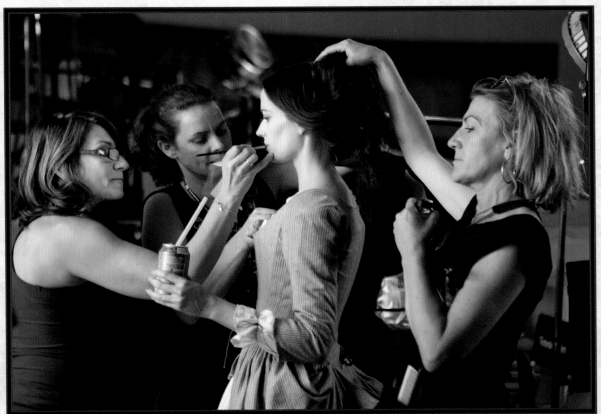

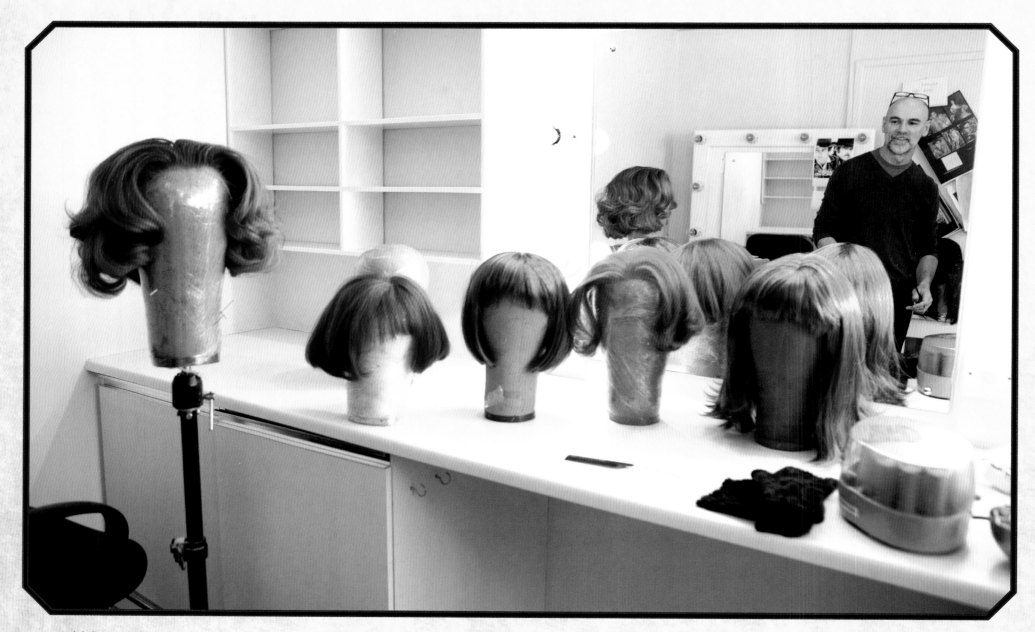

"Helena likes to use wigs because they give such a big character change," says hair stylist Paul Gooch. "It also saves having to color, cut and do all that to the person's own hair. For Dr. Hoffman we went with a tangerine-orange color. She's an alcoholic and smoker, so it's a rather deconstructed look. Her makeup's quite heavy, very much of the period, with garish colors. Helena's great because she doesn't mind looking a mess."

Depp's makeup took between two and two-and-a-half hours to apply each day, and around 45 minutes to remove, and included a wig, a false nose, and false ears. "I wanted to make his ears bigger just because that harkens back to Jonathan Frid," says prosthetics supervisor Joel Harlow. "His ears were a little larger than Johnny's and I thought we could give him a little bit of a point which sort of designates a vampire." The nose was Depp's idea. "To change his profile," says Harlow. "He's always wanted to have a fake nose. He tried it on *Sweeney Todd*. He's always trying to cover up his beauty, frankly," laughs Helena Bonham Carter. "It was hilarious to see how much camouflage he got away with." That camouflage amounted to numerous coats of rubber mask grease paint "to lighten me," notes Depp, "that chalky white, then deathly darkness around the eyes would hollow me up, sort of cadaverous." The final result was, for Harlow, "one of the most satisfying makeups I've done, because it's elegant — it's a character-driven makeup. Personally, Barnabas is the feather in my cap. Not just on this, but for a great number of films, because it is an elegant painting."

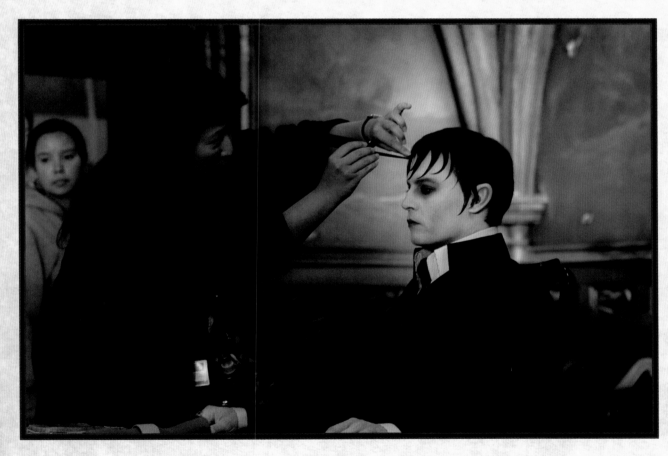

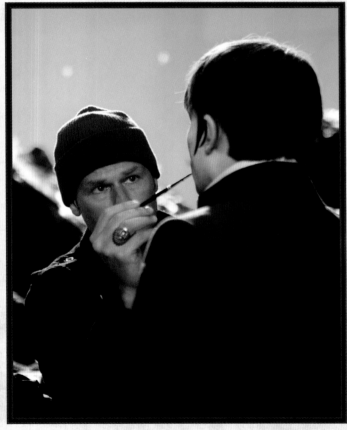

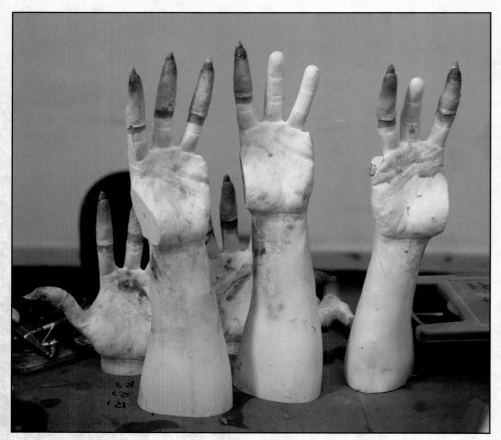

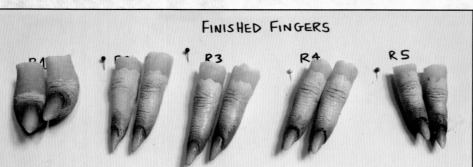

FINISHED FINGERS

R1 R3 R4 R5

Burton wanted Barnabas to have elongated fingers once he becomes a vampire. "There was something about the fingers that was important to me, in the way a vampire touches things and feels things," he says. "It helped with the emotional quality of what the character was." Adds Depp, "The fingers really made the character. Just extending the fingers by two or three inches added a whole other opportunity. I learned how to touch things or pick things up about three inches from where my fingers actually were. It took a little while but I got used to it, but it made the look."

"Tim wanted him 'tactile'," recalls makeup artist Joel Harlow of Barnabas. "His hands sort of lead the way, like they're feeling things out. He sees with his fingers, so they have to be perfect. Trying to achieve that was a challenge. They may seem like a very easy thing to do, but it's probably one of the most complicated makeups I've ever been involved in. It has to look elegant, slim and be seamless, but when you add anything to a finger, to any kind of a makeup, you're adding bulk. It's got to be rigid enough so if he touches something, they don't bend, because that blows the illusion instantly. I thought if I glued a golf tee on the tip of your finger, then put a silicone prosthetic over it, what you have is a bone and skin."

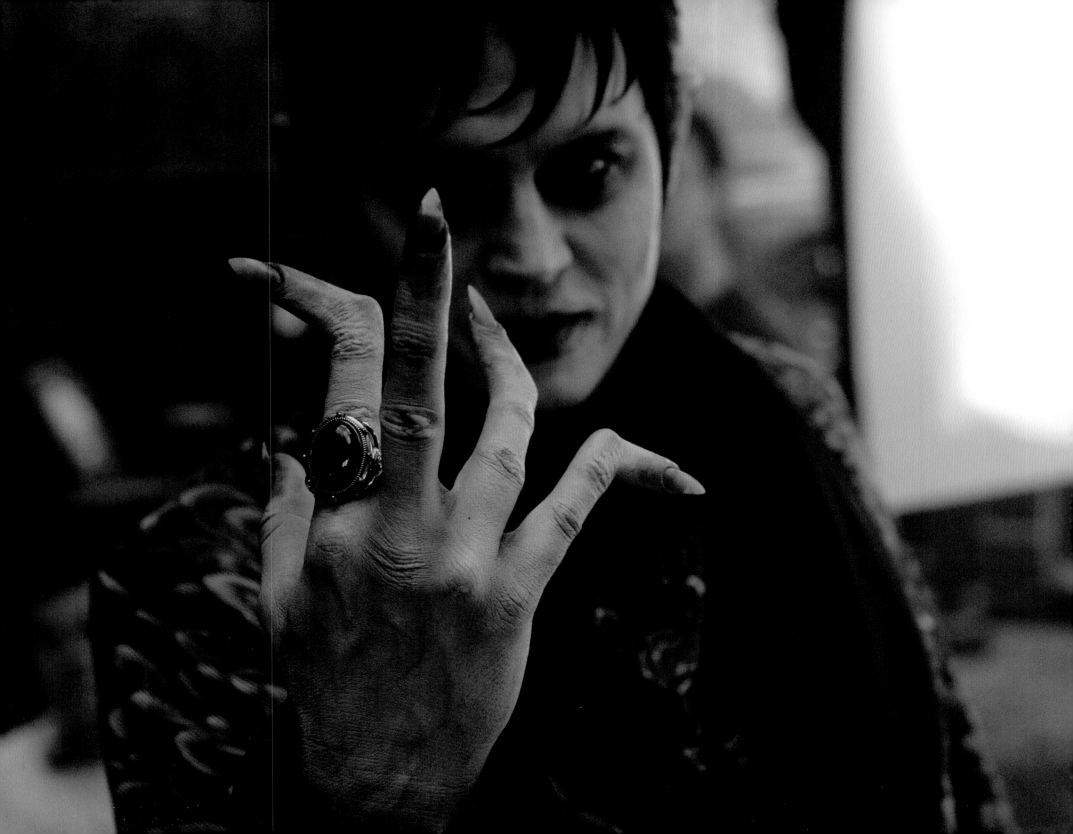

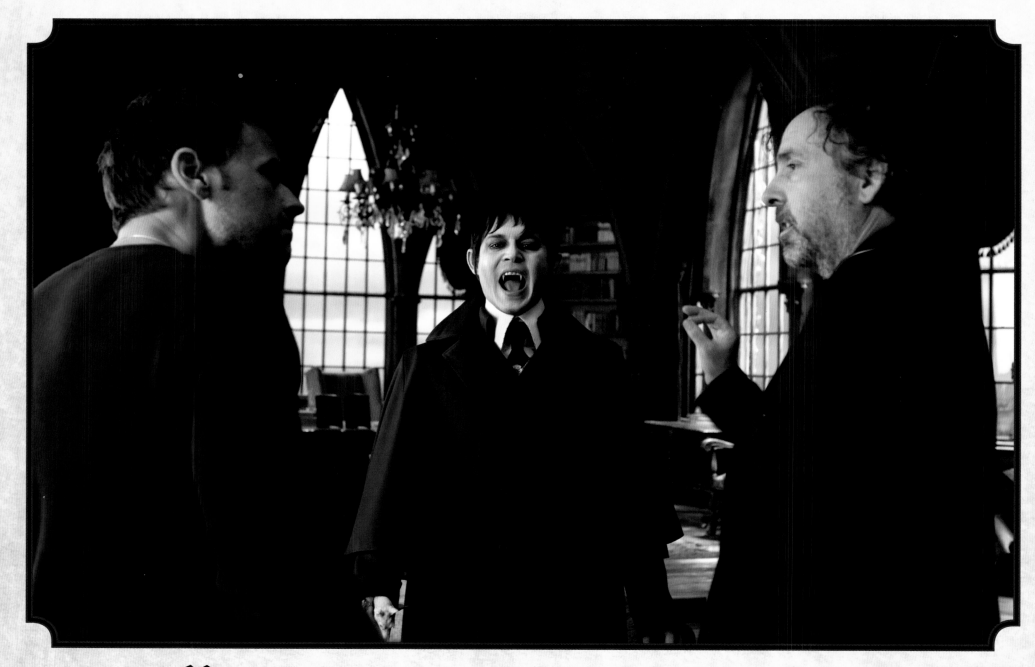

No self-respecting vampire would be complete without a set of fangs and Depp had several. "We did curved canines, we did straight, we did short, we did long," says Joel Harlow. "We even had a set that were more like rattlesnake fangs, that came down from behind the teeth. We also had a set that were activated by him opening his mouth. The fangs would drop down into place."

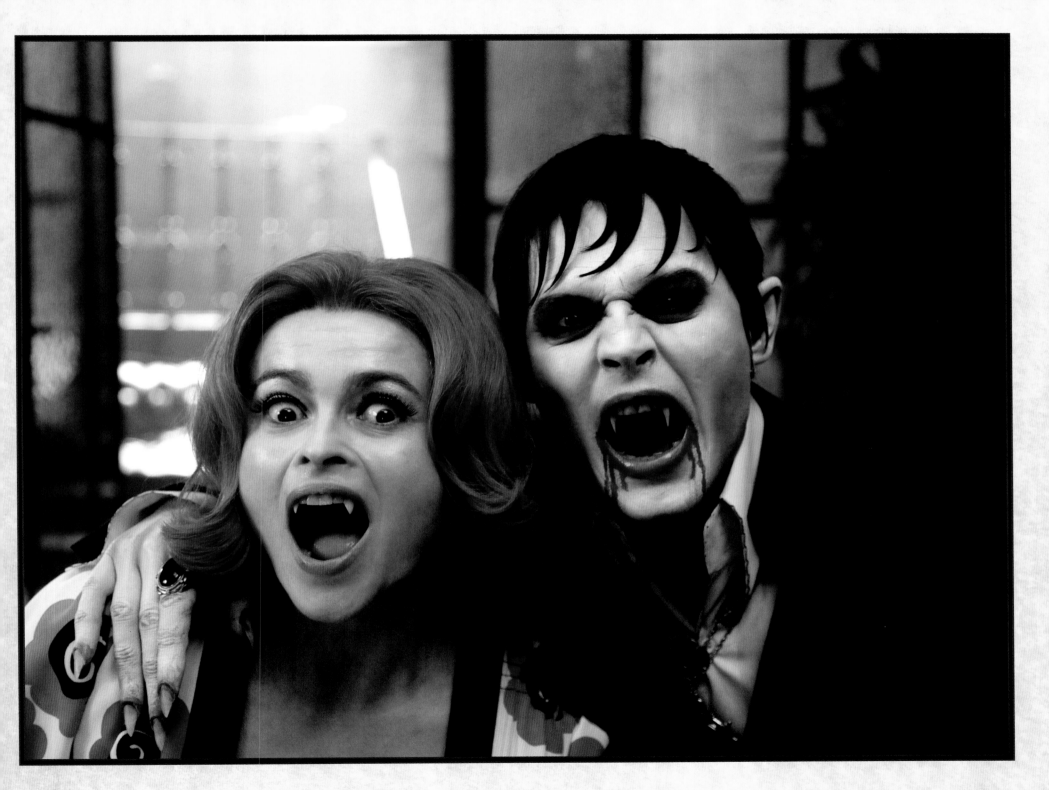

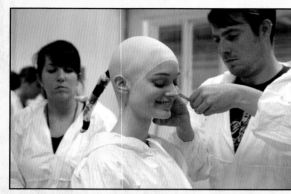
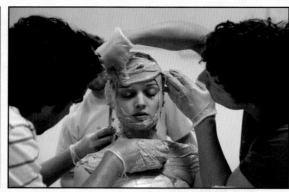
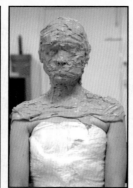
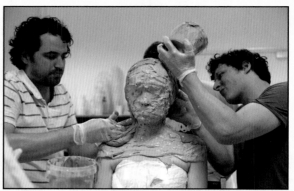
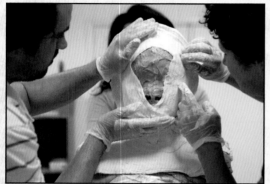
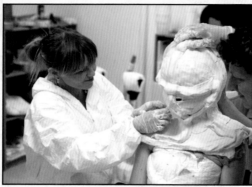
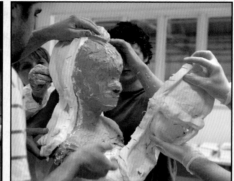
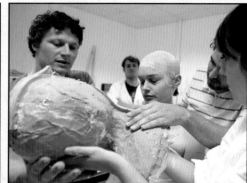
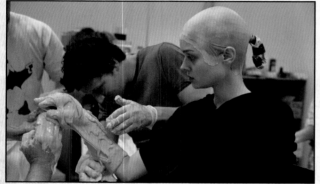
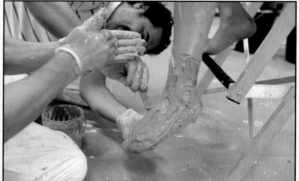
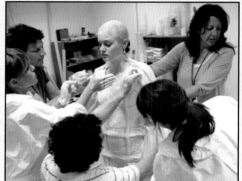
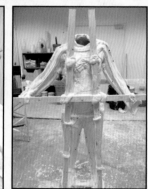
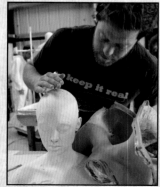
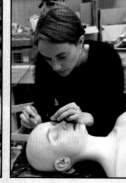
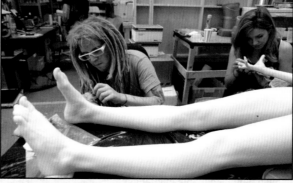
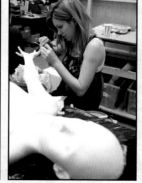
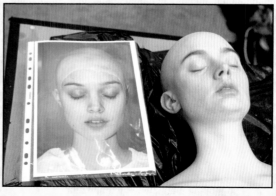

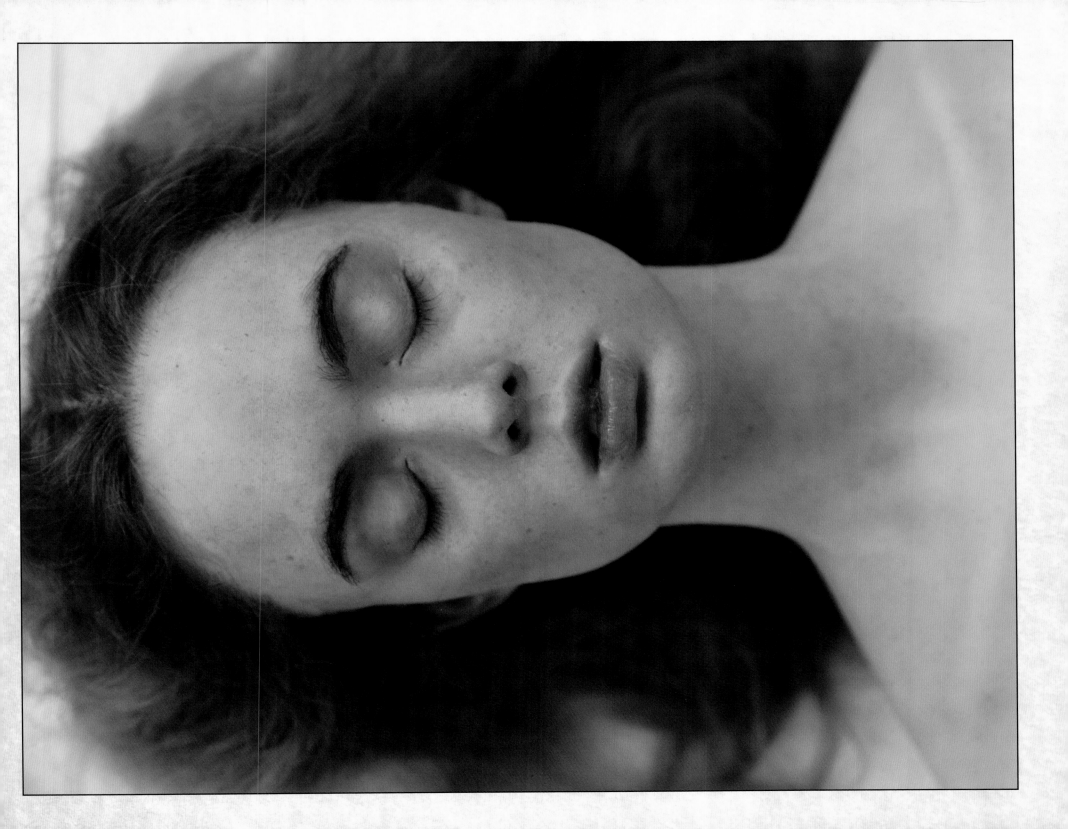

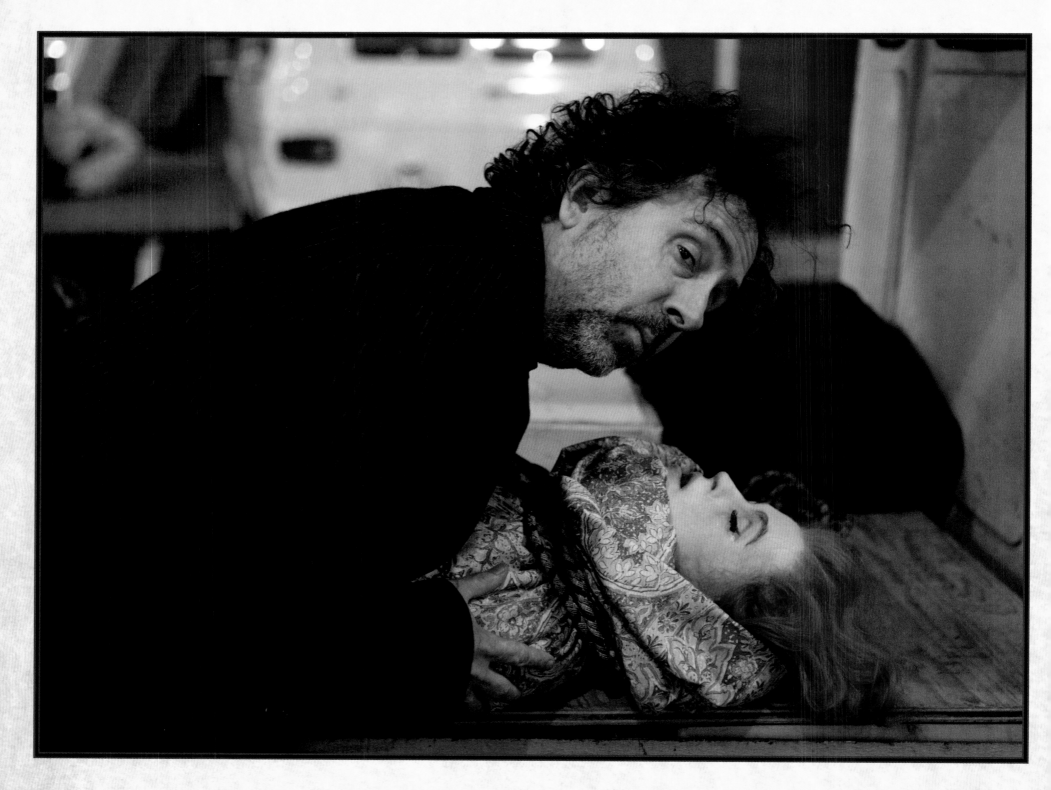

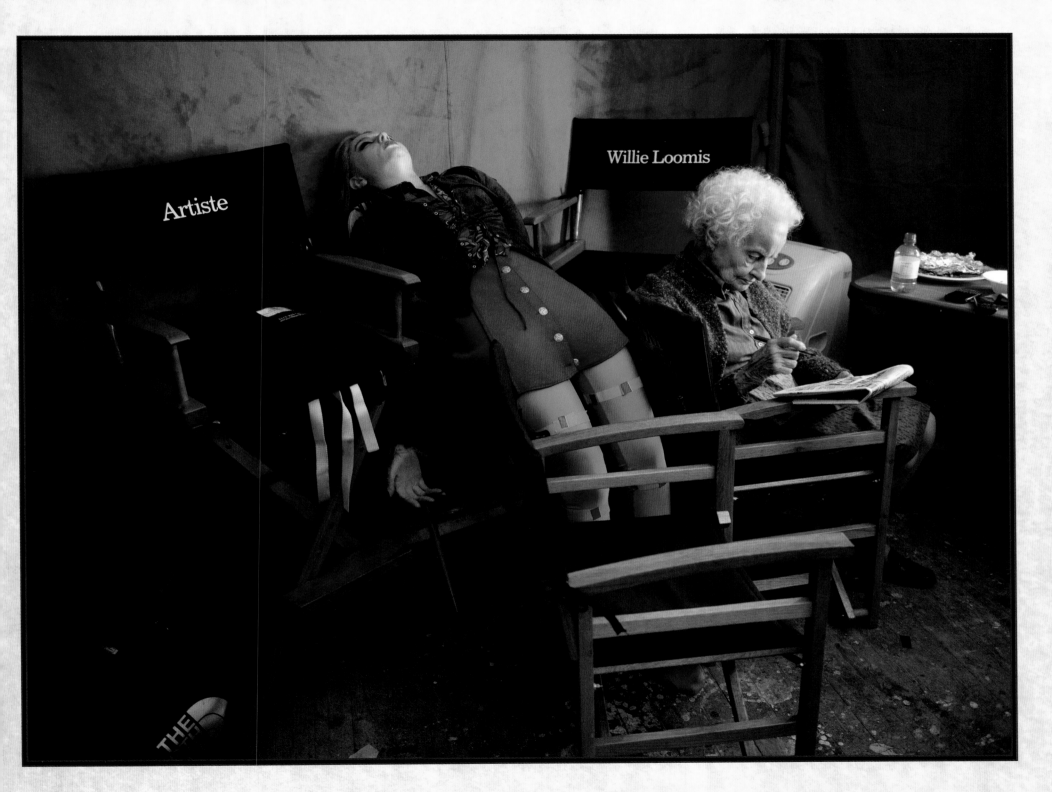

CHAPTER 4

CINEMATOGRAPHY

STUNTS

SPECIAL EFFECTS

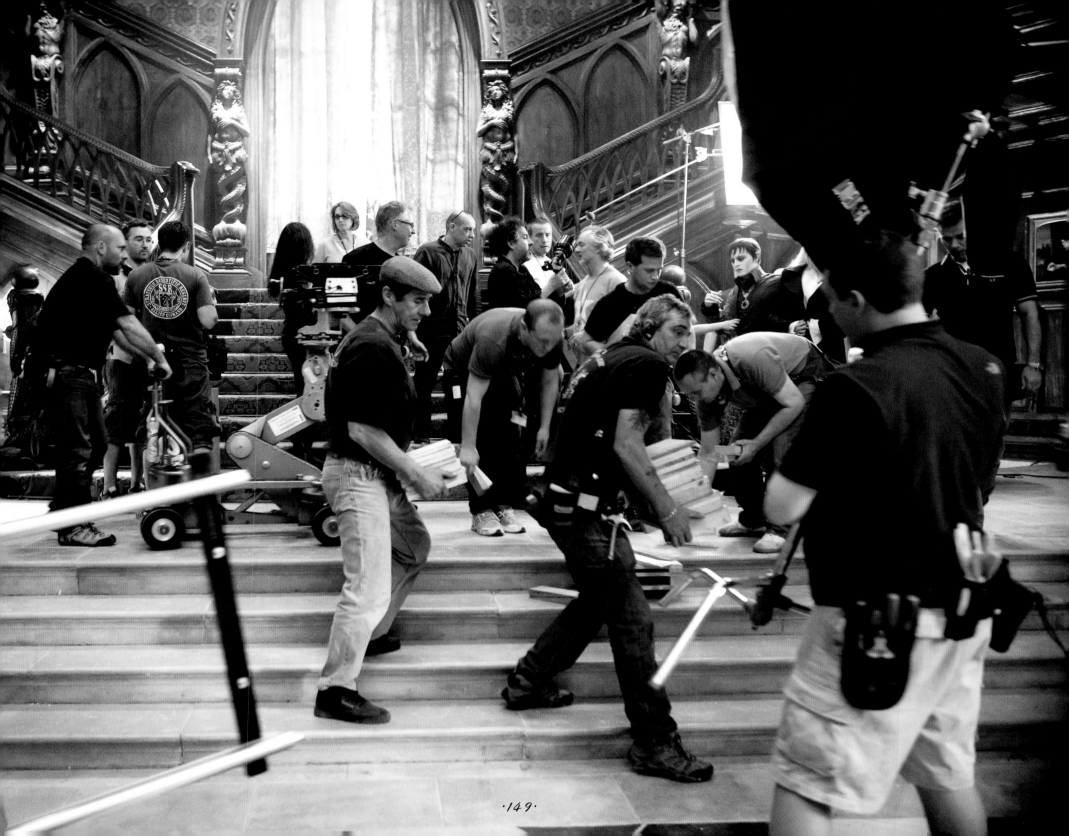

Cinematography

isually Burton wanted *Dark Shadows* to feel like a '70s film, and showed his French director of photography Bruno Delbonnel several classic vampire movies from the period, among them *Blacula*, *Scream Blacula Scream* and *Dracula A.D. 1972.* "We talked about '70s movies, the look of them, the feel of it, the feel of the color scheme. It was more of a vibe," Burton explains. "I really enjoyed working with Bruno. He's very artistic, one of those DPs who every film he does he loves to make it different. He seems to really try and get in there and latch into what it is you're trying to do. He didn't know *Dark Shadows*, and you're not going to look at that show and go, 'That looks nice.' He was always trying to go from a character standpoint, and not from a look standpoint. He was a really good collaborator on that level. We ended up with something I like. It's very '70s in the quality of the look of it." Observes Depp, "We wanted the film to have a certain richness to it, but at the same time this kind of shocking '70s color scheme, psychedelia, because the light can affect an emotion. Bruno is one of those perfect examples of someone literally painting with light."

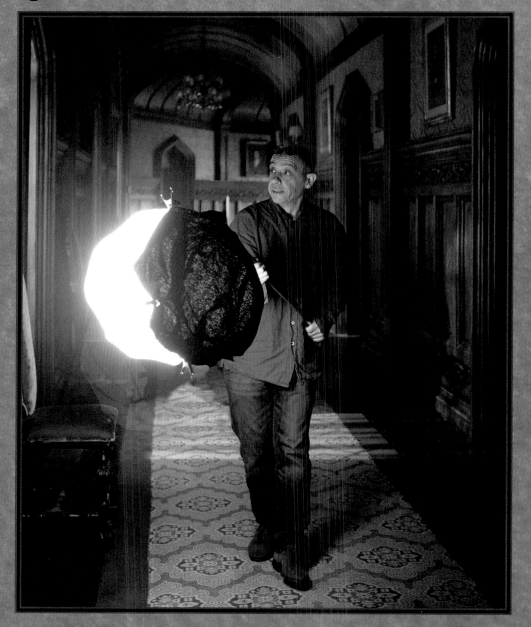

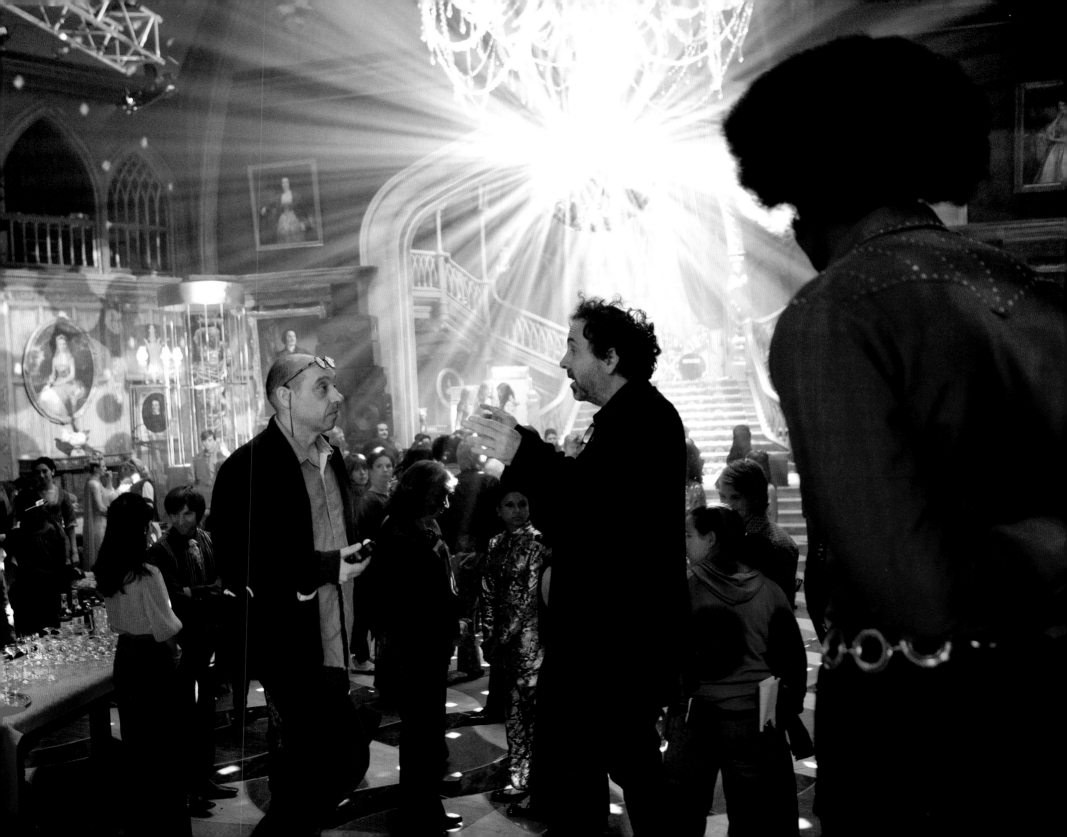

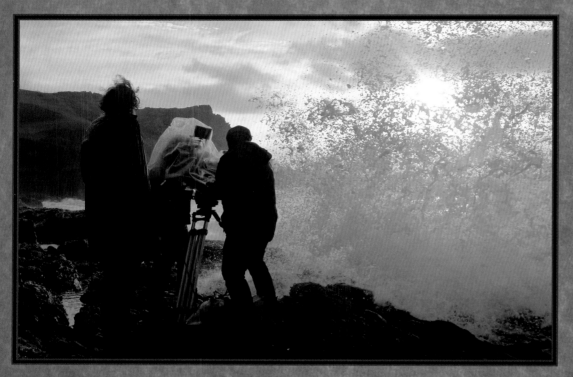

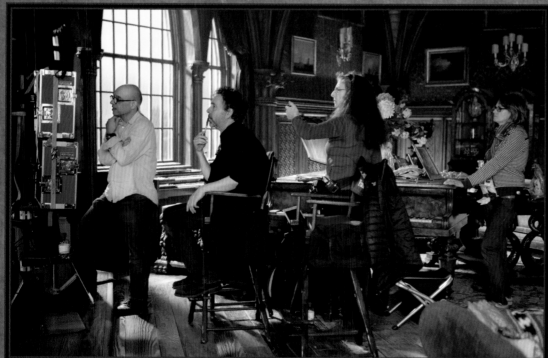

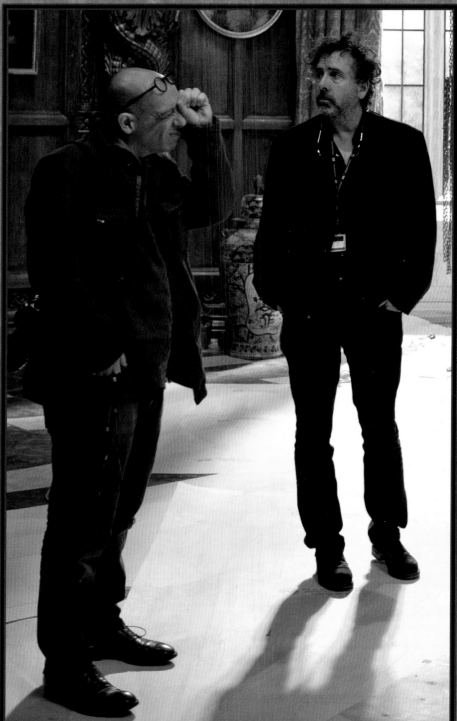

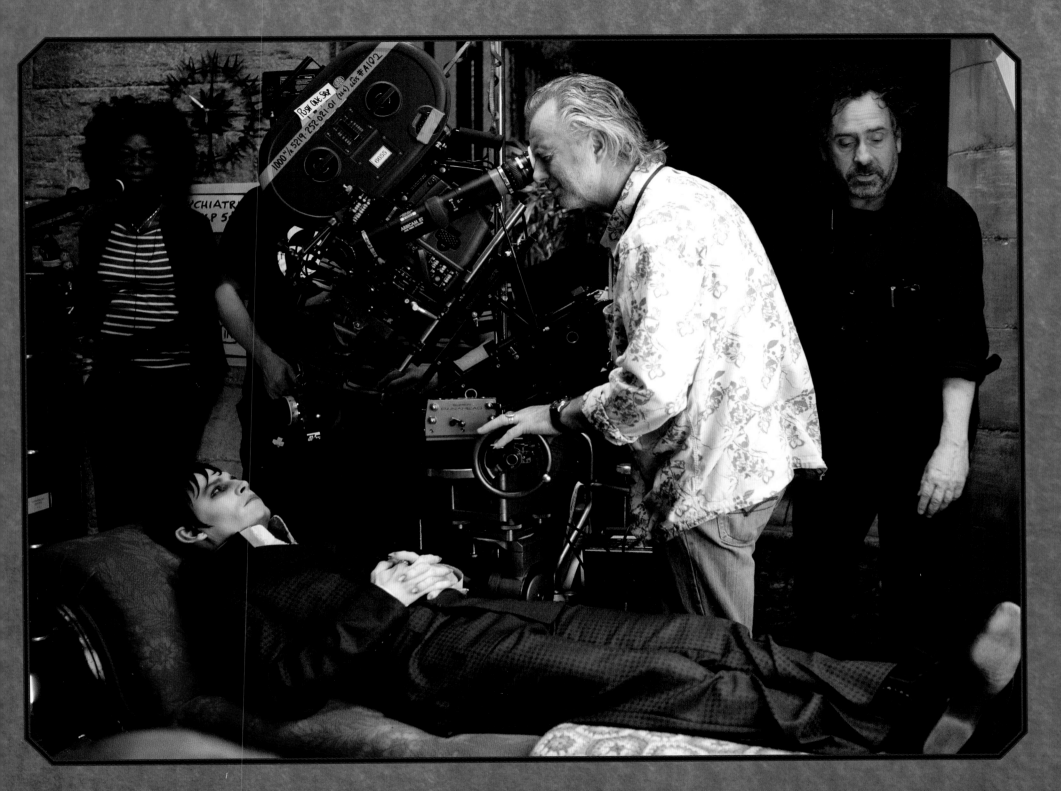

·153·

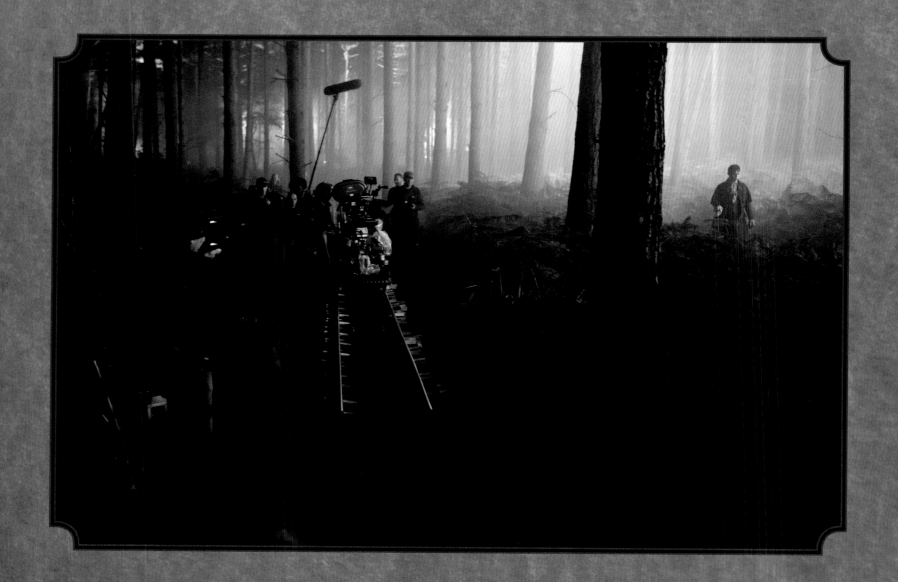

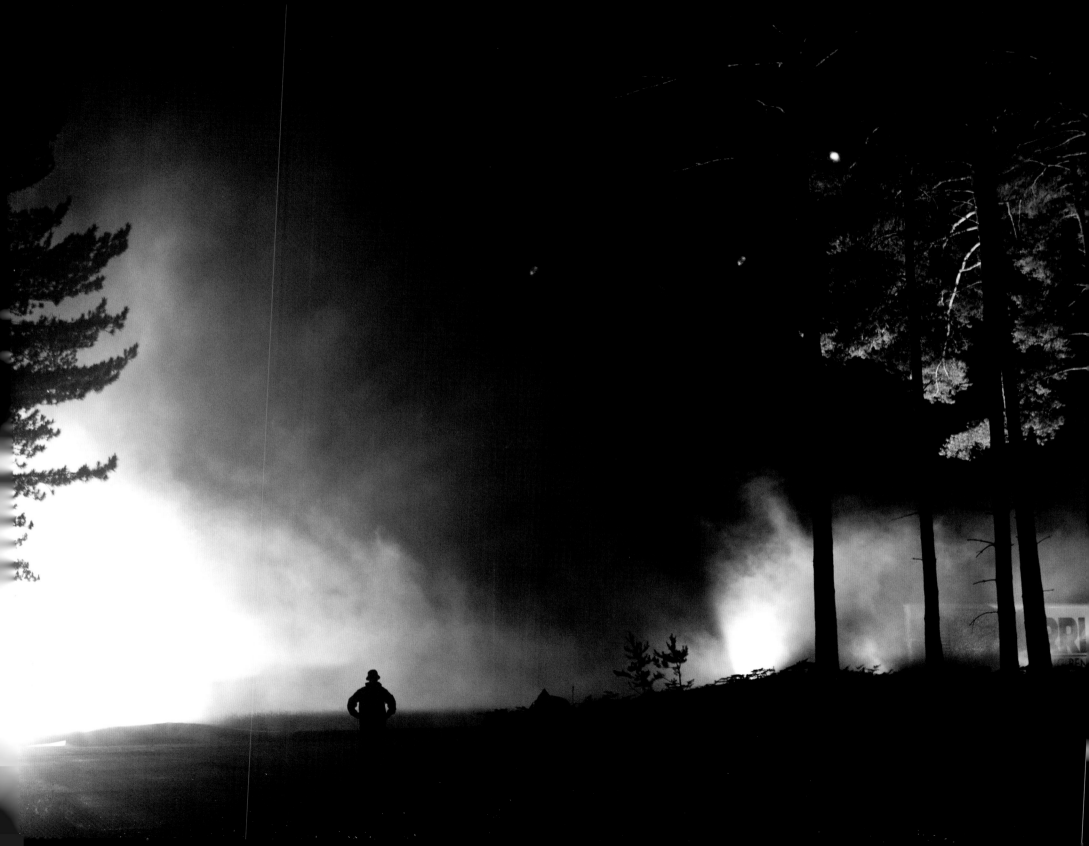

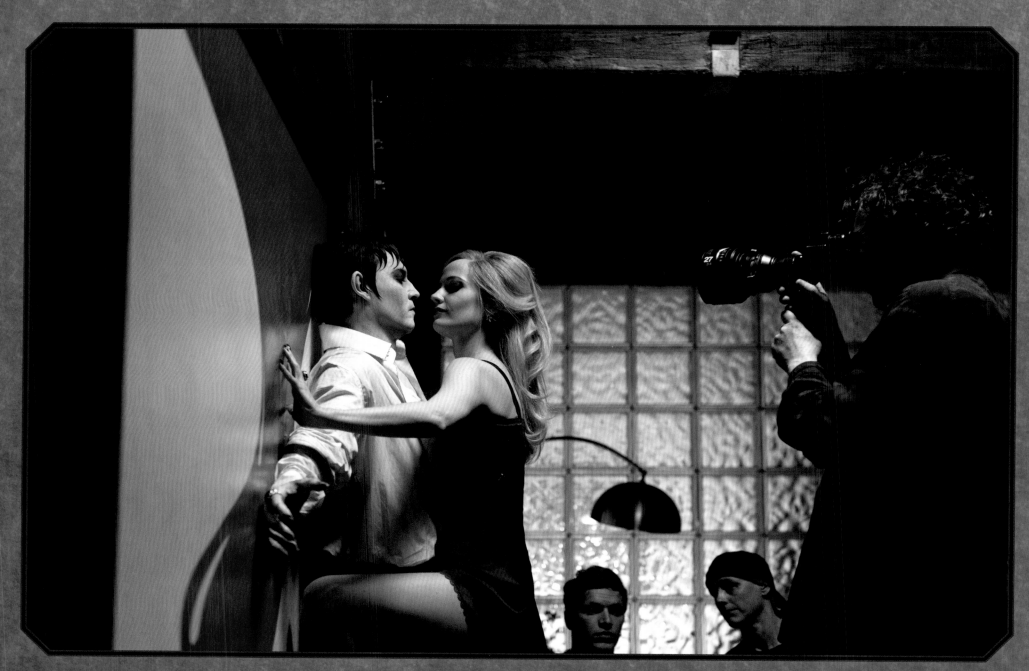

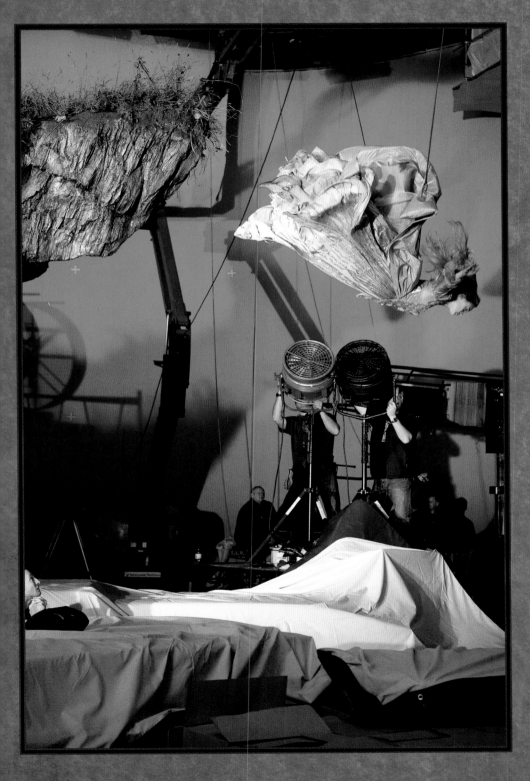

Angelique's office was the stage for a particularly physical workout between her and Barnabas. The actors worked with stunt coordinator Eunice Huthart for the sequence, and wore wire harnesses that enabled them to spin through the air. "Being on wires was not my favorite thing because I'm afraid of heights. But I would do anything for Tim," admits Green. "The sex scene, it took a while to shoot," recalls Depp. "There were times where, literally, I was on a harness and they would pull me back, [and] you have no control whatsoever. Eva was harnessed up and wired to me, so I'm laying on the couch on top of her, wired to Eva Green, which is like every man's dream. I've definitely had more difficult jobs. Then it would be one of those, 'Three. Two. One,' kind of things. It must have scared the hell out of her at first, because the deal was for them to yank me backwards having no idea where I was going to land, and have to stay upright because she was attached to me, and catch her. We did that quite a few times. That was pretty funny." Bella Heathcote also spent time on wires for the scenes in which Josette and Victoria fall from Widow's Peak, into the sea. "I've been skydiving, I love that kind of stuff, so the day I got to fall off the cliff, they were, 'Are you good to go again?' and I'm like, 'Yeah! Yeah! Get me back up there.'"

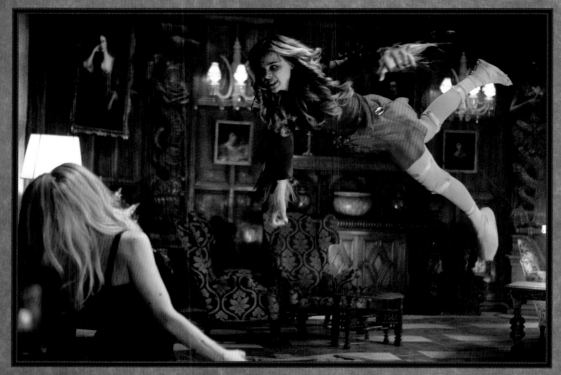

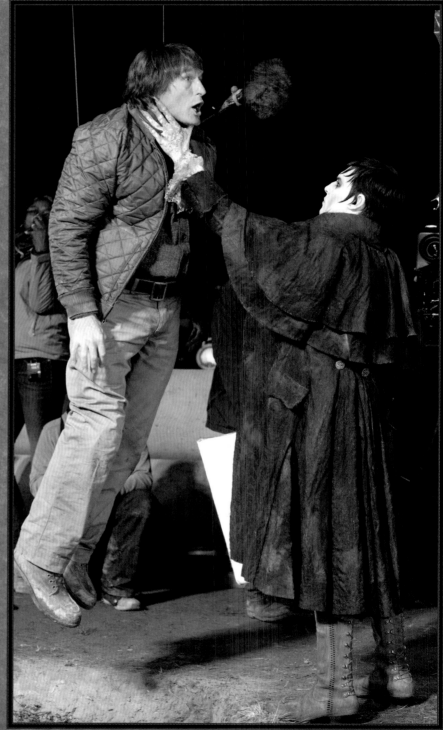

During the film's climax, dubbed the "battle royale" by cast and crew, Carolyn finally lets loose her inner werewolf. Her transformation was a combination of practical and visual effects as well as stunt work. "The end battle was so fun to shoot because I love stunts," says Moretz, who wore werewolf hands in addition to being strapped into a harness so she could walk on all fours. "Eunice, the stunt coordinator, was like, 'Let's string you up and see what you can do.' I got up on the wire and did this leap through the air. I did it three times really well and Eunice was, 'Wow, you're like a mini Angelina.' I was like, 'What, Angelina Jolie?' It was a little hard, because I had fake hands on. But it went really well. The set was on fire."

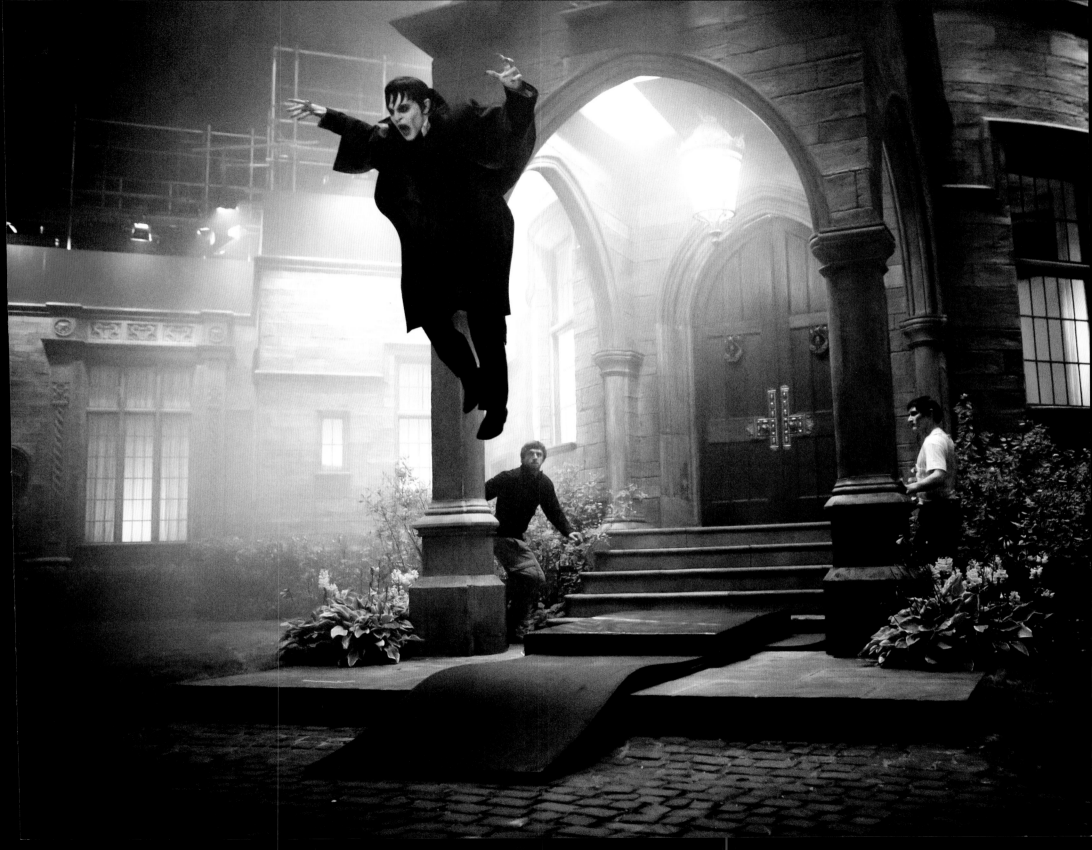

Special Effects

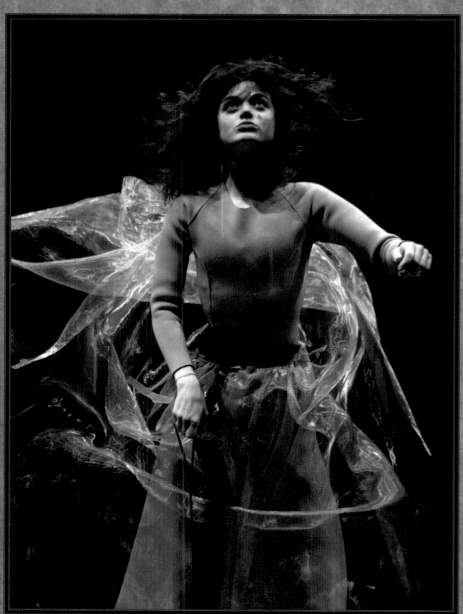

While *Dark Shadows* isn't an effects-heavy film, Burton tried to minimize the amount of CGI by shooting as many effects in camera as possible. To give Josette's ghost an ethereal quality he shot Bella Heathcote in Pinewood's Underwater Tank then removed the water in post-production. "That was really fun," says Heathcote. "There was something really soothing about being underwater. Everything slows down for you. Usually on set everything needs to be hurried along but when you're dealing with water it's a different beast. I felt completely calm in there. I'd take a breath from the regulator, do the action for as long as I could, then make the signal for cut." Costume designer Colleen Atwood also created a dress that was a replica of an 18th century one but made, instead, from an aluminum fabric, printed with metal, and adorned with ribbons that moved in the wind to help with the ghostly feel. Quite by chance, the dress looked great underwater, too. "We made the costume way before we knew it was going to go in," she reveals. "I knew light played amazing on it and it looked cool in the wind, but it's serendipitous it also worked in water."

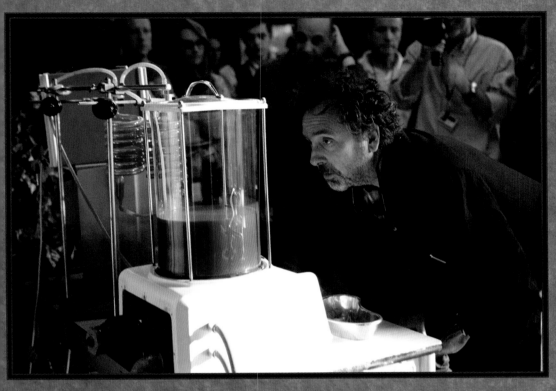

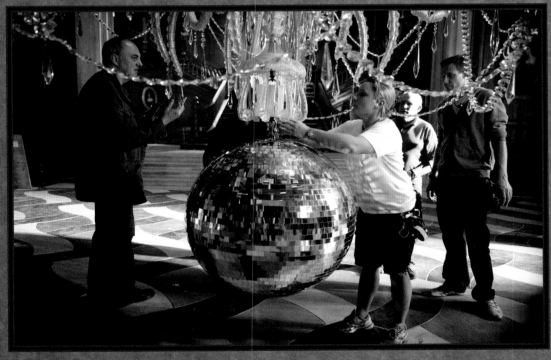

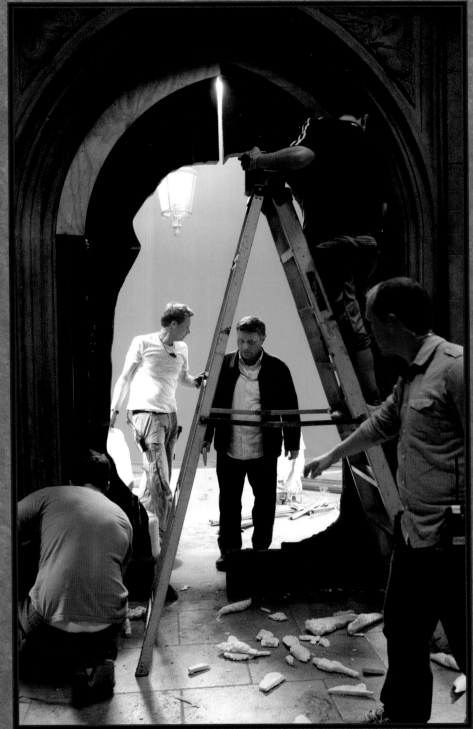

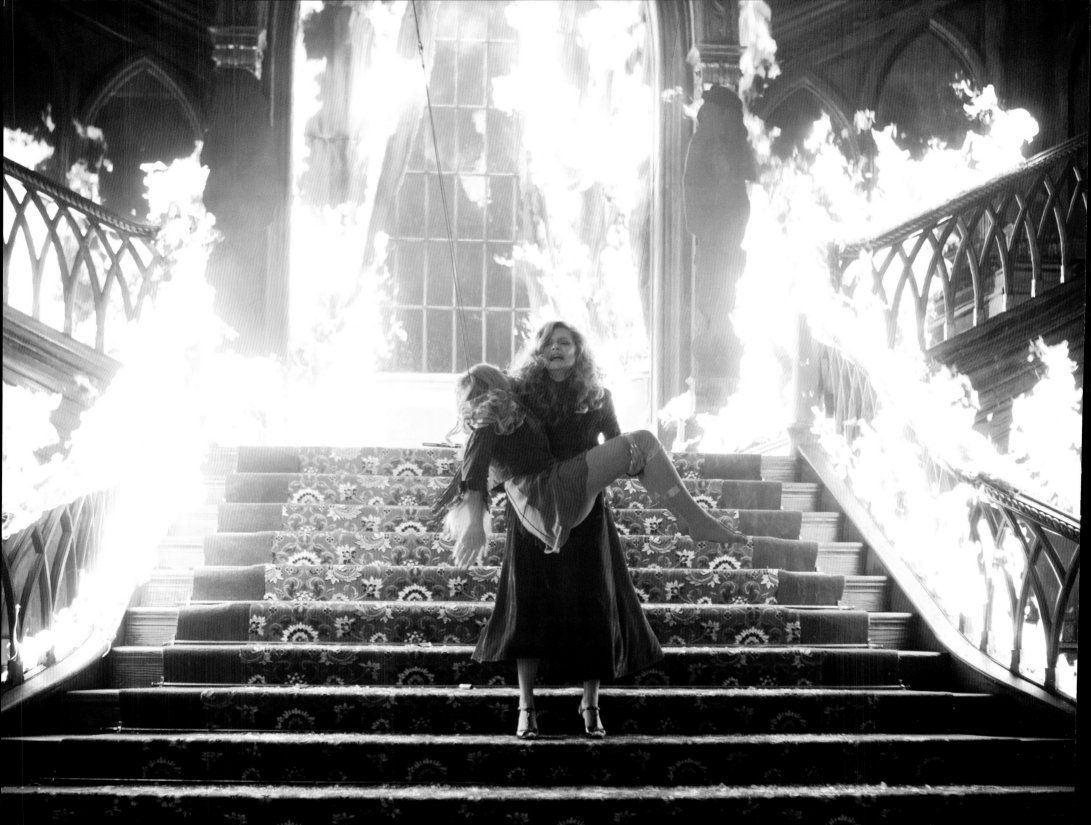

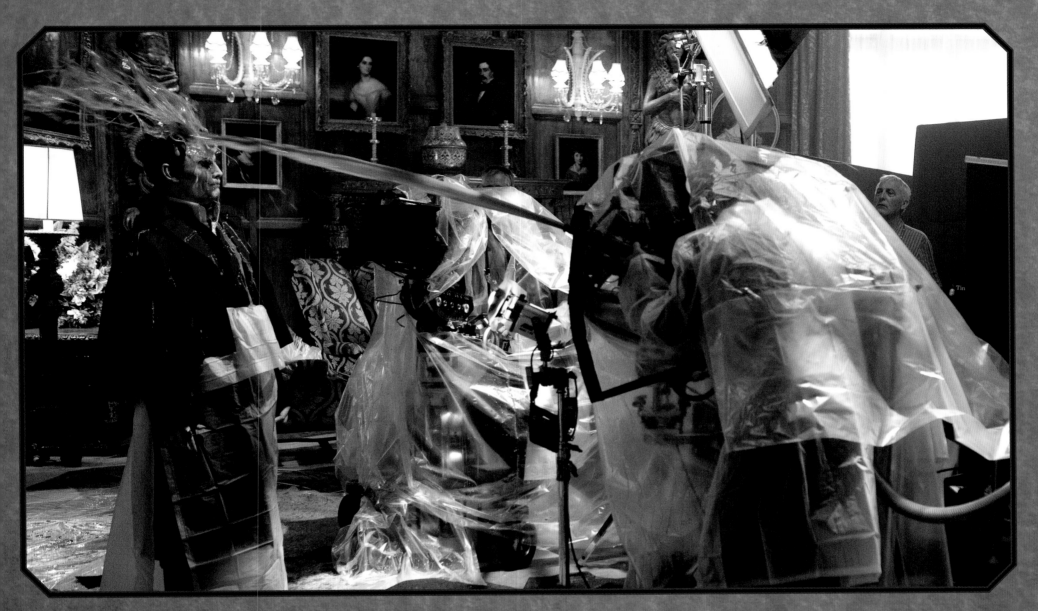

One particularly yucky moment during the "battle royale" involved Angelique spewing green, projectile vomit at Barnabas, a practical gag mounted by special effects supervisor Joss Williams, who built an air ram that was attached via a plastic tube to a puke gun. "We had different types of nozzles. We had straight jets. But Tim liked the helix one," recalls Williams. "You loaded the thing up and fired it. I learned a little trick on a few movies with Tim, which is to give Tim the gun, especially if it's splattering Johnny, so none of us can get the blame. We gave it to Tim and he smacked Johnny straight in the face with it." While the exact ingredients involved in making the vomit are a trade secret, according to Williams "it's pretty much the same as chocolate, except it's not brown. It's green. Water and a very carefully chosen dye because, obviously, I didn't want Johnny Depp to end up green for a week."

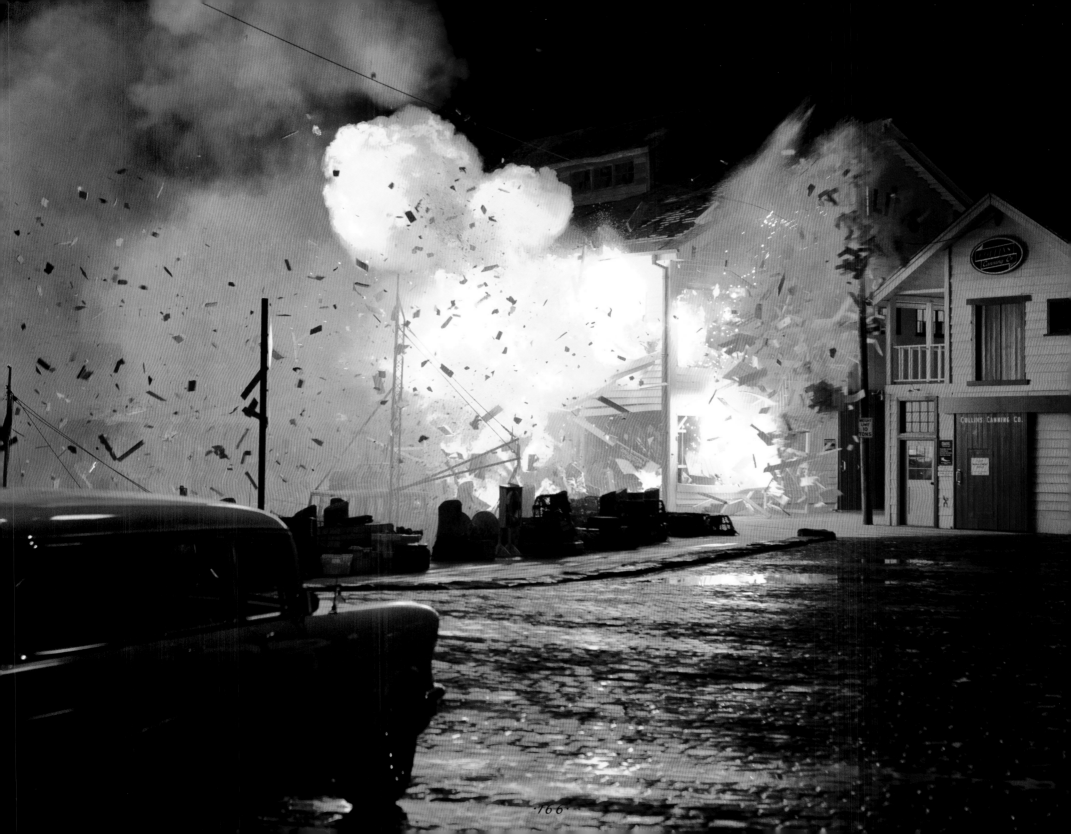

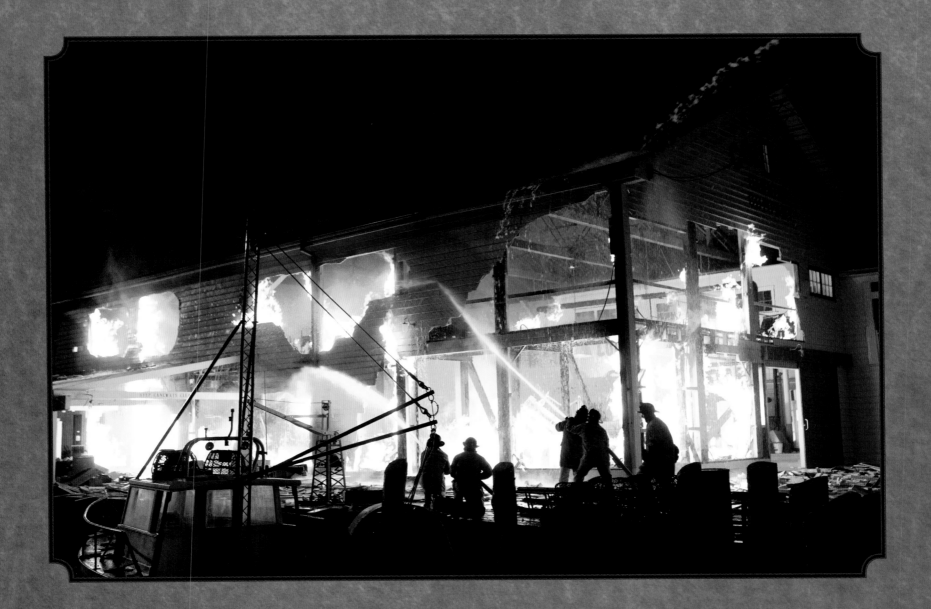

CHAPTER 5

VISUAL EFFECTS

EDITING

SCORING

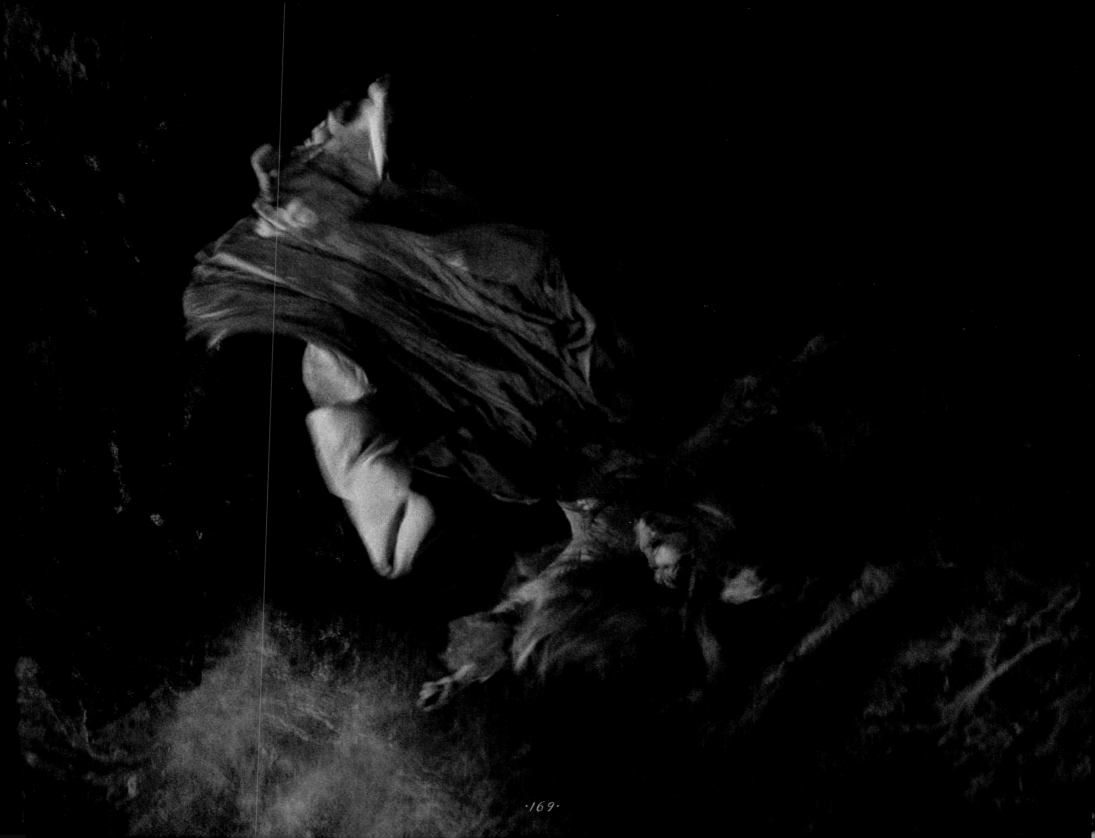

During the climactic battle royale between Barnabas and Angelique, Eva Green's face cracks like a broken doll. Working closely with Burton, concept artist Dermot Power provided the visual effects department with frame-by-frame reference of how Green's face should crack. "I wanted it to be more poetic and not overly special effecty," says Burton of Green's disintegration. "I wanted it to be emotionally based."

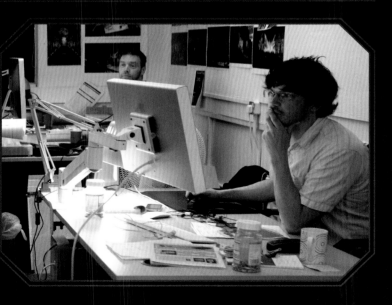

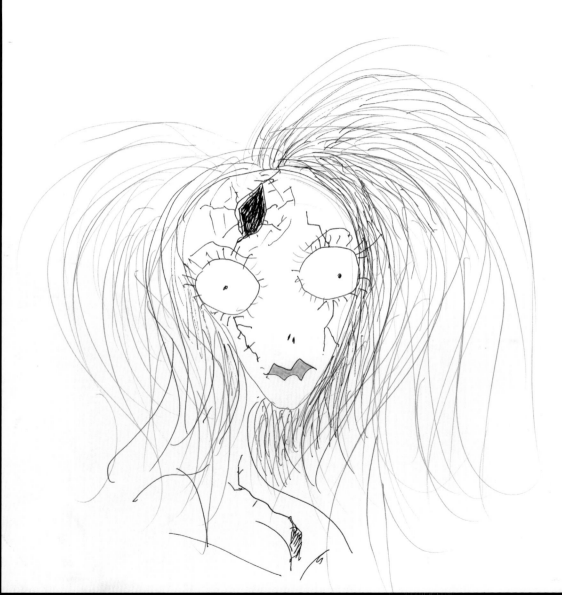

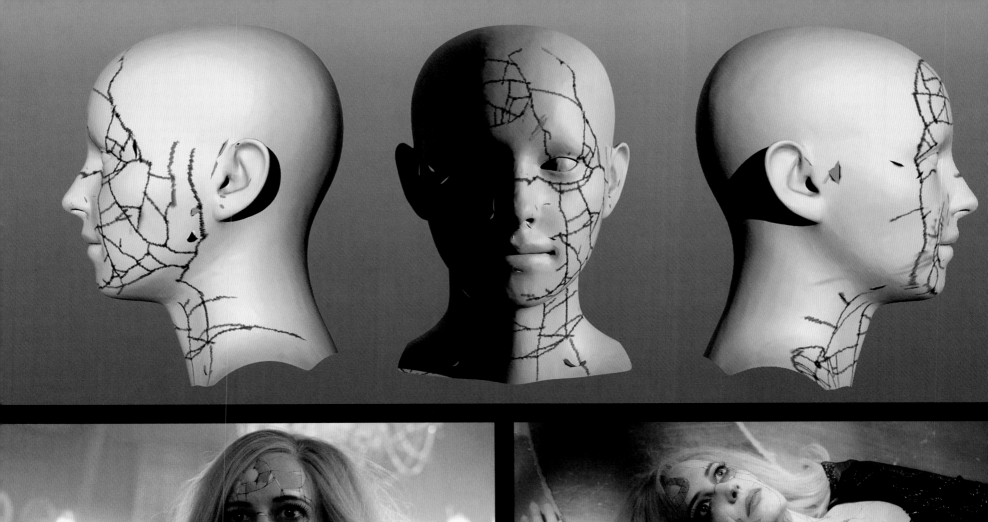

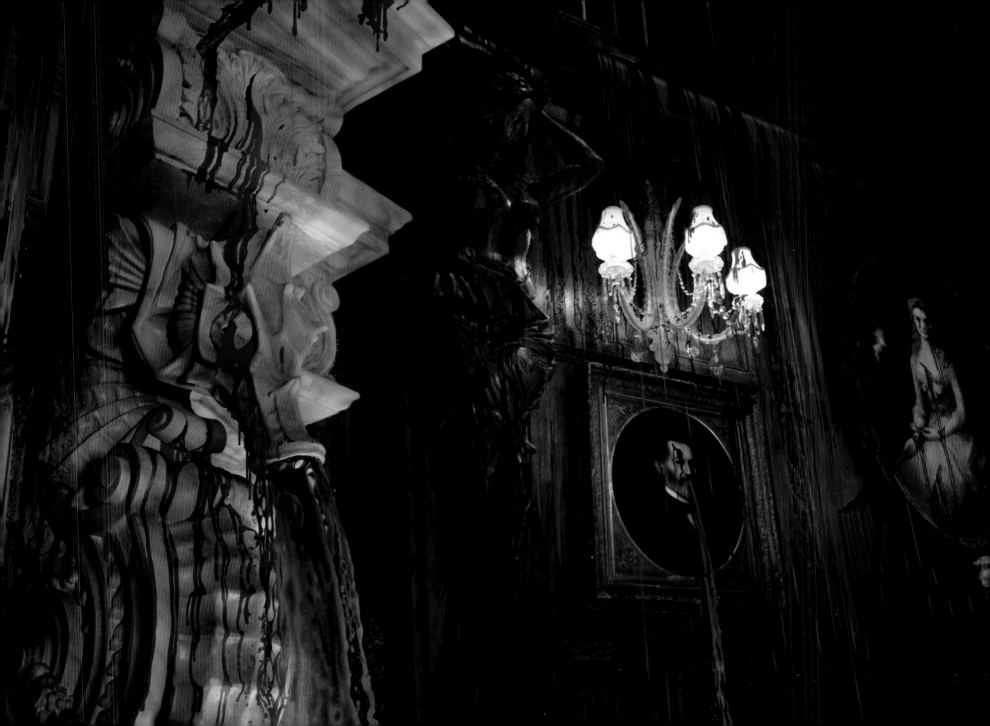

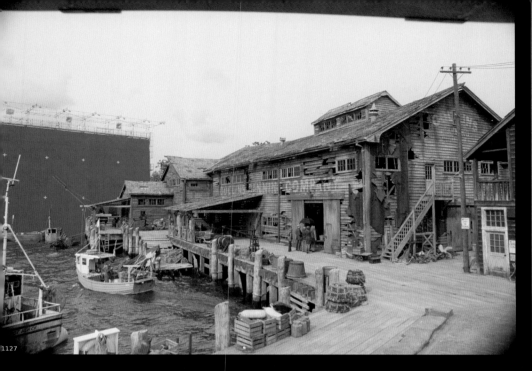
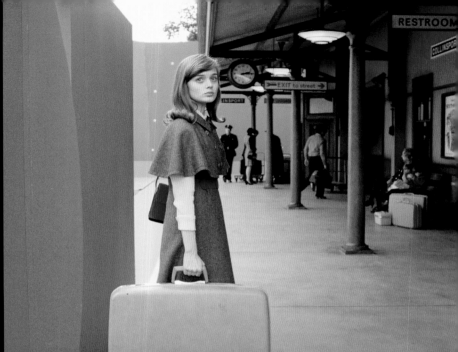
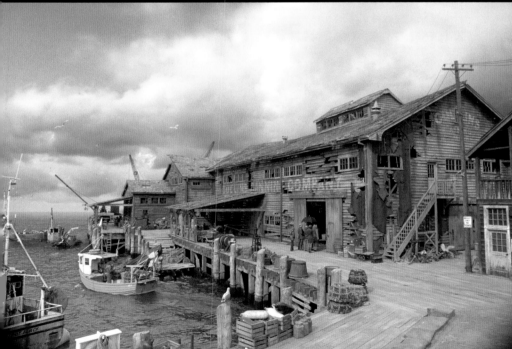
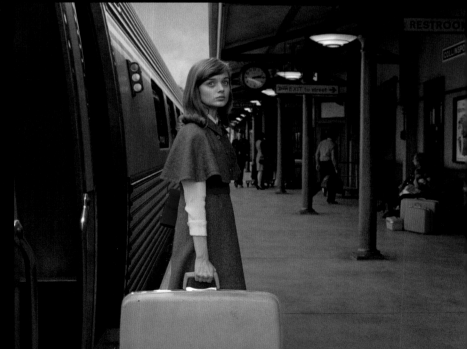

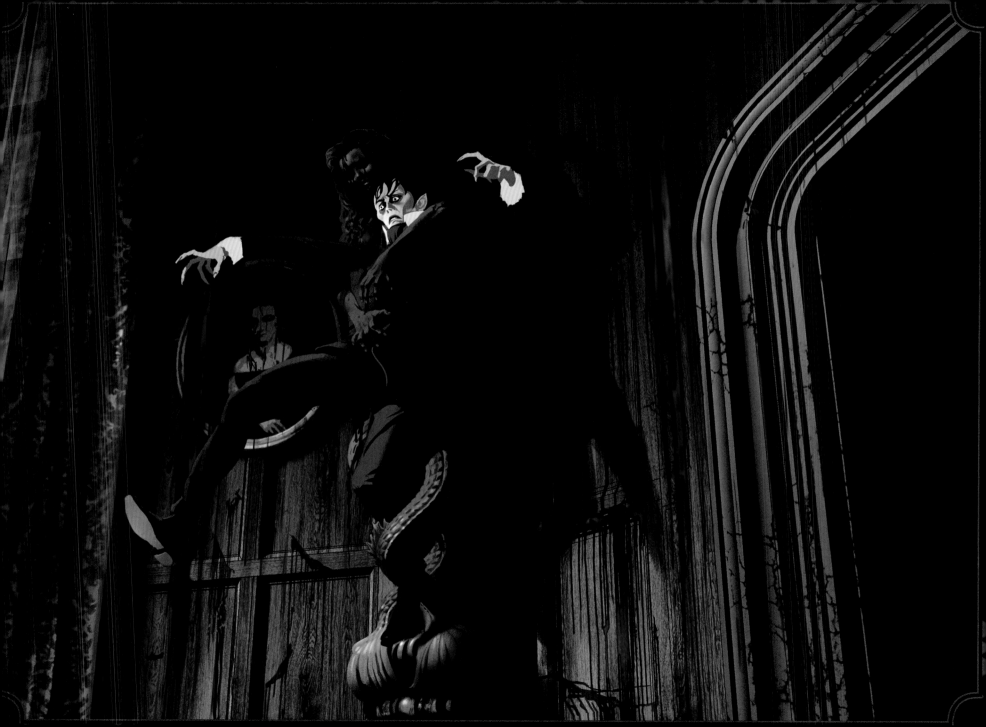

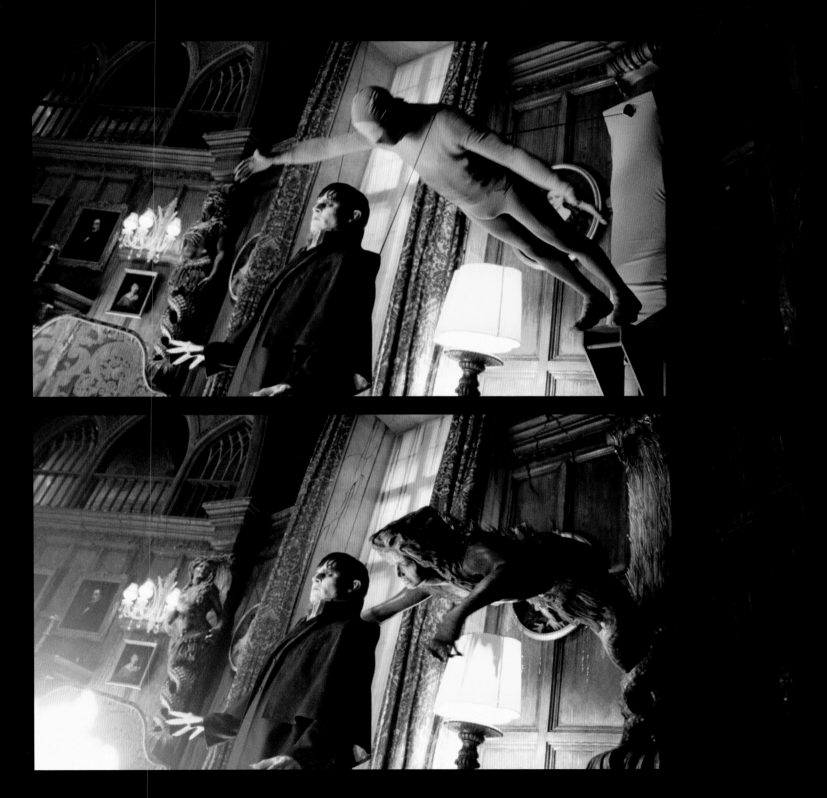

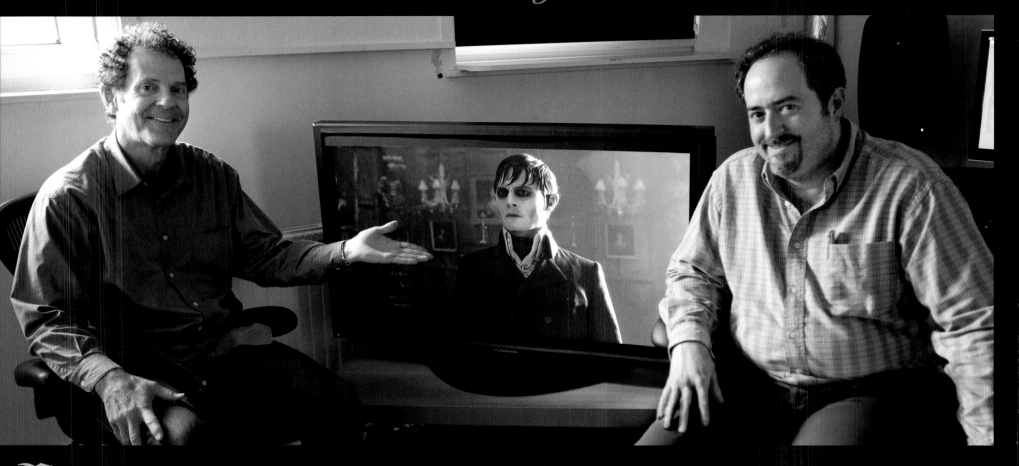

Editor Chris Lebenzon worked out of an office on the Pinewood lot, which allowed Burton to visit several times a day. "Tim's constantly back and forth and we're honing the cut as we go. He shoots around the cut at times and gets angles we need, and eliminates things as well, so it's a very efficient process. I only do it with Tim. I've never done it with other directors," reveals Lebenzon. "Usually on these movies it's such a scamper to get all the film you need and make your day, which means most directors stay on set and shoot as much as they can and now and again they'll look at the cut. I didn't bother looking at the old series too much at all. I could have dove in and done research, but I like to stay very obscure, very clean, like an audience would, so I try not to get too involved in the subject. I more respond to the material as it's coming in, and try to put myself in the seat of someone who's paying for a ticket."

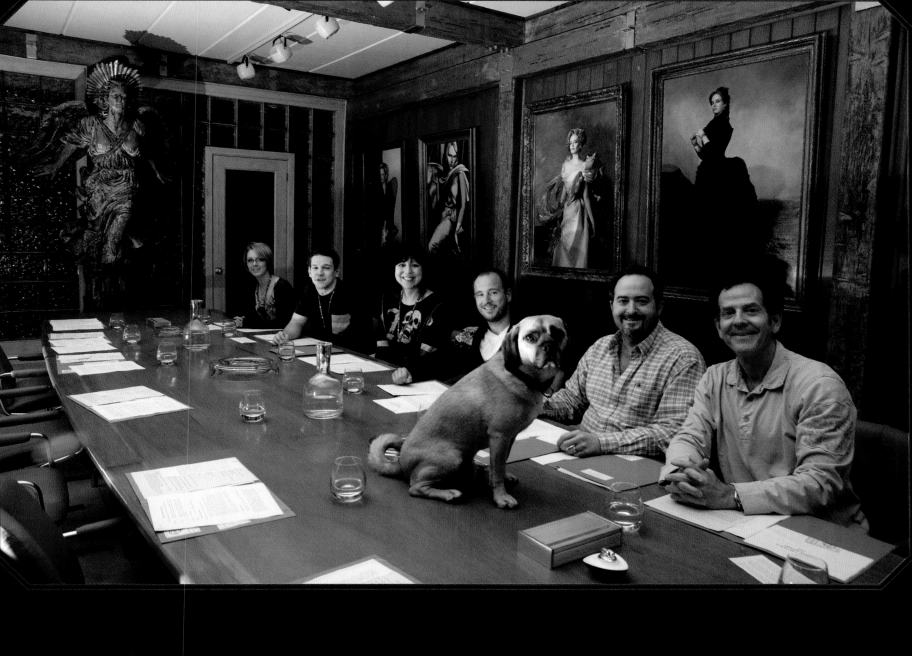

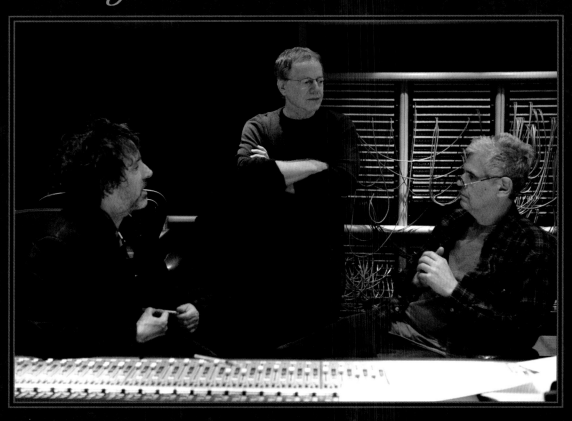

Providing the film's music was Burton's long-time collaborator Danny Elfman. "Danny composed a terrific score, and the source pieces played an equally crucial role," says producer Richard D. Zanuck. "They help establish the time frame and also express the feeling Tim wanted to convey." Elfman elaborates, "I knew the bigger, dramatic scenes would be underscored in a rather theatrical manner, but the real treat was tapping into the retro musical palette Tim had imagined. He wanted a sound that was evocative of both the original TV series, as well as '70s-era horror films. For that we kept it minimal, eerie, and atmospheric, with only electronics and a few solo instruments carrying the melodies."

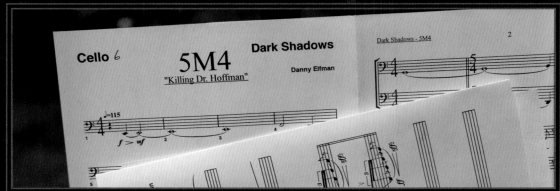

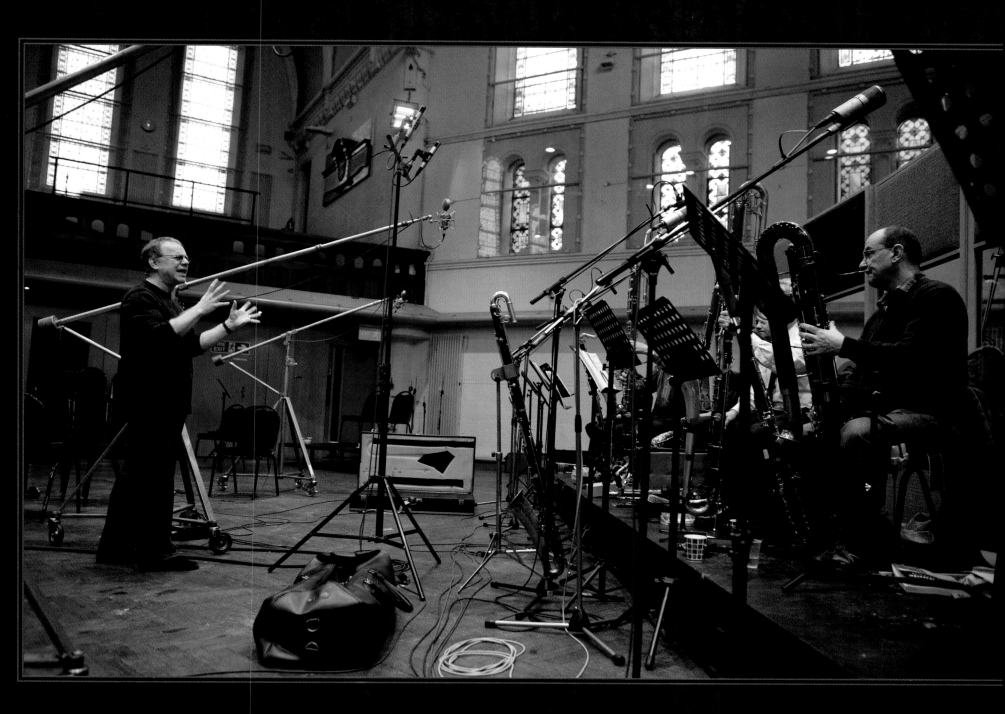

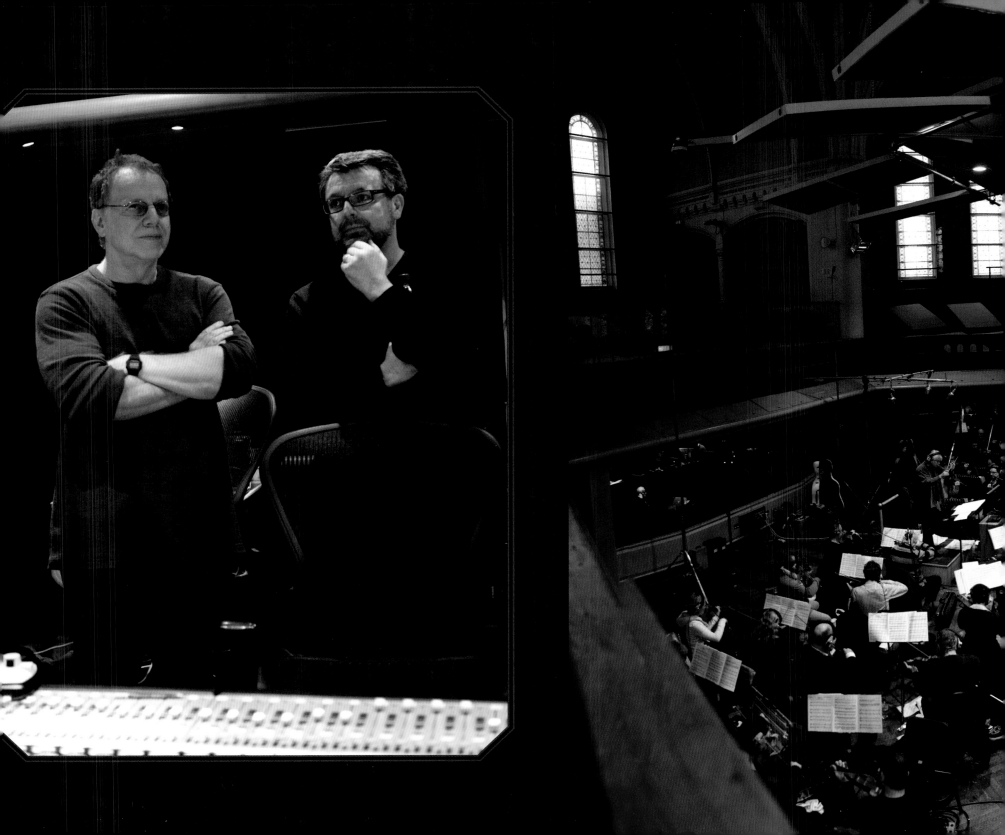

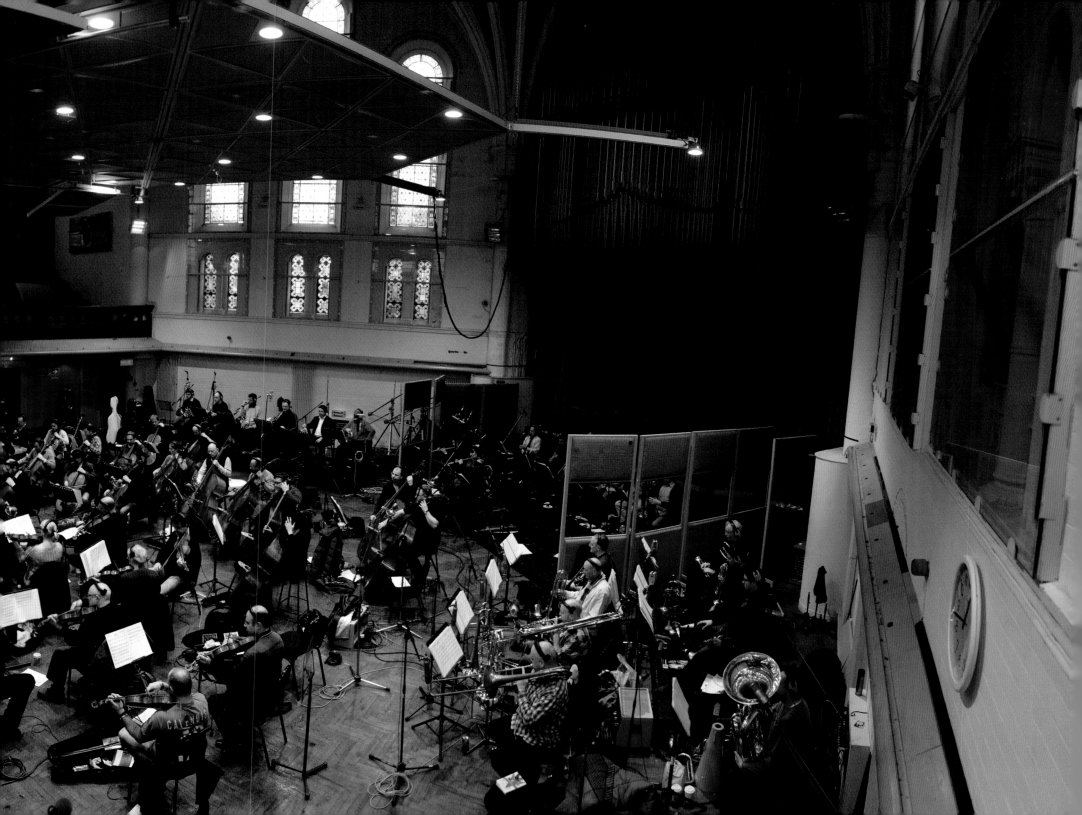

When Tim and Johnny along with millions of other young teenagers were rushing home from school to catch the 4pm TV soap opera, *Dark Shadows,* I was running 20th Century Fox and, frankly, had never seen the show. Not until Johnny had secured the rights and presented the project to Tim did I catch up and run as many of the old shows as were available. Again, frankly, I didn't quite understand what all the fuss was about, but I was viewing the show from a 2009 perspective and anyway if Tim and Johnny wanted to do the phone book, I'd be in.

Dark Shadows is my sixth film with Tim and each one has been a very rewarding learning experience. I've always tried to imagine how he would attack and present each scene, and I've always been wrong. Tim always does the unexpected and that is the reason all of his films are so absorbing. He messes with our senses!

The entire cast of *Dark Shadows* is without question the finest and most diverse team of actors I have ever experienced. Each one was as if the character he or she was playing was written specifically for them by Seth Grahame-Smith. I've never seen anything quite like that. Each character just came to life.

I can honestly say that there has never been a film with so many diversified elements all working in harmony. *Dark Shadows* cannot be compared with any other film as it creates its own genre. It is an outstandingly entertaining film and I am very proud to have been a part of it.

Richard D. Zanuck

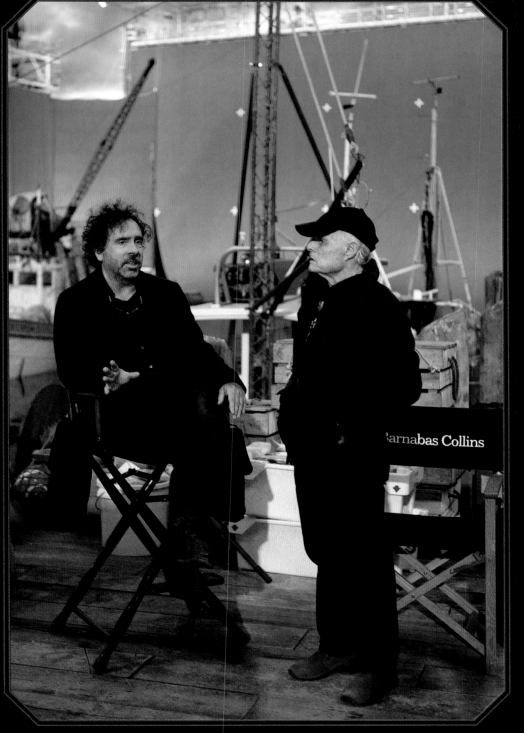

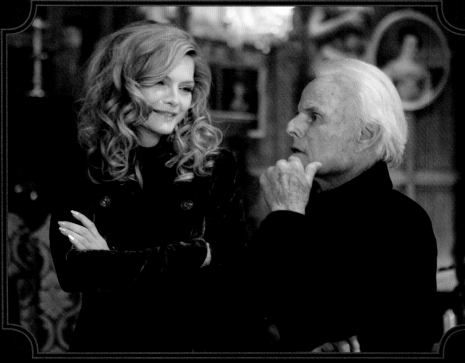

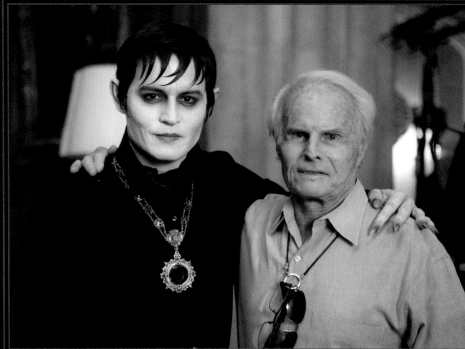

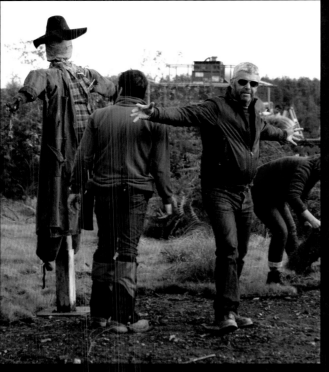
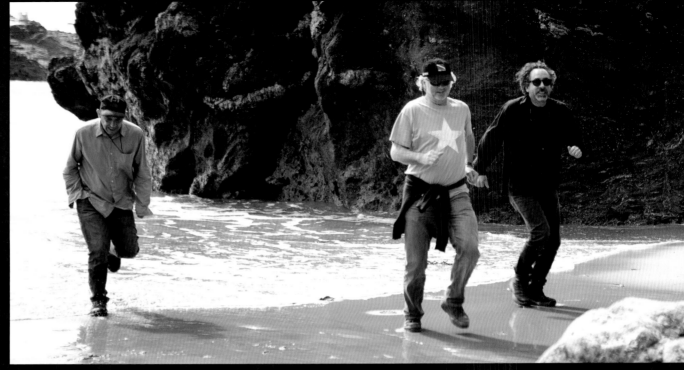
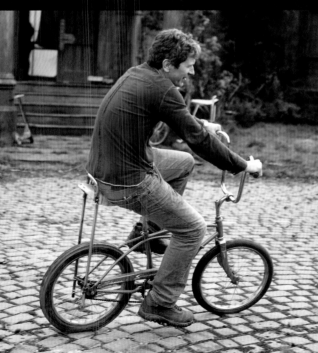
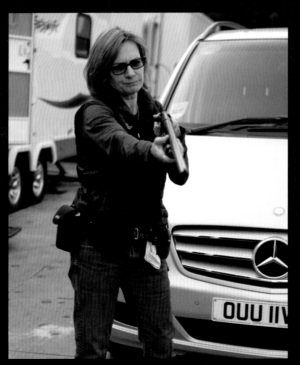
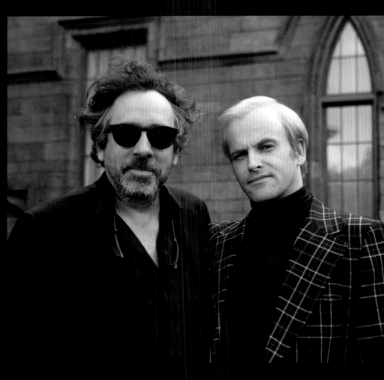

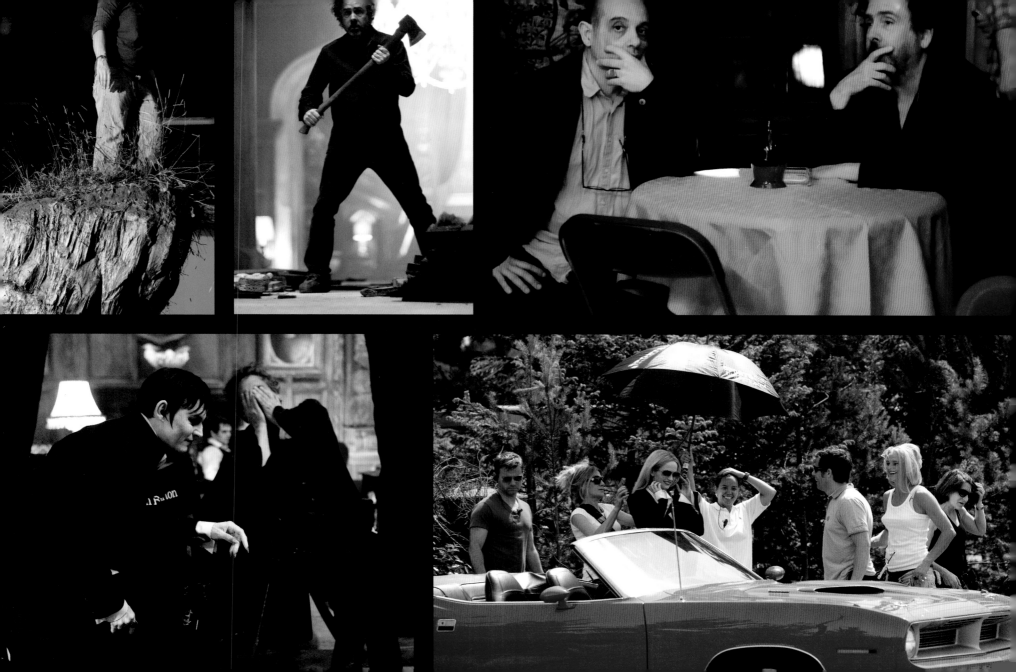

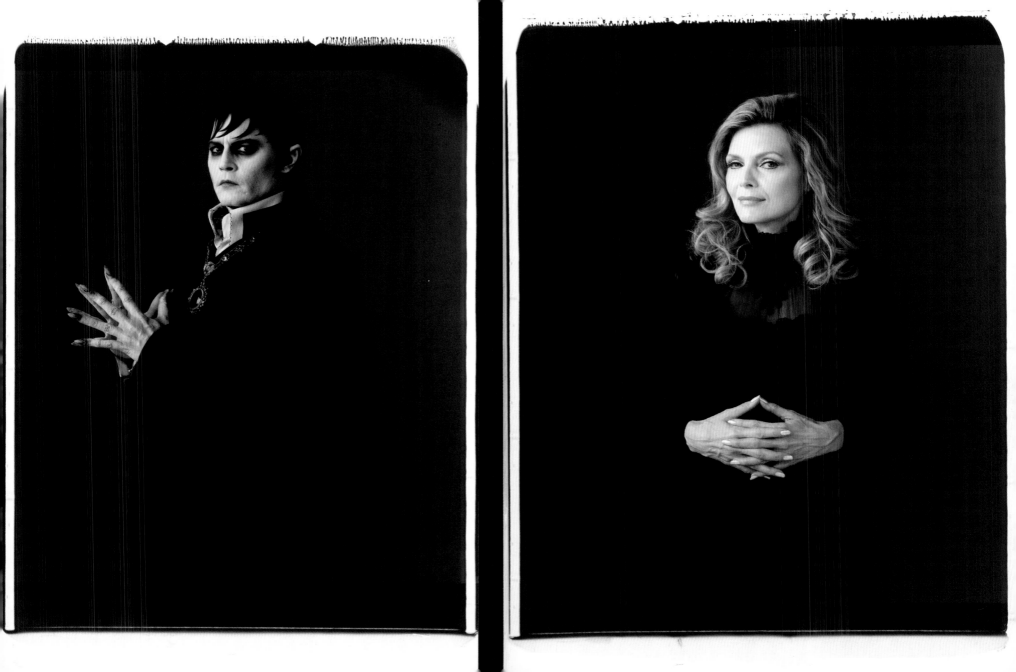

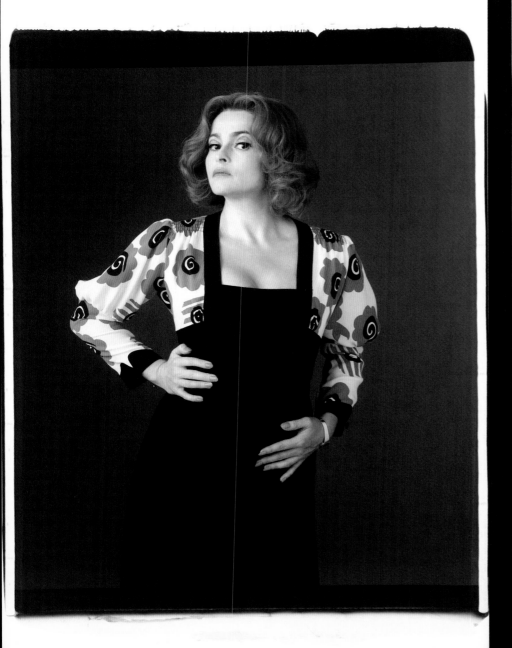
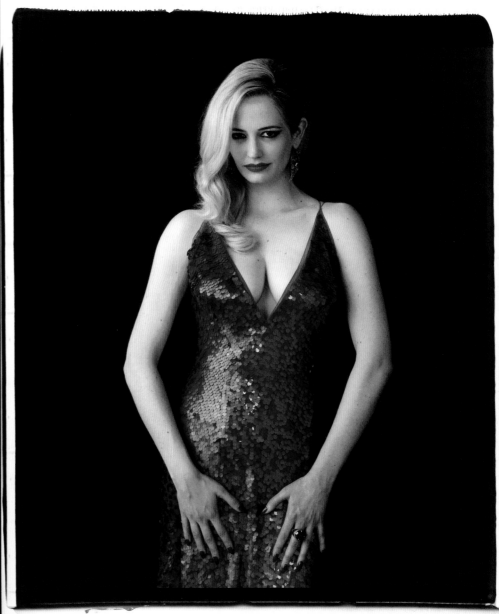

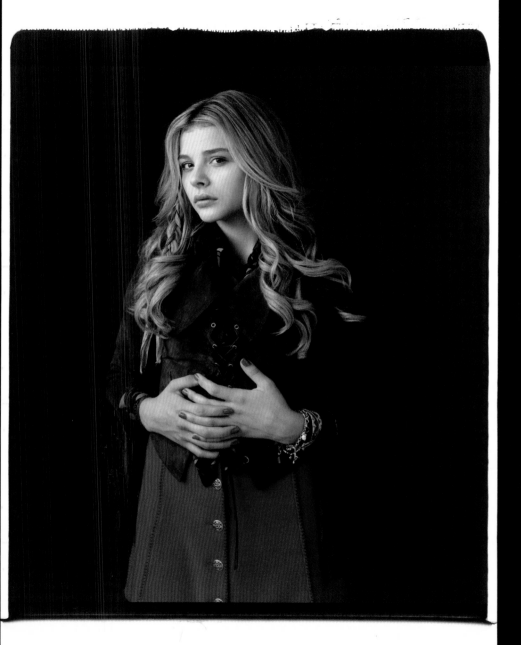
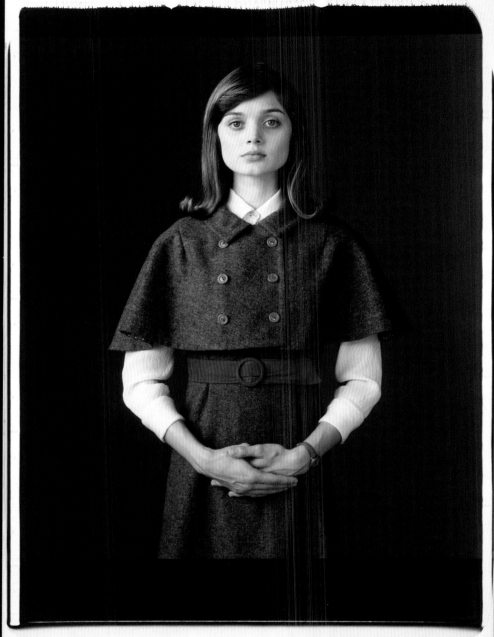

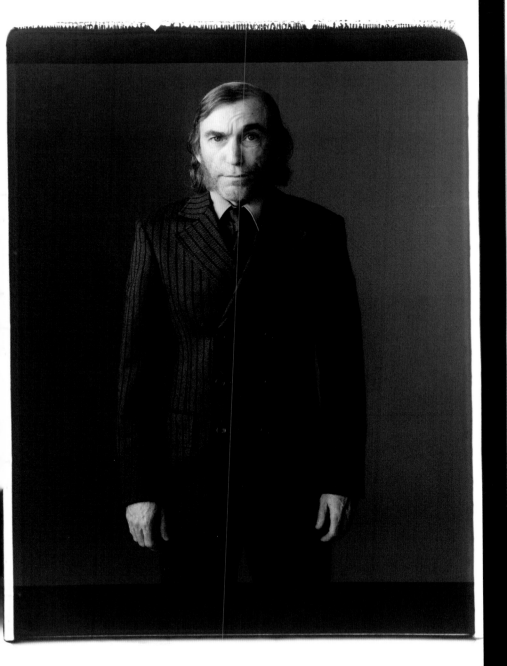
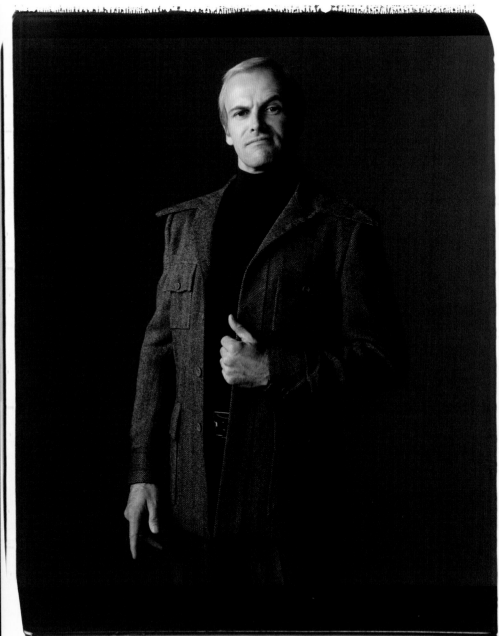

Index of Captions

DARK SHADOWS: THE VISUAL COMPANION
ISBN: 9781781162552
LIMITED EDITON ISBN: 9781781162569

Published by
Titan Books
A division of Titan Publishing Group Ltd.
144 Southwark St.
London
SE1 0UP

First edition: October 2012

10 9 8 7 6 5 4 3 2 1

MARK SALISBURY is editor of the critically acclaimed *Burton On Burton*, as well as author of movie books *Alice In Wonderland: A Visual Companion*, *Prometheus: The Art Of The Film*, *Sweeney Todd: The Demon Barber Of Fleet Street*, *Tim Burton's Corpse Bride: An Invitation To The Wedding* and *Planet Of The Apes: Reimagined By Tim Burton*. A former editor of *Empire* magazine, his other books include *Writers On Comics Scriptwriting* and *Artists On Comics Art*.

For Laura, Milo and Mum, if family is the only real wealth, then I am a very rich man indeed.

WARNER BROS. PICTURES PRESENTS
IN ASSOCIATION WITH VILLAGE ROADSHOW PICTURES AN INFINITUM NIHIL/GK FILMS/ZANUCK COMPANY PRODUCTION A TIM BURTON FILM JOHNNY DEPP "DARK SHADOWS"
MICHELLE PFEIFFER HELENA BONHAM CARTER EVA GREEN JACKIE EARLE HALEY JONNY LEE MILLER CHLOË GRACE MORETZ BELLA HEATHCOTE
MUSIC BY DANNY ELFMAN CO-PRODUCER KATTERLI FRAUENFELDER COSTUME DESIGNER COLLEEN ATWOOD FILM EDITOR CHRIS LEBENZON, A.C.E. PRODUCTION DESIGNER RICK HEINRICHS DIRECTOR OF PHOTOGRAPHY BRUNO DELBONNEL, A.F.C., A.S.C.
EXECUTIVE PRODUCERS CHRIS LEBENZON TIM HEADINGTON AND BRUCE BERMAN BASED ON THE TELEVISION SERIES CREATED BY DAN CURTIS STORY BY JOHN AUGUST AND SETH GRAHAME-SMITH
SCREENPLAY BY SETH GRAHAME-SMITH PRODUCED BY RICHARD D. ZANUCK GRAHAM KING JOHNNY DEPP CHRISTI DEMBROWSKI DAVID KENNEDY DIRECTED BY TIM BURTON

VILLAGE ROADSHOW PICTURES
GK films
Soundtrack Album on WaterTower Music
www.darkshadowsmovie.com
MAY 11
PG-13 PARENTS STRONGLY CAUTIONED
Some Material May Be Inappropriate for Children Under 13.
COMIC HORROR VIOLENCE, SEXUAL CONTENT,
SOME DRUG USE, LANGUAGE AND SMOKING

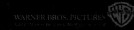

WARNER BROS. PICTURES

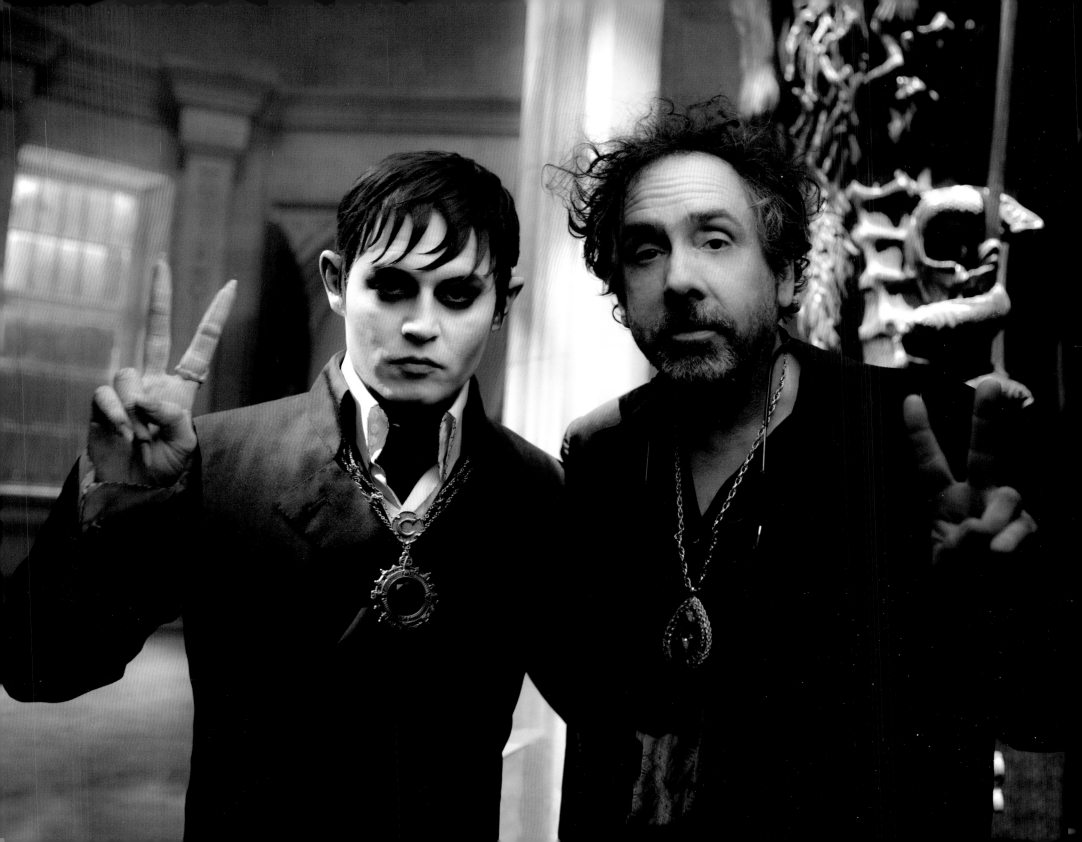